WORK AND PLAY ON THE SHAKESPEAREAN STAGE

Time and again, early modern plays show people at work: shoemaking, basket-weaving, grave-digging and professional acting are just some of the forms of labour that theatregoers could have seen depicted on stage in 1599 and 1600. Tom Rutter demonstrates how such representations were shaped by the theatre's own problematic relationship with work: actors earned their living through playing, a practice that many considered idle and illegitimate, while plays were criticised for enticing servants and apprentices from their labour. As a result, the drama of Shakespeare's time became the focal point of wider debates over what counted as work, who should have to do it, and how it should be valued. This book describes changing beliefs about work in the sixteenth century and shows how new ways of conceptualising the work of the governing class inform Shakespeare's histories. It identifies important contrasts between the way the work of actors was treated in plays written for the adult and child repertories. Finally, it examines whether different playing companies depicted work and workers in different ways in the decade between the reopening of the playhouse at St Paul's in 1599 and the move of the King's Men to the Blackfriars.

TOM RUTTER is Senior Lecturer in Renaissance Literature at Sheffield Hallam University. He has published articles in journals, including *Medieval and Renaissance Drama in England* and *Studies in English Literature*, and is a regular reviewer for *Modern Language Review* and *Early Modern Literary Studies*. This is his first book.

WORK AND PLAY ON THE SHAKESPEAREAN STAGE

TOM RUTTER

CAMBRIDGE
UNIVERSITY PRESS

CAMBRIDGE UNIVERSITY PRESS
Cambridge, New York, Melbourne, Madrid, Cape Town, Singapore, São Paulo, Delhi

Cambridge University Press
The Edinburgh Building, Cambridge CB2 8RU, UK

Published in the United States of America by Cambridge University Press, New York

www.cambridge.org
Information on this title: www.cambridge.org/9780521884860

First published 2008

Printed in the United Kingdom at the University Press, Cambridge

A catalogue record for this publication is available from the British Library

Library of Congress Cataloguing in Publication data
Rutter, Tom.
Work and play on the Shakespearean stage/Tom Rutter.
p. cm.
Includes bibliographical references and index.
ISBN 978-0-521-88486-0
1. Shakespeare, William, 1564-1616–Characters. 2. English drama–Early modern and Elizabethan, 1500-1600–History and criticism. 3. Work in literature. 4. Play in literature. 5. Professions in literature. 6. Literature and society–England–History–16th century. 7. Acting in literature. I. Title.
PR2989.R88 2008
822.3'3–dc22
2008011345

ISBN 978-0-521-88486-0 hardback

To Sophie, Cædmon, and Aphra

Contents

Acknowledgements *page* viii
Note on texts and dates x

Introduction 1

1 Work in sixteenth-century England 11

2 'Vpon the weke daies and worke daies at conuenient times': acting as work in Elizabethan England 26

3 'Though he be a king, yet he must labour': work and nobility in Shakespeare's histories 55

4 'We may shut vp our shops, and make holiday': workers and playhouses, 1599–1601 87

5 'Work upon that now!': labour and status on the stage, 1599–1610 119

Conclusion 153

Notes 158
Bibliography 182
Index 200

Acknowledgements

This book developed out of my Ph.D. thesis, 'Playing Work: The Uses of Labour on the Shakespearean Stage', which was completed with the help of a postgraduate award from the Arts and Humanities Research Board and a Fourth Year Fellowship from the English Department of University College London (UCL). The same two bodies, along with the UCL Graduate School, also helped me to attend the seminar, 'Working Women/Women's Work: The Role of the Working Woman in Shakespeare's England' at the Twenty-Ninth Annual Meeting of the Shakespeare Association of America in 2001. I would like to acknowledge the assistance of the Faculty of Arts and Human Sciences at London South Bank University in enabling me to give a paper at the British Shakespeare Association's biennial conference in 2005. The Humanities Research Centre at Sheffield Hallam University gave me the resources to consult manuscripts at the National Archives and the British Library; I would also like to thank the librarians at both of those institutions and at the libraries of Sheffield Hallam University, Sheffield University, UCL, the University of London and the Warburg Institute.

Material from Chapter 2 appeared as 'The Actors in *Sir Thomas More*' in *Shakespeare Yearbook*, n.s., 16, 227–44. I want to thank the Editor, Douglas A. Brooks, and the Editorial Board for granting me permission to reprint that material here. Material from Chapter 4 appeared as 'Fit Hamlet, Fat Hamlet, and the Problems of Aristocratic Labour' in *Cahiers Elisabéthains* 68 (Autumn 2005), 27–32. Again, I would like to thank the Editorial Board for granting me permission to reprint it.

It is a pleasure to record numerous debts to individuals. Foremost among those is René Weis, who supervised my Ph.D. with exemplary care and generosity and from whom I continue to learn. Henry Woudhuysen provided much guidance in the early stages, and, as secondary supervisor, Helen Hackett read successive drafts of my thesis and made numerous invaluable suggestions. Ann Thompson and Richard Dutton were benevolent but scrupulous examiners, and their comments were a great help when I came to redevelop the material as a book. My colleagues at Sheffield Hallam University, Annaliese Connolly, Lisa Hopkins and Matt Steggle, graciously agreed to read parts of the final draft, and I have benefited from discussions with Eva Griffith, Andrew Gurr, Farah Karim-Cooper, Roslyn Knutson and Lucy Munro. Writing books is not exactly hauling coal, but it's arduous in its own way, and I have been sustained by the companionship of Alice Bell, Robin Deacon, Kevin De Ornellas, Ricardo Domizio, Michelle Dowd, Caroline Gordon, Rowland Hughes, Margaret Kinsman, Sonia Massai, Gordon McMullan, Dinah Roe, Suzanne Scafe and Sarah Wood. Andrew Dewdney, Steve Earnshaw, Chris Hopkins, Danny Karlin, Anna Reading and Hillegonda Rietveld deserve thanks for helping to make their institutions congenial places to do research in. I would like to thank Sarah Stanton at Cambridge University Press (CUP) for believing in this project, Rebecca Jones and Jodie Barnes, for helping it to press, and CUP's anonymous readers for their input, which has made this a better book. I also want to thank Marianthi Makra and Liz O'Donnell for their work on its production. My approach to early modern drama owes a great deal to John Pitcher, in whose undergraduate seminars and tutorials this project's origins lie.

To three people, incalculable thanks are due. They are my parents, Bill and Rowena, who have provided continual encouragement to me in my academic career, and my wife Sophie, who has been an unfailing source of love and support in the face of extreme provocation. To her, and to our children Aphra and Cædmon, this book is dedicated.

Note on texts and dates

Speech prefixes in quotations from plays have been standardised throughout. Except where indicated, in-text references to the works of Thomas Dekker, Ben Jonson, John Marston and William Shakespeare use the following editions:

THOMAS DEKKER, *The Dramatic Works of Thomas Dekker*, ed. Fredson Bowers, 4 vols. (Cambridge: Cambridge University Press, 1953–61).
BEN JONSON, *Ben Jonson*, ed. C. H. Herford and Percy and E. M. Simpson, 11 vols. (Oxford: Clarendon Press, 1925–52).
JOHN MARSTON, *The Plays of John Marston*, ed. H. Harvey Wood, 3 vols. (Edinburgh: Oliver & Boyd, 1934–39). As Wood does not supply lineation, volume and page number are given.
WILLIAM SHAKESPEARE, *The Riverside Shakespeare*, ed. G. Blakemore Evans (Boston, Mass.: Houghton Mifflin, 1974).

Except where indicated, dates of performance throughout this book are from Alfred Harbage, *Annals of English Drama 975–1700: An Analytical Record of All Plays, Extant or Lost, Chronologically Arranged and Indexed by Authors, Titles, Dramatic Companies, &c.*, rev. S. Schoenbaum (London: Methuen, 1964).

Introduction

In his Preface to *The Oxford Book of Work*, Keith Thomas notes the imbalance between the time and energy we expend on work and its comparatively meagre presence in literature: 'for all its centrality to human existence, work has never been a popular literary theme. By comparison with love or warfare, the business of getting a living has been relatively neglected by poets and novelists.' According to Thomas, classical ideas of aesthetic decorum meant that workers tended to be marginalised, ridiculed or, at best, idealised into pastoral, while popular literature has usually sought to carry readers away from their daily working lives. Furthermore, because work is 'a long, continuing process, rather than a discrete act', it is difficult to capture its essence within the formal confines of a literary text.[1]

On this basis, the treatment of work in the drama of Shakespeare's time ought to be an unpromising subject for a book. Admittedly, the principle of decorum was never wholeheartedly observed on the Renaissance stage, to the dismay of commentators such as Sir Philip Sidney, who lamented plays' 'mingling Kinges and Clownes'.[2] However, the English drama was evidently popular, speaking to a broader audience than any purely literary art was able to: according to one opponent of the theatre writing in 1582, the former playwright Stephen Gosson, 'the common people which resort to Theatres' consisted of 'Tailers, Tinkers, Cordwayners, Saylers, olde Men, yong Men, Women, Boyes, Girles, and such like'. Gosson went on to complain that on the stage 'those thinges are fained, that neuer were', and three decades later another dramatist, Ben Jonson, could similarly criticise the escapist character of English plays, 'wherein, now, the Concupiscence of Daunces, and Antickes so raigneth, as to runne away from Nature, and be afraid of her, is the onely point of art that tickles the *Spectators*' (*The Alchemist*, To the Reader, 5–8).[3] Apparently, the men and women of early modern England went to the theatre seeking something different from their everyday lives; indeed, the very word 'play' implies that to speakers of English, there is something about drama that is fundamentally at odds with the workaday world. And to move on to Thomas's last point, the formal properties of a play, filling just 'the space of two houres and an halfe' by Jonson's estimate (*Bartholomew Fair*, Induction, 79), make it perhaps ill-equipped to convey the ongoing and repetitious character of work.

In fact, however, a Londoner who regularly visited the theatre around the beginning of the seventeenth century would have been able to view representations of work of many different kinds. At *The Shoemakers' Holiday* (1599), he or she could have watched some actors pretending to make shoes and another pretending to be a young woman working in a shop; characters in *Patient Grissil* (1600) weave baskets and carry logs. In *Thomas Lord Cromwell* (*c.* 1599–1602), the young Cromwell keeps his father's servants awake by studying out loud; the servants then distract him from his work with the noise of their hammers. *Hamlet* (1599–*c.* 1601) depicts a man digging a grave and allows him to speak about the practicalities of his trade: 'your water is a sore decayer of your whoreson dead body' (V. 1. 171–2). The play also includes a theatrical performance by a fictitious troupe of professional actors. And, in an even more striking representation of the labour that goes into the making of art, *Satiromastix* (1601) includes a barely veiled parody of Ben Jonson at work on a poem that had been written by the real Ben Jonson:

> O me thy Priest inspire.
> For I to thee and thine immortall name,
> In – in – in golden tunes,
> For I to thee and thine immortall name –
> In – sacred raptures flowing, flowing, swimming, swimming:
> In sacred raptures swimming,
> Immortall name, game, dame, tame, lame, lame, lame,
> Pux, ha it, shame, proclaim, oh –
> In Sacred raptures flowing, will proclaime, not –
> O me thy Priest inspyre!
> For I to thee and thine immortall name,
> In flowing numbers fild with spright and flame,
> Good, good, in flowing numbers fild with spright & flame.
> (I. 2. 8–20)

The poem's claim to visionary inspiration is tellingly counterpointed by the play's depiction of the hesitations, false starts and authorial labour that have gone into its composition.

This book will argue that the drama of Shakespeare's time was actually very much concerned with the topic of work, for a number of reasons.

Some of these had to do with broader social and cultural developments of the period: as I argue in Chapter 1, while the dominant social theory of the Middle Ages had tended to assume that work was carried out only by one part of society, by the end of the sixteenth century it had become much more common for the idea of work to be invoked when describing the activities of a wide range of groups, from actors to the nobility. I ascribe this partly to demographic factors and the changing nature of England's economy but also to cultural changes such as the Protestant Reformation, with its stress on the idea of vocation, and to the concepts of civic service and statecraft that humanist writers derived from Classical texts. Then, in the final part of the chapter, I address some of the theoretical problems that surround any attempt to locate theatrical production in relation to such developments. How methodologically valid is it to relate early modern play texts to their supposed historical context, when our sense of that context is itself the product of other texts? And what sorts of relationship can be identified between the surrounding culture and the drama, which was not only shaped by wider cultural forces but was also a significant cultural force in its own right?

In Chapter 2, I go on to suggest that one important reason why broader developments and debates concerning work in early modern society came to be played out on stage was because of the drama's own problematic relationship with the idea of work. As the amateur religious drama of the Middle Ages gave way, albeit in irregular fashion and for a variety of reasons, to a more professionalised theatre whose plays, especially around London, were performed regularly and in purpose-built spaces, actors were increasingly accused of earning a living without labouring in a vocation. I examine the way this charge was made both in correspondence between London's civic authorities and the Privy Council and in printed works against the theatre from the 1570s onward. I then turn my attention to the public stage of the 1590s, identifying a number of plays that respond to this criticism by emphasising the industriousness and skill of professional actors.

In Chapter 3, I argue that during the early modern period the concept of work was inextricably linked to social status in that a gentleman was by definition someone who did not perform manual (or, it was often argued, commercial) work. However, while in the Middle Ages this social group had predominantly been conceptualised as *bellatores* or defenders of the realm, its changing social role, as well as the social and cultural changes referred to in Chapter 1, encouraged a redefinition of its activities in terms of work, a phenomenon whose effects are particularly evident in sermons, religious commentary and the Book of Homilies. In the latter part of the chapter, I focus on Shakespeare's histories of the 1590s as the group of plays most obviously influenced by this new discourse; however, rather than passively echoing it, Shakespeare sets it up against other conceptions of nobility as a means of characterisation and in order to generate dramatic excitement. More complicatedly, in the two parts of *Henry IV* and in *Henry V*, Shakespeare presents Hal as an individual who artfully manipulates ideas of work and idleness in his creation of a public self, thereby suggesting that such ideas are shifting and contingent rather than immutable or universal.

In Chapter 4, I discuss the relationship between the London theatre at the beginning of the seventeenth century and these linked concepts of work and social status, arguing that it was both complex and conflicted. On the one hand, plays such as *The Shoemakers' Holiday* and *Julius Caesar* engaged with the question of whether manual workers should be present in theatre audiences, intervening in a broader debate within the City of London over servants' and apprentices' rights to free time. On the other hand, dramatists writing for the revived companies of child actors playing at St Paul's and the Blackfriars attempted to identify them with the social elite, and, to do so, they invoked the still-prevalent association of gentility with idleness, representing their playhouses as places from which workers were absent and stressing the amateurism of their actors. I compare *Hamlet* and *Patient Grissil* as very different responses to this strategy by dramatists writing for the adult companies; I then go on in Chapter 5 to consider whether the pattern established around 1600, whereby different playing companies positioned themselves in different ways in relation to the concepts of work and social status, is one that persisted during the first decade of the seventeenth century. I end by examining *Coriolanus*, suggesting that in the characterisation of its hero Shakespeare brings together contrasting discourses about work that I have associated with the adult and child companies respectively.

It will have become apparent from the above synopsis that, in this book, I treat the concept of work as a decidedly ambiguous one whose relationship with any given activity is far from stable. Acting is considered by some commentators to be work, by others not; gentlemen and nobles are represented as workers who serve the realm through non-manual labour, but the idea that to be a gentleman is to be idle remains widespread. It might be argued that these instances reflect particular moments of transition in the history of the theatre or of the English class system, but I would suggest that they also reflect the inherently problematic nature of work as a concept: as Thomas observes, '"Work" is harder to define than one might think'. If we define working as 'purposively expending energy', in Thomas's paraphrase of the entry in the *Concise Oxford Dictionary*, then this is to include strenuous recreations such as tennis; if we say that 'work is what we do in our paid employment', then this excludes slave labour. 'It seems odd ... to say that writers have ceased to work when they leave their word-processors and go to do some overdue digging in their gardens'.[4] This confusion is paralleled on the semantic level, where the word 'work' proves to be extremely broad in its range of applications. It comes from the old English *weorc* and has denoted an action 'involving effort or exertion directed to a definite end, esp. as a means of gaining one's livelihood; labour, toil; (one's) regular occupation or employment' (*OED* 'work', *sb*., I. 4) since the ninth century: in Ælfric's Exodus, 20:9 (*c*. 1000), the Israelites are commanded, 'Wyrc six da[y]as ealle ðine weorc'. However, the *OED*'s more general definition, 'Something that is or was done; what a person does or did; an act, deed, proceeding, business' ('work', *sb*., I. 1), is of similar antiquity: in his Homilies, I, 318, Ælfric writes, 'þæt weorc wæs begunnen on[y]ean Godes willan'. The verb is equally flexible: in Alfred's translation of Boethius's *De consolatione philosophiae* (*c*. 888), XLI we are asked, 'Hwy sceall þonne æni[y] mon bion idel, ðæt he ne wyrce?' ('work', *v*., II. 24), but in the Prologue to *The Canterbury Tales*, line 497, Chaucer's Parson gives this example to his flock: 'That firste he wroghte, and afterward that he taughte' ('work', *v*., II. 21). In particular, the transitive verb means primarily 'To do, perform, practise' ('work', *v*., I. 1): in *Beowulf*, line 930, Hrothgar says that God can 'wyrcan wunder æfter wundre'.[5] 'An Homilie against Idlenesse', one of the homilies added in 1563 to the Book of Homilies first printed under Edward VI, is an important example of how both noun and verb could be used in their narrower and in their more general senses during the Elizabethan period. It talks of 'labouring men, who bee at wages for their worke', but also tells us that 'we are commanded by *Iesus Sirach*, not to hate painefull workes'. St Paul's second letter to the Thessalonians responds to the news that among them 'there were certaine ... which did not worke', but 'the best time that the diuell can haue to worke his feate, is when men bee asleepe'.[6]

What is it that stops an activity from being just 'something that is or was done' and gives it the more specific status of work? Sociologists who have focused on work find it difficult to say, Richard Hall noting 'how slippery the concept of work is' and Keith Grint writing of the 'ambiguous nature of work' and 'the enigmatic essence of work'. The problem is that, as Grint points out, the 'difference between work and non-work seldom lies within the actual activity itself and more generally inheres in the social context that supports the activity': there is nothing inherent in digging a garden, to use Thomas's example, that makes it work rather than leisure. Rather, a task's status as work comes from the social context in which it is done, a fact that is implicitly acknowledged in Hall's tellingly circular definition: 'Work is the effort or activity of an individual that is undertaken for the purpose of providing goods or services of value to others and that is considered by the individual to be work.'[7] Ultimately, an activity is work because we consider it to be so.

This view of work as socially contingent, even socially constructed, is an important point of difference between my approach and that of Maurice Hunt in one of the few other book-length studies of work in the early modern drama that I know of, *Shakespeare's Labored Art: Stir, Work, and the Late Plays.* Hunt argues that 'Shakespeare's dramatization of labor in his late plays ultimately reflects the ambiguous, bifurcated attitudes of different segments of his culture': the early modern period inherited the medieval conception of work as a curse, but the Reformation precipitated a more positive view of work both as a sign of election, in the case of good works, and as having salutary, disciplining effects. In *Pericles* and *Cymbeline,* Shakespeare 'satirizes the sloth of certain (upper) Jacobean social classes' and shows how physical work 'proves redemptive for afflicted characters such as Pericles and Imogen'. In *The Winter's Tale, The Tempest* and *Henry VIII,* the working mind, often represented in terms of birth labour, 'take[s] precedence over physical labor'. Hunt describes Shakespeare's as a 'labored art', not only because it is 'an art recommending the virtues of work of all kinds, from physical labor to the work of the mind', but also because of its highly wrought, 'Mannerist' style.[8] As succeeding chapters will show, my own book shares with Hunt's an assumption that while an animus against labour was still in evidence in parts of the early modern social elite, the Reformation precipitated a change in attitudes towards work, particularly among the middling sort. However, I feel that Hunt may underestimate the extent to which a disdain for work continued to be prevalent even outside the aristocracy. The speaker of Sonnet III expresses a strong sense of its power to degrade ('my nature is subdu'd / To what it works in, like the dyer's hand'), while Shakespeare's own acquisition of a coat of arms for his father (and therefore himself) implies a more complex attitude towards the social elite than mere distaste at their idleness. More fundamentally, while Hunt explores the social and intellectual contexts for Shakespeare's plays, he neglects to discuss their dramatic context – the fact that they were written for a medium that was inextricably implicated in contemporary debates over what constituted legitimate forms of work and recreation. Finally, I would question Hunt's assumption that there is a relatively unproblematic concept of work towards which one can gauge changing attitudes. Rather, I would argue that the whole notion of work is inherently unstable and that ideas of what work means, and what activities constitute work, vary greatly in different times and cultures.

An important example of how the status of a given practice as work or non-work is socially constructed rather than immutable is that of women's work. Even today, women's work inside the home tends to go unpaid, and to some extent unrecognised, while outside it, it remains more poorly paid than that of men.[9] During the early modern period, ideas about women's work often reflected the legal subordination of married women to their husbands. As Amy Louise Erickson summarises the situation:

> Under common law a woman's legal identity during marriage was eclipsed – literally covered – by her husband. As a 'feme covert', she could not contract, neither could she sue nor be sued independently of her husband ... The property a woman brought to marriage – her dowry or portion – all came under the immediate control of her husband.[10]

This subordination was reinforced by religious doctrine: in Ephesians 5:22, St Paul calls upon wives to 'submit your selues vnto your housbands, as vnto the Lord'.[11] The implications of this are evident in numerous books on marriage printed during the sixteenth and early seventeenth centuries in the tradition established by Heinrich Bullinger's *Der Christlich Eestand* (1540), translated by Miles Coverdale in 1541. When the proper division of labour in the marital relationship is discussed, the work of wives, like their goods, is seen as their husbands' property; rather than working for herself, a wife is her husband's 'helper'.[12] As the author of *Covnsel to the Husband: To the Wife Instruction* (1608) puts it, the good wife 'laboureth in her place for her husbands quiet, for his health, for his credit, for his wealth, for his happines in his estate more then for her selfe, and counteth his in all those respects her owne'.[13] Also, while a man's work is assumed to be productive and carried out outside the home, his wife's activities are supposed to lie within the home and consist of saving or spending what he has brought in. Lorna Hutson has shown how this gender division of labour derives 'from a text entitled *Oeconomicus*, written by the Socratian philosopher

Xenophon, and from its derivative, a pseudo-Aristotelian text of the same name'; as well as informing Protestant marriage literature, these texts are closely followed in works as varied as Castiglione's *Il Cortegiano* (translated 1561), Sir Thomas Smith's *De republica anglorum* (1583) and Thomas Heywood's *Gynaikeion* (1624). As Smith puts it,

> The naturalest and first conjunction of two toward the making of a further societie of continuance is of the husband and the wife after a diverse sorte ech having care of the familie: the man to get, to travaile abroad, to defende: the wife, to save that which is gotten, to tarrie at home to distribute that which commeth of the husbandes labor for nurtriture of the children and family of them both, and to keepe all at home neat and cleane.[14]

In Smith's account, only the practices of the husband are described as labour; the task of the wife is to save and distribute their fruits. From her activities, the idea of work is withheld.

Perhaps because women's work, both in the early modern period and today, has exemplified so graphically the way in which definitions of work are shaped by wider forces in society, critics who have addressed this topic have tended to be free of what I see as Hunt's overly straightforward sense of what work actually means. In the first chapter of *The Usurer's Daughter*, Lorna Hutson examines the construction of women's work in Protestant household manuals, arguing that it served as a site onto which the more morally disreputable aspects of husbandry – the 'ethical stigma of the calculating outlook' – could be placed.[15] In an article on *The Shoemakers' Holiday*, Ronda A. Arab similarly shows how an attempt to valorise the labour of men involves the marginalisation and denigration of women's work. Thomas Dekker's 'exaltation of male artisans' systematically devalues the contribution of women to Simon Eyre's household, and Eyre's wife Margery is repeatedly made the target of sexualised verbal abuse.[16] The dramatic depiction of women's work outside the home has also attracted critical attention. In the course of her wide-ranging survey, *Women and the English Renaissance: Literature and the Nature of Womankind, 1540–1620*, Linda Woodbridge notes that the drama of the period 'is full of women who mind the store – shopkeepers' wives who serve customers, often in their husbands' absence'. Because, other than servants, 'the only other city women who worked and brought in money were whores', plays that depicted such characters tended either to exploit them for the ends of anti-citizen satire or to insist defensively on their chastity.[17] More specifically, Garrett A. Sullivan Jr. suggests that plays likened women's work outside the home to prostitution because they were influenced by a broad historical trend away from masters relying on the aid of their wives and towards the employment of hired labourers.[18] Although Sullivan sees Marston's *The Dutch Courtesan* (1603–4) as an expression of anxieties about the place of women in the urban economy rather than a conscious attempt at propaganda, Mary Wack's study of the treatment of alewives in the mystery plays of sixteenth-century Chester shows how the drama could be an active participant in the regulation of female labour. She argues that two scenes apparently added to the cycle, one of which shows Mrs Noah refusing to board the ark because she wants to stay drinking with her gossips and the other of which shows Mulier, a tapster and brewster, being dragged back to Hell for trade violations, may have been meant to reinforce and justify laws enacted in Chester during the 1530s which regulated the sale and production of alcohol and forbade women between the ages of fourteen and forty from working as tapsters.[19] Finally, the instability, social marginality and low status of women's work has been a central theme of two recent studies, Patricia Fumerton's *Unsettled* and Fiona McNeill's *Poor Women in Shakespeare*. Fumerton identifies in early modern England a 'conceptual block against multiple or serial and occasional employment as legitimate work (especially when practiced by women)', and this meant that women's work outside the home, when not carried out in a formal context such as apprenticeship, contract or marriage, was often construed as illegitimate, leaving its practitioners vulnerable to prosecution for vagrancy.[20] McNeill contrasts the bureaucratic invisibility and low status of women's work with its economic ubiquity and fundamental importance in the development of capitalism, a state of affairs mirrored in the drama: 'Representations of poor women are everywhere in early modern drama, if not at the center ... They are represented at the peripheries of early modern drama just as they were pushed to the peripheries of early modern culture.'[21]

Although I have written on the topic of women's work elsewhere,[22] I have chosen not to focus on it in this book, partly because I want to concentrate on the narrower question of the relationship between work and social status and partly because this is one aspect of the subject of work that has already attracted considerable critical attention. However, critics such as those referred to above, though varied in their approaches, supply me with three of the basic assumptions of this study: first, as I have already said, that an activity's status as work is not a given, but socially constructed; second, that to see something as work is not necessarily to validate it, as is the case with women's work outside the home; and third, that as in Chester in the 1530s, the stage itself did not just reflect broader changes in the nature and understanding of work but also was an agent, sometimes wittingly, sometimes unwittingly, in bringing them about, not least because its own problematic position in relation to concepts of work and play made its treatment of those concepts ideologically overdetermined. This final point is one to which I will return repeatedly in the course of this book; first, however, I want to explore more fully the ways in which notions of work were changing during the early modern period.

CHAPTER 1

Work in sixteenth-century England

I suggested in the Preface to this book that as a way of categorising behaviour, work is both fluid and ambiguous. Activities that might be designated work in one historical or social context might not in another; thus, the meaning of work is something that changes between times and places. In this chapter, I want to suggest that work meant something different in the early modern period to what it had during the Middle Ages.[1] I shall argue in subsequent chapters that this change of signification had important implications both for the status of acting and for the way the idea of work was used in the drama. Before going on to do so, however, it will be necessary to address some methodological questions about how criticism of the drama might relate it to the broader ideological and social developments I discuss, and this will be the focus of the second part of the current chapter.

WORK AND SOCIAL THEORY: MEDIEVAL TO EARLY MODERN

In his essay, 'Imagination and Traditional Ideologies in *Piers Plowman*', David Aers identifies what he calls 'the major social ideology' of the late Middle Ages:

> This envisaged society as a static hierarchy of estates, fixed in occupations which were organically related, mutually beneficial, harmonious and divinely ordained. Society was often presented as a human body, with head and hands as king and nobility, feet as peasantry, and so on. As common was the tripartite division into those who pray, those who fight and those who labour to maintain fighters and praysters.[2]

The corporeal metaphor and the tripartite division are often combined: as one Dominican preacher put it, 'God has ordained three classes of men, namely, labourers such as husbandmen and craftsmen to support the whole body of the Church after the manner of feet, knights to defend it in the fashion of hands, clergy to rule and lead it after the manner of eyes.'[3] Both the extraordinary longevity and the wide currency of this trope are demonstrated by Georges Duby in *The Three Orders: Feudal Society Imagined*, which begins by giving post-medieval examples of it from 1610 and as late as 1951. While Duby largely confines his study to northern France, he does note that the earliest recorded instance comes from Anglo-Saxon England. In the ninth-century version of Boethius's *De consolatione* ascribed to King Alfred, the translator interpolates a commentary at Book 2, Chapter 17, noting that a king should 'have a well-populated land; he must have men of prayer, men of war, men of labor [*sceol habban gebedmen and fyrdmen and weorcmen*]'. A century later, the same tripartite division is used both by Ælfric and by Wulfstan; Duby suggests that the insistence on fighting and praying being carried out by different groups was a response to pressure on Anglo-Saxon monks and clerks to take up arms against the Danes. Subsequent formulations of the scheme in eleventh-century France similarly reacted to perceived threats to the distinction between the religious and the secular life, on the one hand from heretics who saw priests as unnecessary, on the other from Cluniac attempts to import monastic values into lay society. However, it was later pressed into the service of the medieval monarchy, with the king depicted as 'umpire' between the three estates.[4]

For my purposes, what is most noteworthy about the tripartite division of society is its restriction of work to only one of these estates. The toil of the *laboratores* supports the praying of the *oratores* and the warfare of the *bellatores*: as Stephen of Fougères put it in a sermon presented to Henry II of England, 'Knights and faultless clerks / Live by what the peasants work.' Conversely, the other two estates enjoy luxurious lives exempt from work: as Benedict of Saint-Maure wrote for the same king, clerks

> have to eat
> To dress and shoe their feet
> Far more lavishly
> More peacefully and more securely
> Than those who work the earth.[5]

The writers who conceptualised society in this way were obviously informed by Christian theology, and, indeed, they presented the scheme as ordained by God and, hence, immutable. It is natural to wonder, therefore, how the idleness of two groups was reconciled with the Judaeo-Christian notion that work is the common punishment of all for the sins of our first parents:

Also to Adam he said, Because thou hast obeied the voyce of thy wife, and hast eaten of the tre (whereof I com*man*ded thee, saying, Thou shalt not eat of it) cursed is the earth for thy sake: in sorowe shalt thou eat of it all the dayes of thy life.
Thornes also, and thystles shal it bring forthe to thee, and thou shalt eat the herbe of the field.
In the sweat of thy face shalt thou eat bread, til thou returne to the earth: for out of it wast thou taken, because thou art dust, and to dust shalt thou returne. (Genesis 3:17–19)[6]

In practice, however, Adam's curse was not believed to lie with equal weight upon all members of society. As Thomas Aquinas would explain in the *Summa theologica*, 'not everyone sins that works not with his hands, because those precepts of the natural law which regard the good of the many are not binding on each individual'.[7] Original sin meant that some people had to work for the general good; it did not oblige everyone to eat bread in the sweat of his or her face.

Evidently, this rationalisation of class division was not universally accepted. Its apparent inconsistency with the implications of Genesis is expressed in the rhyme attributed to John Ball from the time of the Peasants' Revolt: 'Whan Adam dalf, and Eve span, / Wo was thanne a gentilman?'.[8] Furthermore, as Jacques Le Goff argues, as early as the end of the twelfth century the tripartite schema was becoming incompatible with an increasingly urbanised and commercialised society, in which new social groups were evolving. Nevertheless, the model 'continued to be used as a literary and ideological theme for a long time to come'.[9] Aers finds in *Piers Plowman* a sense of the gap between this established ideology and the diverse, fragmented society Langland saw around him; however, the conventional formula is the 'normative paradigm' consciously subscribed to by the poet, who assumes 'the total relevance of the chief and traditional social model to his world and his poem':

The Kyng and Knyghthod and Clergie bothe
Casten that the Commune sholde hem communes fynde.
The Commune contreved of Kynde Wit craftes,
And for profit of al the peple plowmen ordeyned
To tilie and to travaille as trewe lif asketh. (Prologue, 116–20)

The idea of work is restricted to those who labour with their hands to provide for the other estates. Similarly, when in Passus VI Piers establishes the respective duties of himself and the knight, the language of labour is applied only to his own:

'By Seint Poul' quod Perkyn, 'ye profre yow so faire
That I shal swynke and swete and sowe for us bothe,
And othere labours do for thi love al my lif tyme,
In covenaunt that thow kepe Holy Kirke and myselve
Fro wastours and fro wikked men that this world destruyeth.'
(Passus VI, 24–8)[10]

The knight's defence of commons and Church justifies his exemption from work. The same notion is expressed in other late medieval texts such as John Wyclif's *On the Duty of the King* (1378–9):

It is clear that it is necessary for the parts of the kingdom to be coordinated in quantity and number, since if all were to be lords, who would be workers or servants? If all were to be presbyters, who would be the lords governing or functioning secularly? Therefore, it is necessary for there to be a three-fold hierarchy in the kingdom through which all are arranged into one person of one heart, namely, the priests or those who pray, the secular lords or defenders, and the common people or labourers.[11]

Once again, it is axiomatic that labour, prayer and government should be kept separate, divided between the estates. And, in a 1388 sermon at Paul's Cross, Thomas Wimbledon compares the Church to a vine that requires cultivation:

To priesthood it falleth to kut away the void braunches of sinnes with the swerd of her tong. To knighthode it falleth to letten wrongs and thefftes to ben done, and to maintaine Goddis law and them that ben techers thereof, and also to kepe the londe from enemies of other londes. And to labourers it falleth to travail bodelich and with their sore swete geten out of the earth bodilich lifelode for hem and other partes.[12]

By the Elizabethan period, however, this model of society appears to have lost much of its currency. The Homily against Idleness, one of the twenty-one new homilies added in 1563 to the Book of Homilies first published in 1547, opens by giving a very different picture of the place of work in the commonwealth:

Forasmuch as man, being not borne to ease and rest, but to labour and trauaile, is by corruption of nature through sinne, so farre degenerated and growne out of kinde, that hee taketh Idlenesse to bee no euill at all, but rather a commendable thing, seemely for those that be wealthy, and therefore is greedily imbraced of most part of men, as agreeable to their sensuall affection, and all labour and trauaile is diligently auoyded, as a thing painefull and repugnant to the pleasure of the flesh: It is necessary to bee declared vnto you, that by the ordinance of GOD, which hee hath set in the nature of man, euery one ought, in his lawfull vocation and calling, to giue him selfe to labour: and that idlenesse, being repugnant to the same ordinance, is a grieuous sinne, and also, for the great inconueniences and mischiefes which spring thereof, an intolerable euill: to the intent that ye vnderstand the same, ye may diligently flee from it, and on the other part earnestly apply your selues, euery man in his vocation, to honest labour and businesse, which as it is enioyned vnto man by GODS appointment, so it wanteth not his manifold blessings and sundry benefits.

The idea that a class of people may be exempt from the duty to labour by virtue of its wealth is quickly rejected as a symptom of our sinful corruption. Instead, idleness is both a sin in itself and a precursor to other sins; God has ordained that every man must labour, 'euery man in his vocation'. As the homilist goes on, this does not mean that all men should 'vse handy labour'; rather, 'as there be diuers sorts of labours, some of the minde, and some of the body, and some of both: So euery one ... ought both for the getting of his owne liuing honestly, and for to profite others, in some kind of labour to exercise himselfe'.[13] The medieval assumption that work is the business only of one class of people has vanished.

The Homily against Idleness is by no means alone in assuming that the duty to labour lies not only upon one class in society but upon all humankind: repeatedly, writers from the sixteenth century onward present non-manual occupations as forms of work. Thomas Elyot stresses the work carried out by the ruling class, writing, 'they that be gouernours ... do imploye all the powers of theyr wittes, and theyr diligence, to the only preseruation of other theyr inferiours'.[14] Charged with idleness, the clergyman in *A Compendious or Brief Examination of Certayne Ordinary Complaints* (1549?) insists that 'albeit we labour not much with our bodies ... yet yee know wee laboure *with* our mindes'.[15] Members of the secular professions, too, stressed the labour they had undergone in acquiring expertise: John Cotta wrote that a physician's education must be 'watered with the dew and sweate of painfull studie', while William Fulbecke emphasised the 'extreame diligence' needed to study law.[16] It was now possible for Hugh Latimer to preach, as he did before Edward VI in 1549, that '[e]very man must labour; yea, though he be a king, yet he must labour'.[17]

Of course, as will become apparent during the course of this book, Latimer's dictum was not universally accepted. For one thing, while some gentlemen and nobles used the idea of work as a way of representing their role as governors, work still retained many of the demeaning associations it had possessed during the Middle Ages: it was a commonplace to say that a gentleman should be able to 'live idly and without manuall labour'.[18] For another, some groups in society chose to earn a living by practices that not everyone considered to be legitimate. Actors are one example; merchants are another, in that commentators were often troubled by the mysterious nature of commercial profits. In his essay 'Of Riches', Francis Bacon wrote that while the '*Gaines* of *Ordinary Trades* and *Vocations*, are honest', 'the *Gaines* of *Bargaines*, are of a more doubtfull Nature; When Men shall waite upon Others Necessity, broake by Servants and Instruments to draw them on, Put off Others cunningly that would be better Chapmen, and the like Practises, which are Crafty and Naught'.[19] Finally, an undercurrent of opinion evidently held it unacceptable that any class should be exempt from the duty of manual labour (although such ideas could not be expressed in print before the Civil War), as in this example from Gerrard Winstanley's *The Law of Freedom in a Platform* (1652):

> Traditional Knowledg ... is an idle, lazy contemplation the Scholars would call Knowledg, but it is no knowledg, but a shew of Knowledg, like a *Parrat* who speaks words, but he knows not what he saith: This same shew of knowledg rests in reading or contemplating, or hearing others speak, and speaks so too, but will not set his hand to work: And from this Traditional Knowledg and Learning rise up both Clergy and Lawyer, who by their cunning insinuations live meerly upon the labor of other men, and teach Laws which they themselves will not do, and layes burdens upon others which they themselves will not touch with the least of their fingers.[20]

As Christopher Hill argues, in the sixteenth century such ideas had 'circulated only in the heretical underground: now they could suddenly be freely discussed'.[21] Nevertheless, much as Aers sees the tripartite model as the dominant ideology informing *Piers Plowman* even as the poem highlights its shortcomings, so the assumption that 'euery one ought, in his lawfull vocation and calling, to giue him selfe to labour' might be seen as the official ideology of early modern England. The Preface to the Book of Homilies enjoins 'all Parsons, Vicars, Curates, and all other hauing spirituall cure' to read one of them to his congregation 'euery Sunday and Holyday in the yeere'.[22]

What brought about this reconceptualisation of work, from being a painful duty carried out by those who laboured with their hands to being an obligation incumbent upon all? One way of answering this question is to consider it in terms of the *longue durée*. In his essay, 'Licit and Illicit Trades in the Medieval West', Jacques Le Goff identifies a gradual trend towards urbanisation in Europe between the ninth and the thirteenth centuries: 'New trades came into being or developed, new professional categories made their appearance or grew more substantial, and new socioprofessional groups, strong in numbers and by virtue of their roles, demanded and won esteem and even a prestige appropriate to their strength.' Whereas in the earlier Middle Ages, 'the whole class of *laboratores*, or workers, the mob of lower orders, was an object of contempt', as this class grew in numbers and influence, 'labor became meritorious' rather than 'grounds for contempt and a mark of inferiority'.[23] While this is convincing as a description of a long-term development, however, it does not explain why there should be such a gap between the social theory of Langland, in the fourteenth century, and that of Latimer, in the sixteenth. On the other hand, more local economic changes did take place during the Tudor period in England which might have been the stimulus to new attitudes.

The question of whether the sixteenth century can actually be called a period of economic growth in England is a contentious one, as Sybil M. Jack's survey shows.[24] More certainly, however, it was a period of growth both in population and in prices. In 1500, England's population seems to have stood at a little over 2 million, as compared to 5 or 6 million in 1300; by the 1550s it had risen to 3 million, by 1600 to 4 million, by the 1630s, perhaps, to 5 million.[25] The country's failure to produce enough food for its population was noted by Tudor observers such as Thomas More, who attributed it to the enclosure of arable land in order to graze sheep, and Thomas Starkey, who cited the large number of idle servants and religious, as well as the 'neclygence of the plowme*n* & artyfycerys'.[26] Whether or not they were accurate in identifying the cause, it is evident that these commentators saw productivity as an important social issue. Christopher Hill has suggested that, slightly later in the century, England's economic stagnancy impelled Puritan thinkers into deliberately fostering the notion that all members of the commonwealth had a duty to work:

> So long as there are few consumer goods within the purchasing power of the mass of the population, there is little incentive to earn more than the subsistence minimum wage ... Prices must be kept up if men are to be made to labour. Until men work harder there will be no cheap consumer goods. An ideology advocating regular systematic work was required if the country was to break through this vicious circle to economic advance.[27]

Hill's formulation might be criticised, as it appears to ascribe a rather teleological motivation to the Puritans: they knew that England needed to modernise its economy and so decided to create a work ethic. However, the economic changes of the sixteenth century may have given greater currency to an 'ideology advocating regular systematic work'. A predictable effect of the failure of productivity to keep pace with population growth was price inflation: while wages rose approximately threefold between the start of the sixteenth century and the middle of the seventeenth, the price of cereals rose sevenfold, with dire effects for wage labourers and for landlords who lived off their rents. Conversely, the beneficiaries of inflation were, first, those able to market their surplus produce and, second, the economically enterprising: as D. C. Coleman puts it,

> The adventurous or the lucky, the ruthless or the greedy did better than those who, for reasons of laziness, inertia, or misfortune, were unwilling or unable to depart from old ways ... The gainers were to be found in all ranks of life but more especially amongst enterprising yeomen and landowning gentry, amongst traders, merchants, and lawyers.[28]

Whereas the Middle Ages had been dominated by the ideology of classes – the nobility, the clergy – who had not seen themselves as workers, sixteenth-century price inflation augmented the wealth and power of groups whose position depended not on an army of feudal retainers but on the industry of themselves and their employees. The bigger merchants, particularly those involved in the lucrative export of cloth, which trebled between the mid-fifteenth and mid-sixteenth centuries, became important as a source of finance to the Crown, especially when the fall of Antwerp closed down Europe's main money market.[29]

The landless poor, however, and those whose land holdings were not large enough for their profits from the sale of produce to offset rising rents, did badly as a result of price inflation. Their numbers were increased not only through general population growth and rent increases but also through enclosures; and many were forced into vagrancy and unemployment. The fact that significant numbers of people had no work was seen by Tudor governments as a worrying threat to order and stability.[30] This concern is reflected in legislation such as the 1563 Statute of Artificers (5 Eliz. I. c. 4), which required unretained workers in certain occupations to labour for a master, prescribed minimum periods of employment, restricted geographical mobility and made both dismissal and voluntary departure from service more difficult. The 1576 Acte for the Setting of the Poore on Worke, and for the Avoyding of Ydlenes (18 Eliz. I. c. 3) compelled the poor either to work on 'a competent Store and Stocke of Woole Hempe Flaxe Iron or other Stufe', to be provided for them in towns and cities, or to enter houses of correction so that they 'shall not for want of Worcke goe abrode eyther begginge or committinge Pilfringes or other Misdemeanor lyvinge in Idlenes'; the wording of the Act suggests that order, rather than productivity, was its principal concern.[31]

The problem of feeding a rising population, the 'growing social importance of the industrious sort of people' and the perceived link between idleness and social unrest are three developments that may have contributed to a heightened sense of the social importance of work in the early modern period.[32] In particular, the increasing wealth and power of merchants and yeomen, groups who worked themselves and whose income depended on the industry of others, may have encouraged the expression of a belief that all in the commonwealth had a duty to labour. Changing attitudes to work, however, can be attributed not only to new material conditions but also to new intellectual and religious ones. Max Weber's argument that the Reformation created a moral and religious climate favourable to the growth of capitalism has been criticised as positing too straightforwardly causal a link between religious and economic change; however, it might more cautiously be ventured that some doctrines of the Reformers may have facilitated the expression of new attitudes towards work and economic life.[33] Luther's denial that there was a separate and superior clerical estate gave a new dignity to manual work: 'A shoemaker, a smith, a farmer, each has his manual occupation and work; and yet, at the same time, all are eligible to act as priests and bishops.' Again, while good works do not save the soul, they have the beneficial effects of preventing idleness and encouraging discipline, as well as being an inevitable condition of living in society.[34] R. H. Tawney stresses Luther's distrust of mercantile work but argues that Calvin and his followers 'seized on the aptitudes cultivated by the life of business and affairs [and] stamped on them a new sanctification'. In other words, the merchants and tradesmen who found Calvinism attractive were able to use certain features of it – personal discipline, rejection of established church teaching – to validate existing aspects of their conduct such as industriousness and, under some circumstances, the taking of usury. Tawney sees this as ultimately giving rise to the Puritan temper, whereby 'mundane toil becomes itself a kind of sacrament'; but it must be emphasised that this derives only partly from a specific 'conception of the nature of God and the destiny of man' and 'partly from the obvious interests of the commercial classes'.[35]

While new attitudes towards work were not inherent in the doctrines of Luther and Calvin, Protestants were able to take from them a framework in which manual and commercial work could be favourably represented. Furthermore, in the context of the English Reformation, Protestant writers used ideas such as that of the vocation as a means of attacking the monastic system. Thomas Becon, for example, provides this gloss on the Parable of the Talents (Matthew 25:14–30):

Worke, labour, toyle, and occupy my money therfore, sayeth our master Christ, till I come. Be not sluggish: be not idle: be not carelesse: Lyue according to your vocation & calling ... And albeit these wordes of Christ be generally spoken to al orders of people, to all states and degrees without excepcion: yet do they specially concerne the spiritual Pastores, ye Ministers of Gods worde.[36]

He goes on to criticise monks and friars for living idly and in no vocation. However, while his recourse to the doctrine of the calling seems to be motivated primarily by anti-monasticism, it has the further effect of giving currency to the notion that all in the commonwealth must work. Similarly, in *A Treatise of the Vocations* (1603), William Perkins uses the idea of the calling to attack monastics, and also vagabonds, on the basis that God 'would not that men ... should be as wandring Rechabites, tied to no certaine place or calling'. However, he stresses much more emphatically than Becon that '[e]uery person of euery degree, state, sexe, or condition without exception, must haue some personal and particular calling to walke in'; even 'the life of a king is to spend his time in the gouerning of his subiects, and that is his calling'. Furthermore, 'to them which imploy their gifts more is giuen, and from them which imploy them not, is taken that which they have: and labour in a calling is as pretious as golde or siluer'.[37] Perkins gives a wider application to a doctrine originally used to attack Catholicism.

Early modern culture also derived ideas from Classical literature that may have affected attitudes towards work. As Lorna Hutson has shown, some Reformers were themselves indebted, in their conceptualisation of domestic relationships, to the scheme elaborated in Xenophon's *Oeconomicus*, and in a work of the same title once wrongly ascribed to Aristotle, whereby a man's effective management of his household both equips him for and is testimony to his abilities as a civil governor.[38] Though Hutson is particularly concerned with the repercussions of this for the literary representation of women, Xenophon's emphasis on the relationship between husbandry and statecraft – as embodied in the figure of Cyrus of Persia, a successful military leader and diligent gardener – may have made it easier for early modern writers to imagine government in laborious terms.[39] Various Latin writers also stressed the duty of the social elite to take part in the business of government, an attitude typified by Cicero's *De officiis*, 'one of the most published secular works of the sixteenth century in England', which was 'securely established in the curricula of the English schools'.[40] Cicero not only recommends that 'those whom Nature has endowed with the capacity for administering public affairs should put aside all hesitation, enter the race for public office, and take a hand in directing the government'; he insists that a young man should be 'trained to toil and endurance of both mind and body [*in labore patientiaque et animi et corporis*], so as to be strong for active duty in military and civic service'.[41]

However, of more far-reaching significance than either of these notions was the conception of society and of government that humanists were able to derive from Classical literature. As Brendan Bradshaw argues, 'the perception which dominated the cultural ethos of late medieval Europe' regarded 'Man as fallen from grace, corrupt in nature, and in need of redemption'; accordingly, 'government was perceived as an instrument of coercion and punishment necessary for the maintenance of justice and order in the domain of corrupt human nature'. By contrast, the humanists took from the Classical tradition 'a perception of human nature as perfectible and disposed to virtue', and, consequently, a view of society not as divinely ordained but as something that could be rationally ordered to humane ends.[42] Perhaps the fullest expression of these new assumptions is in Thomas More's *Utopia*, a depiction of a state where 'affairs are ordered so aptly that virtue has its reward, and yet, with equality of distribution, all men have abundance of all things'. Because society is arranged for the common good rather than the benefit of the few, the burden of labour is equally shared, and no one is allowed to 'sit idle'. However, because everybody works, a working day of six hours is 'not only enough but more than enough for a supply of all that is requisite for either the necessity or the convenience of living'.[43]

DRAMA AND SOCIAL CHANGE

Though the paragraphs above are only a brief account of some factors that may have shaped early modern perceptions of work, they do provide an indication both of the multiplicity of those factors and of the diversity of their effects. Socio-economic developments such as the crisis of productivity and the phenomenon of masterless men and women may have heightened the importance of work in the eyes of the ruling class, while some of those whose livelihood depended on their own work were growing in wealth and influence. At the same time, the way in which these developments were conceptualised was affected by new ways of thinking such as humanism and Protestantism: merchants justified their profits with reference to Calvinist teaching, and Thomas More diagnosed the problems of Henrician England with reference to Classical conceptions of the State. The picture created in the Homily against Idleness of a commonwealth where all labour in their vocations should be seen as embedded within this complex of social and cultural forces. However, it is important to stress that while the Homily may have expressed the official ideology of Elizabethan England, it conflicted with other very different ways of thinking about work. For example, a radical undercurrent that would eventually achieve expression after the start of the Civil War decried the idleness of those who did not labour with their hands, while the medieval assumption that work was the degrading lot of the socially inferior retained currency.

As critics and literary historians often note, any attempt to locate the early modern drama in relation to such developments carries with it significant theoretical and methodological problems. Louis A. Montrose has written that historicist literary scholars are concerned with both 'the historicity of texts and the textuality of history', thereby emphasising, first, that the writing and the reading of texts are culturally determined and, second, that our access to the past is by necessity textually mediated.[44] This makes binaries such as drama and society, text and context, difficult to sustain: not only is the drama indivisible from the society that produced it, but the context of dramatic texts can only be apprehended through yet more text. Harold Veeser makes a similar point to Montrose:

> New Historicism seeks less limiting means to expose the manifold ways culture and society affect each other. The central difficulty with these terms lies in the way they distinguish text and history as foreground and background: criticism bound to such metaphors narrows its concern to the devices by means of which literature reflects or refracts its contexts.[45]

Although this appears to support the practice of reading dramatic texts alongside other material such as *A Treatise of the Vocations* or the Book of Homilies, as the present study does, it also suggests that it may be illegitimate to differentiate between the former (as texts) and the latter (as historical documents). However, critics who have attempted a more theoretically self-aware form of historicism such as that recommended by Montrose and Veeser have themselves been criticised for the eclecticism with which they link canonical and non-canonical texts. One example that has been repeatedly cited is Stephen Greenblatt's *Shakespearean Negotiations*, which parallels Shakespeare's plays with other early modern texts such as Thomas Harriot's description of the first Virginia colony, a book on hermaphrodites and childbirth by the French physician Jacques Duval and an account by Hugh Latimer of his doctrinal correction of a condemned woman. Rather than positing a direct influence of these texts on Shakespeare, Greenblatt writes in more nebulous terms of a 'circulation of social energy', of 'negotiations and exchanges' between the theatre and 'surrounding institutions, authorities, discourses, and practices'.[46] David Perkins complains that here, 'the arbitrary choice of context, inherent in all historical contextualising, becomes obvious and extreme': 'any discourse can be brought into conjunction with any other, so long, that is, as the essayist can construct an interrelation between them'.[47] A similar point is made by Walter Cohen, who observes that 'New historicists are likely to seize upon something out of the way, obscure, even bizarre: dreams, popular or aristocratic festivals, denunciations of witchcraft, sexual treatises ... This strategy is governed methodologically by the assumption that any one aspect of a society is related to any other.'[48] It appears that rejection of the text–context binary for a less hierarchical methodology of reading different discourses alongside one another may be achieved only at the expense of a clear notion of how those discourses relate; a theoretically informed historicism must still ask the basic question, 'how – by what paths, processes, or chain of events – does the context have its impact on the text?'[49]

Although, as we have seen, problems inherent in the notions of 'text' and 'context' may preclude a satisfactory answer to this question, an underlying argument of this book is that one way of relating the early modern drama to the culture around it is through focusing on the institutional structures within which it was made and consumed. Over recent decades, practices such as patronage, censorship, theatrical finance and repertory formation have attracted significant critical attention, and perhaps one reason for this is that they enable commentators to identify specific instances where extra-dramatic forces influenced the making of plays. To give three examples: in *The Queen's Men and their Plays*, Scott McMillin and Sally-Beth MacLean argue that the ideological content of plays in the repertory of the Queen's Men was shaped by the political agenda of the Earl of Leicester and Francis Walsingham, whom they take to have been behind the company's formation.[50] Richard Dutton has explored the role of successive Masters of the Revels in the regulation of the drama, and his discussion of individual cases where their work is visible (as with George Buc's annotation of *The Second Maiden's Tragedy* in 1611) seems to show them striving to make plays performable according to the Privy Council's standards of acceptability.[51] Finally, in *The Repertory of Shakespeare's Company, 1594–1613*, Roslyn Lander Knutson shows how the dramatic output of theatre companies was shaped by the demands of the repertory system, which (in the context of a varied overall offering) encouraged repetition of successful formulae, sequels and spin-offs.[52]

While my own book is informed by these and other accounts of the institutional contexts of the early modern drama, it attempts to highlight two ways in particular in which the material circumstances wherein drama was produced can be seen as having mediated between it and wider debates and anxieties about work in early modern England. The first, which I shall discuss in the next chapter, relates to the position of actors themselves. In Elizabethan London, where playing was carried out with increasing regularity and in purpose-built theatres, the business of acting began to look more and more like other forms of work; however, a criticism frequently made against actors was that theirs was an illegitimate way of earning a living, scarcely different from begging. As a result, actors were directly implicated in some of the controversies over the nature of work that I have discussed over the preceding pages, and the effects of this can, I argue, be discerned in several plays from the 1590s. The second aspect of dramatic production on which I focus is the practice not of playing but of playgoing. As I shall explain in Chapter 4, the fact that playing companies were in the business of providing entertainment to audiences that were often socially diverse meant that they became involved in a current debate over the rights of workers, especially servants and apprentices, to free time; again, several plays, particularly from the years 1599–1601, can be seen as engaging in this controversy. One factor that may have helped make the presence of workers in theatre audiences particularly noteworthy during those years is the revival of companies of child actors at St Paul's and the Blackfriars and the attempts of dramatists writing for those companies to align them with the social elite by presenting their theatres as places where workers were not welcome. In doing so, they exploited long-standing assumptions about the incompatibility of work with high social status; thus, an extra-dramatic discourse relating to work and gentility was brought onto the stage as a result of two acting companies' striving for self-definition.

It would, however, be absurd to argue that the only way in which wider discourses concerning work were mediated into the drama was through its own problematic institutional position: this denies the makers of plays any agenda other than the defence of the practices whereby they made their living. Instead, this book suggests that playwrights made use of such discourses for dramatic purposes such as characterisation and the creation of conflict, as I shall argue of Shakespeare's histories in Chapter 3. I also examine, in Chapter 5, the question of whether the various London playing companies consistently articulated different ideological positions with regard to work, possibly reflecting a 'stratified social scale divided amongst different playhouses'.[53] Finally, I suggest that in specific plays – the two parts of *Henry IV*, *Henry V*, *Hamlet*, *A Woman Killed with Kindness*, *Eastward Ho!* – dramatists appear to engage with and to question the ideological assumptions underpinning notions of work within their culture: the central binary of work and idleness, and its relationship with the gradations of social status that structured early modern drama and society.

CHAPTER 2

'Vpon the weke daies and worke daies at conuenient times': acting as work in Elizabethan England

The sixth edition of Sir Thomas Overbury's character book *The Wife* appeared in 1615, two years after Overbury's death. Amongst other additions, it contains a character of 'An excellent Actor', possibly by John Webster, which appears to be a reply to John Cocke's 'A common Player', printed earlier that year in John Stephens' *Satyrical Essayes Characters and Others*. Cocke's player is 'A daily Counterfeit', a servile crowd-pleaser given to drink and of loose sexual morality. The author of 'An Excellent Actor', however, praises his subject's skill and the moral worth of his profession:

> Whatsoeuer is commendable in the graue Orator, is most exquisitly perfect in him; for by a full and significant action of body, he charmes our attention: sit in a full Theater, and you will thinke you see so many lines drawne from the circumference of so many eares, whiles the *Actor* is the *Center* ... By his action he fortifies morall precepts with example; for what we see him personate, we thinke truely done before vs: a man of deepe thought might apprehend, the Ghosts of our ancient *Heroes* walk't againe, and take him (at seuerall times) for many of them.[1]

Clearly, the two characterists have very different ideas about the value of theatre and about what theatrical entertainers tend to be like as people. It is also notable, however, that the writer who seeks to disparage his subject calls him a *player*, and the one who seeks to praise him, an *actor*. Whereas the word 'player' had been used to mean 'one who acts a character on the stage' for at least a century and a half by 1615, it was relatively novel to use 'actor' in this sense: the first usage recorded in the *OED* comes from Sidney's *A Defence of Poesie*, written around 1580. Sidney uses the word metaphorically, to contrast the creativity of the poet with the dependence upon nature that limits practitioners of other sciences: 'There is no Art delivered unto mankind that hath not the workes of nature for his principall object, without which they could not consist, and on which they so depend, as they become Actors & Plaiers, as it were of what nature will have set forth.'[2] Sidney here seems to be using the words 'actor' and 'player' interchangeably: since they are joined by 'and' rather than 'or', the effect is one of rhetorical amplification rather than a broadening of his field of reference. The author of 'An Excellent Actor', however, seems to have been more alert to the two words' contrasting implications. 'Player' suggests recreation and frivolity; 'actor', however, asserts the value of personation as a form of action, and it is therefore appropriate that this word is chosen when a positive, approving characterisation is to be given.[3]

The fact that these two words, with their rather different overtones, could be used to denote the same activity is testimony to one of the central arguments of this chapter: that the status of acting as a form of work was decidedly uncertain in the early modern period. As I shall suggest elsewhere in this book, this made the stage a symbolically charged arena in which to address the theme of work: the status of its inhabitants as workers or non-workers was itself vexed and problematic. Here, I shall make the case that the practice of acting underwent a reorientation in relation to work during the sixteenth century. The period saw both a decline in amateur playing within the context of civic festivity and the rise of a commercial theatre centred in London; but, paradoxically, as acting became more like other forms of work, it also attracted increasing opposition as an illegitimate way of earning a living. As I shall argue in the latter part of this chapter, in representations of actors on the public stage of the 1590s, theatre professionals made a conscious effort to respond to this charge, portraying actors as skilled and industrious craftsmen.

ACTING AND WORK IN THE SIXTEENTH CENTURY

As historians of the theatre have frequently noted, the status of the actor and the nature of his work changed over the course of the sixteenth century. The thriving commercial theatre that was in evidence in London by 1600 simply had not existed 100 years before; E. K. Chambers wrote in 1923 that by this date acting had begun 'to take its place as a regular profession, in which money might with reasonable safety be invested, to which a man might look for the career of a lifetime, and in which he might venture to bring up his children'. However, the nature of this change no longer seems as straightforward as once it did. Chambers attributed it to direct interventions by the executive in the theatre industry, such as the formation of the Queen's Men in 1583 and the assumption by the Government of 'direct responsibility for the regulation of the stage throughout the London area' in 1597.[4] Muriel C. Bradbrook similarly argued that when in 1572 the right to license acting troupes was restricted to noblemen and justices, the effect was to 'define the actors' status, restrict the number of licensed troupes, and so by a process of concentrating ability to foster the growth of professionalism'.[5] The assumptions underlying the views of Chambers and of Bradbrook, however, are open to question. First, their teleology is dubious. The word 'profession' is invoked by both but, strictly speaking, early modern actors can only be called professionals in the broad sense that distinguishes them from amateurs: they earned money through playing. Acting in the early modern period never became a profession according to Wilfrid R. Prest's definition of professions as 'non-manual, non-commercial occupations sharing some measure of institutional self-regulation and reliance upon bookish skills or training'; though players needed to be literate in order to learn lines, their skills were primarily physical and practical as well as being exercised before a paying public.[6] Nor, for that matter, did actors have a great deal in common with urban tradesmen. While, according to Gerald Eades Bentley, the 'basic hierarchy' of individual acting companies resembled that of the guilds, they lacked 'professional organization and structure':

> they had no central organization of all troupes in the profession, like that of the Lord Mayor and Council, and nothing like the tight organization of the regular guilds such as the Ironmongers or Stationers with their own system of Master and Court and set regulations for all units of the same trade.[7]

David Kathman has recently shown how actors took advantage of the convention that 'freemen were under no obligation to practice the trades of their companies' and that 'a freeman could train his apprentices in his actual profession, whatever that might be, and they could still be legally bound and freed by his livery company'; thus, despite the lack of an actors' guild, actors who were members of livery companies were able to bind as apprentices boys whom they then trained for the stage.[8] Nevertheless, such boys were, strictly speaking, acting apprentices rather than apprentice actors; and it remains the case that without an actors' guild there was no body to formalise the status of London actors, to say who could and could not be an actor, to enforce a standard for theatrical production, to prescribe uniform conditions of apprenticeship, and so on. Instead, actors derived their social position from their attachment, however much a 'legal fiction', to the retinue of a member of the nobility.[9] This seems effectively to have been the case even before it was explicitly made a prerequisite for legitimate playing in 1572: with one exception, all the acting companies recorded as visiting Norwich between 1540 and 1572 are referred to as servants of nobles or of members of the royal family, suggesting that the authorities there considered other actors to be vagrant according to existing laws.[10] Indeed, the fact that the 1572 Act partly served to codify an existing state of affairs points to a second assumption shared by Chambers and Bradbrook: that it was executive intervention in the form of legislation directed at actors that brought about the changes they perceive. The research of David M. Bevington, Glynne Wickham and others, however, has shown how the evolution of the early modern theatre was more organic than this.[11] Professional actors, for example, were not a new phenomenon in Tudor England. Bevington points out that Henry VI was entertained by 'interluders' in 1427, and his reading of *Mankind* (1465–70) demonstrates that professional actors also toured away from court.[12] Over the following pages, I want to argue that the change in the status of actors that took place over the course of the sixteenth century can be understood, not simply as a professionalisation but rather as a gradual reorientation in relation to the idea of work brought about by wider social, economic and religious trends.

Arguably, the most important factor in this reorientation was the decline in civic drama (mystery plays in particular) and the growth in the number of touring companies. By its nature, the mystery play worked in harmony with the rhythms of civic life. Taking place on a religious festival, such as Corpus Christi, it did not disrupt economic production; based on the Scriptures, it amplified religious teaching. It was acted by members of the craft guilds and, therefore, did not inflict a class of professional players on the social structure. In different ways, Anne Barton (writing as Anne Righter) and Michael D. Bristol argue that this form of theatre should not, or not simply, be seen as recreational. Barton sees it as an extension of religious ritual, a ceremony whose audience were participants rather than spectators: 'While the performance lasted, audience and actors shared the same ritual world, a world more real than the one which existed outside its frame.'[13] Bristol argues that structurally it occupied the position of carnival in medieval society: 'Because of its capacity to create and sustain a briefly intensified social life, the theater is festive and political as well as literary – a privileged site for the celebration and critique of the needs and concerns of the *polis*.'[14] The decline of this theatre took place at different points of the sixteenth century in different cities – and for different reasons. In Coventry, for example, the demise of the Corpus Christi cycle was connected to a more general drop in that city's prosperity: in 1539, Mayor Coton complained to Henry's chief minister Thomas Cromwell that 'at Corpus chr*ist*i tide / the poore Co*m*ene*rs* be at suche charges w*ith* ther playes & pagyont*es* / that thei fare the worse all the yeire after'.[15] However, it seems also to be the case that, as Harold C. Gardiner and Glynne Wickham have separately argued, the mystery plays were 'deliberately extirpated' as papist relics under Henry, Edward and Elizabeth.[16] In her recent survey of civic playing in York, for example, Alexandra F. Johnston shows Matthew Hutton and Edmund Grindal, the Dean and Archbishop of York respectively, to have been instrumental in its suppression between 1568 and 1579, concluding, 'The struggle had clearly been a doctrinal one.'[17] In 1572 and 1575, mayors of Chester were summoned before the Privy Council to explain why they let the mystery cycle be performed, in the latter instance against the express wishes of Grindal and the President of the North.[18] Popular feeling in Chester may also have militated against the plays: the Mayors List records that in 1571 they were played despite the fact that 'manye of the Cittie were sore against the setting forthe therof', though it does not record whether their scruples were religious or financial.[19]

The decline of civic drama coincided with an increase in the use of drama for a variety of purposes by monarchs and the nobility. Suzanne R. Westfall shows that as well as retaining players and dramatists for their private entertainment, Tudor nobles encouraged them to tour, both to defray the cost of keeping them fed and clothed and to 'ensure that [their own] political, economic, and artistic prominence was visibly represented throughout the land'. The content of the plays was itself of political import:

> During the consolidation of Tudor power, when the role and even the definition of nobility were undergoing cataclysmic revision, the interludes provided effective opportunities for the noble patron to express his philosophical or political views, in an attempt to reinforce his particular perception of the social order.

With the advent of the Reformation, powerful Protestants used the drama to discredit the Pope and to assert Henry's religious authority. In the 1530s, for example, John Bale wrote plays with the titles *Super vtroque regis coniugio*, *De sectis papisticis*, *De traditionibus papistorum*, *Contra corruptores verbi dei*, and *De traditione Thomae Becketi* for his patron John de Vere, Earl of Oxford, and the extant anti-Catholic plays *Three Laws* and *King Johan* for Thomas Cromwell.[20] John Foxe later wrote that players, printers and preachers had been the 'triple Bulwark against the triple crown of the Pope, to bring him down'.[21] It is difficult to say how far plays like Bale's encroached upon the popular stage, because records of nobly sponsored companies playing at civic (as opposed to household) venues tend to specify only the companies' patrons rather than the drama performed. Furthermore, we cannot be sure from the records when such companies started to become a familiar presence in the English towns; as Westfall points out, 'the absence of payment does not automatically connote the absence of players, for in times of financial hardship, players may have depended upon the townspeople's donations rather than on municipal expenditure for their reward'.[22] However, in general terms, a growing penetration of the towns by nobly or royally sponsored acting companies, with or without designs of religious reform, can be clearly identified. In Norwich, for example, the Chamberlains' Accounts record payments to one named group of players in 1539–40, to two in 1544–5, to three in 1556–7 and to five in 1560–1, although the increase is not uninterrupted.[23] In Coventry, there is a similarly uneven rise in the number of annual payments to named companies from four in 1574, when the Wardens' Accounts begin, to six in 1577 and eight in 1583 (the figures may be higher depending on whether references to a nobleman's 'gesters' or 'men' indicate playing companies).[24] As I have already argued, a decline in the civic drama seems to have coincided with this trend.

The Reformation also modified the relation between acting and civic life in less direct ways. The dissolution of the monasteries deprived the poor of a vital network of support; in combination with rent increases and land enclosures, this produced 'rising numbers of able-bodied poor', so-called 'masterless men' perceived by governments as a threat to order and stability.[25] How many of this swollen body of the unemployed went on to become actors is unknown. However, it is the case that from 1572 onwards, vagrancy legislation begins for the first time to refer explicitly to the unlicensed actor as vagrant.[26] The fact, noted earlier, that the authorities in Norwich allowed only royally and nobly patronised companies to play there shows that actors were already subject to the vagrancy laws. Nevertheless, the classification of 'Common Players in Enterludes, & Minstrels, not belonging to any Baron of this Realm or towards any other honourable Personage of greater Degree' as 'Rogues, Vagabonds and Sturdy Beggars' in the 1572 Act for the Punishment of Vagabonds and for the Relief of the Poor and Impotent (14 Eliz. I c. 5) implies an increasing perception of actors as part of the problem of masterlessness.[27] Nor was it necessarily an easy matter to tell legitimate actors apart from illegitimate ones. The Chamberlain's Accounts for Norwich in 1590 record a payment of ten shillings to 'the lorde shandos players' and then, immediately after, a further payment of twenty shillings 'in rewarde to a nother Company of his men that cam w*i*th lycens presently after saying y*a*t thos that Cam before were counterfet*es* & not the L*ord* Shandos men'.[28] Even if actors were in effect subject to vagrancy law before 1572, the Act made explicit the narrowness of the line separating legitimate actors from illegitimate masterless men – a narrowness confirmed by the experience of the Norwich authorities.

With the decline of the mystery plays and the expansion of the touring companies, a form of theatre that was an expression of civic life and took place in harmony with civic rhythms was replaced by one that came from outside and may have had propagandistic designs. The former was a holiday, amateur drama which did not provide its performers with a livelihood; the latter was performed on days that may not have been religious festivals, by individuals who may not have had another source of income. In some instances, nobly sponsored drama seems actively to have disrupted civic life: freemen of Norwich were banned in 1588–9 from attending plays because they were acted on the Sabbath, had given rise to brawls and murder and were an allurement to vice.[29] Even when they passed off without violence, however, the visits of playing companies may have given rise to psychological disturbance. Peter Greenfield writes,

> The players' visit to a town provided a temporary escape from the unchanging regimen of work, and of familial and civic duties, imposed by the social order. More dangerous was that the players themselves represented a life of constant festival, of freedom from the authority of master, guild, and city, of freedom to determine one's own time, movements, and actions.[30]

In the provincial towns, drama's status seems to have changed: playing became less of a local ritual, more of a foreign entertainment.

While the relationship between players and polis was just as fraught in the City of London as in the provinces, the situation was crucially different in that, as Andrew Gurr puts it, 'Only London was large enough in population to make it advantageous for the companies to stay any length of time'.[31] Whereas the level of demand for plays in provincial cities permitted only a few performances before a company would have to move on, London's vastly larger size permitted a longer residency. That this was the case by, at the latest, the 1570s is evident from the building of a permanent stage at the Theatre in Shoreditch in 1576.[32] Such a permanent presence gives rise to a very different relationship with civic and religious institutions to that enjoyed by a company that arrives, performs and departs. Whereas the arrival of a touring company constitutes a brief irruption of play into a community's working life, a group of actors with a permanent presence does not so much disrupt working life as compete with it. This repetition of performance itself modifies the status of play, making it less of a festival activity and more like the daily grind of tradesmen: 'If all the year were playing holidays, / To sport would be as tedious as to work' (*1 Henry IV*, I. 2. 204–5). In the following two sections, I will suggest that the growing regularity of playing in London affected the way actors and acting were represented by the theatre's professed opponents, both in printed works and, first, in the ongoing dialogue over control of the drama between the London authorities and the Privy Council.

ACTING AND IDLENESS, I: THE CITY AUTHORITIES

Any attempt to analyse the documents that passed between the Mayor and Corporation of London and the Privy Council in the latter half of the sixteenth century concerning the regulation of the theatre must acknowledge the way recent historians have moved away from, or at least radically reevaluated, E. K. Chambers' assumptions regarding the respective attitudes to the drama of those two bodies:

> The history of play-licensing in London ... really turns upon an attempt of the Corporation, goaded by the preachers, to convert their power of regulating plays into a power of suppressing plays, as the ultimate result of which even the power of regulation was lost to them, and the central government, acting through the Privy Council and the system of patents, with the Master of the Revels as a licenser, took the supervision of the stage into its own hands.[33]

I shall make reference later on to the question of the extent and motives of the Privy Council's support for the drama. As for the attitude of the Corporation, which is my present concern, Chambers' belief that it was driven by religious fervour into attempting to suppress playing altogether has been largely discredited. For one thing, as Richard Dutton has noted, 'the authorities were not simply kill-joys; they had real public order concerns, when as many as 3000 people might attend a single performance, and there was no regular police force to supervise them'. Their argument that theatres spread plague was heeded by the Privy Council at times when contagion was particularly rife, indicating that it was seen as more than a mere pretext.[34] Furthermore, it is not clear that the City authorities uniformly desired the total suppression of plays. Charles Whitney has suggested that attitudes towards the theatre varied with each Lord Mayor, identifying Nicholas Woodrofe (1580), Thomas Blanke (1583), and John Spencer (1594) as particularly vehement opponents of the stage.[35] William Ingram has also argued that what the Corporation wanted was not an end to playing but control over performances and, more particularly, over the revenue that could be accrued from fees and fines; this view informs his reading of an Act made by the Common Council on 6 December 1574 obliging innkeepers and other owners of playing spaces to seek the Council's approval, to present it with play texts for perusal, to post bonds that they would keep good order with the Chamberlain of London and to contribute to poor rates. Ingram sees the Act as more than simply repressive:

> One of the traditional uses of prohibitions has been to provide a context for the profitable granting of exemptions and for the equally profitable issuing of licenses authorizing others to grant exemptions. Given what else we know of City governance, this is a plausible, and not an unnecessarily cynical, construction to place on the act, especially in light of the evidence that companies of players did continue to play in the City after 1574 and that playing in innyards seems, if anything, to have increased after that date.[36]

It seems that we need to look beneath the surface of the City's professed outrage at plays: as Scott McMillin and Sally-Beth MacLean say of the dialogue between Corporation and Privy Council, 'Neither party spoke in directly political terms, and for that reason – politics being obviously the real concern of both – the moral shading of the city and the aesthetic shading of the privy council are to be taken as codes subject to further examination.'[37]

Whatever the motives behind the complaints the Corporation made against plays, however, those complaints seem to have changed in nature during the last decades of the sixteenth century, in a way that may reflect the changing relationship between acting and work that I posit in this chapter. To illustrate this, I want to begin by examining the 1574 Act of Common Council mentioned above. The preamble of the Act makes numerous accusations against plays:

> hearetofore sondrye greate disorders and Inconvenyences have benne found to ensewe to this Cittie by the inordynate hauntyinge of greate multitudes of people speciallye youthe, to playes, enterludes, and shewes namelye occasyon of ffrayes

and quarrelles, eavell practizes of incontinencye In greate Innes, ... inveglynge and alleurynge of maides ... to previe and vnmete Contractes, the publishinge of vnchaste vncomelye and vnshamefaste speeches and doynges, w*i*thdrawinge of the Quenes Ma*ie*sties Subiectes from dyvyne se*r*vice on Sonndaies and hollydayes, At w*hi*ch Tymes suche playes weare Chefelye vsed vnthriftye waste of the moneye of the poore and fond p*er*sons sondrye robberies by pyckinge and Cuttinge of purses vtteringe of popular busye and sedycious matters, and manie other Corruptions of youthe and other enormyties, besydes that allso soundrye slaughters and mayheminges of the Quenes Subiectes have happened by ruines of Skaffoldes fframes and Stagies, and by engynes weapons and powder vsed in plaies.[38]

The preamble goes on to mention the danger of such assemblies in times of plague. As Ingram says, some of these accusations, namely that plays corrupted the young and enticed people away from church in times of divine service, are rather formulaic: 'Thirty years earlier the Common Council had prefaced an earlier proclamation against playing with essentially the same arguments.'[39] The passage also mentions the robbery and sedition that take place when plays are performed, the unchaste speeches that are uttered, the encouragement to the poor to waste their money and the danger from plague and collapsing scenery, most of which arguments the Corporation would repeat in its ongoing dialogue with the Privy Council. By 1580, however, they had been joined by a new complaint against the stage that is absent from earlier documents. In a letter to Lord Burghley of 17 June, Lord Mayor Nicholas Woodrofe complained that plays drew people, not just from the service of God, but from 'honest exersises'.[40] By this, he seems to intend the definition given in the *OED* under 'exercise', *sb.*, 2, 'Habitual occupation or employment; customary practice': in other words, work. The argument that time spent at plays is time lost from work reappears in an Act of the Court of Aldermen dating from between autumn 1582 and 1587 which banned playing in the City and called on their lordships to do so in the suburbs, criticising plays for (amongst other things) 'great wasting both of the time and thrift of many poore people'; as well as 'earnings', 'thrift' may here denote '[m]eans of thriving; industry; labour; profitable occupation' (*OED* 'thrift', *sb.*, 1b).[41] More explicitly, in February 1592 the Lord Mayor complained to Archbishop of Canterbury John Whitgift that because of plays 'the prentizes & seruants' were 'w*i*thdrawen from their woorks' and asked him to intercede with the Master of the Revels to have them banned in London. Petitioning Lord Burghley in November 1594 not to let the Swan be built, he complained that o*u*r apprentices and servants ar by this means corrupted & induced hear by to defraud their Maisters to maintein their vain & prodigall expenses occasioned by such evill and riotous companie whearinto they fall by these kynd of meetings to the great hinderance of the trades & traders inhabiting this Citie.

In July 1597, the Lord Mayor complained to the Privy Council that plays

maintaine idlenes in such persons as haue no vocation & draw apprentic*es* and other seruant*es* from theire ordinary workes and all sort*es* of people from the resort vnto sermons and other Christian exercies to the great hinderance of traides and p*ro*phanation of religion established by her highnes within this Realm.[42]

The new theme present in all of these documents is the notion that plays are bad for productivity, enticing prentices and servants away from their work to the detriment of trade and traders. While the implication that for such people to be outside the supervision of their masters is a risk to public order echoes the concerns of 1574, the allusion to 'hinderance of traides', the idea that the theatre is bad for business, is a new one. What had happened since 1574 to make such accusations valid currency?

I would suggest that the key development was the growing regularity of theatrical performance facilitated by the building of three permanent theatres outside the City around the year 1576: the Theatre, the Curtain and the playhouse at Newington Butts. Admittedly, plays were already being staged fairly frequently by 1564, when Bishop Grindal referred to players ('an idle sorte off people, w*hi*ch have ben infamouse in all goode co*m*mon-weales') setting up 'bylles' – presumably of advertisement – 'daylye, butt speciallye on holydayes'.[43] However, the building of the new theatres was an innovation of both practical and symbolic importance: as Margreta de Grazia writes, hereafter, 'the theater became free to occupy its own time and space'.[44] The freedom to play was no longer subject to the owner of a venue that had been built for another purpose, such as an inn, deciding to turn an afternoon over to drama: players could perform as often as it was profitable to do so, within the limits established by the Privy Council. Ironically, this state of affairs seems to have been hastened by the Corporation's own actions. Ingram, like Glynne Wickham, carefully avoids making an overly schematic link between the 1574 Act of Common Council and the building of three theatres within the suburbs over the next three years; it should also be pointed out that the apparently short-lived Red Lion had already been built by James Burbage and John Brayne in Whitechapel in 1567 (see Note 32). However, given the bureaucratic and financial hoops the Act required owners of playing spaces to jump through, 'it seems a reasonable guess that inkeepers and others addressed by the act, anticipating its enforcement and the penalties for noncompliance, would have had second thoughts about offering their premises to players in light of the sudden escalation of costs and of bureaucratic hassle as well'.[45] In turn, this may have sharpened any existing desire among theatrical entrepreneurs such as Burbage to have access to purpose-built venues outside the Lord Mayor's jurisdiction. A second action of the Corporation that apparently encouraged weekday playing was the decision to complain to Lord Burghley in the wake of the Paris Garden accident of January 1582–3, 'where by ruyn of all the scaffoldes ... a greate nombre of people [were] some presentlie slayne, and some maymed and greavouslie hurte'. Lord Mayor Thomas Blanke presented the incident as God's judgement 'for suche abuse of the sabboth daie', and Burghley accordingly agreed to ban Sunday playing, although the persistence of similar bans after this date suggests that the original measure was not successfully enforced.[46] The Corporation's attempt to restrict playing appears to have backfired: in December 1583, Francis Walsingham corrected the Lord Mayor's assumption that players' license to perform extended 'onely to holy daies and not to other weke daies', informing him they were licensed to play 'vpon the weke daies and worke daies at conuenient times'.[47] The theatre's disruption of the working week thus received the approval of the Privy Council – whose decision in March 1583 to extend its protection (and control) of London playing with the formation of the Queen's Men has been interpreted as a further reaction to the Paris Garden controversy.[48]

The accusation of the City authorities that plays distracted Londoners from their work can thus be seen as deriving, ironically enough, from the fact that playing was becoming more like other forms of labour in London: repetitive, geographically fixed, carried out on weekdays. It was also becoming increasingly integrated within the London economy, in a number of respects. As I noted earlier, in 1574 the Common Council aimed to use money gained from the licensing of playing spaces to pay for poor relief; in 1600, the Privy Council's permission for the building of the Fortune theatre was given only after the inhabitants of Finsbury had sent them a letter testifying that not only was the proposed site near Finsbury Fields, and so no great disturbance but also, 'the erectors of the said house are contented to give a very liberal portion of money weekly towards the relief of our poor'.[49] The building of theatres also caused money to flow between the entertainment industry and the rest of the City in less direct ways. As Kathleen E. McLuskie and Felicity Dunworth point out, it provided work for 'a range of related trades' such as carpenters and painters.[50] The Privy Council's decision to let the Rose theatre be reopened in about 1592 came after Lord Strange's Men had sent them a petition citing their own difficulty in meeting overheads and the fact that 'the vse of *our* plaiehowse on the Banckside, by reason of the passage to and frome the same by water, is a greate releif to the poore watermen theare'. They enclosed a letter from the watermen in support of this.[51] Conversely, it was the wealth of London's merchants and tradesmen that enabled the theatres to be built in the first place. John Brayne, who financed the Red Lion and the Theatre, was 'a successful grocer with a house and business in Bucklersbury', while Philip Henslowe, though nominally a dyer, 'apparently engaged in a variety of business investments including starch making, pawnbroking, and property investment' before investing in the Rose.[52] Given these relationships and parallels between playing and other forms of economic activity in London, it is a further irony that from the 1580s the Lord Mayor and Corporation seem to have become increasingly insistent that acting was not a legitimate way to earn a living. In April 1580, Woodrofe wrote to the Lord Chancellor Thomas Bromley that, 'the players of playes which are vsed at the Theatre and other such places and tumblers and such like, are a very sup*er*fluous sort of men, and of suche facultie as the lawes haue disalowed'.[53] Around 1584, when the Corporation answered a petition sent from players to the Privy Council asking to be allowed to perform in City inns, it refuted the argument that players depended on performance for their livelihood as follows:

> It hath not ben vsed nor thought meete heretofore that players haue or shold make their lyuing on the art of playeng. but men for their lyuings vsing other honest and lawfull artes, or reteyned in honest seruices, haue by companies learned some enterludes for some encreasce to their profit by other mens pleasures in vacant time of recreation.[54]

As I shall argue in the next section of this chapter, it is striking, and perhaps not coincidental, that during the same period of the early 1580s, printed attacks on the theatre began to make use of the same argument: that it was unmeet that players should make their living through the art of playing.

ACTING AND IDLENESS, II: ANTI-THEATRICAL LITERATURE

While Chambers saw the Corporation as 'goaded by the preachers' into the suppression of plays, other critics have conversely argued that after

1576, the Lord Mayor and Corporation encouraged hack-writers and churchmen to continue in print and pulpit their campaign against the theatres. Muriel C. Bradbrook contends that, 'the City Fathers appealed to their clerical mercenaries' to attack plays; Andrew Gurr suggests a little more cautiously that on occasion, 'particularly in the years after the first theaters were established, 1576–84, the Lord Mayor may have financed pamphleteers like the former playwright Stephen Gosson to attack the irreligious iniquities of playgoing'.[55] Certainly, the fact that the first verso of Anglo-Phile Eutheo's *A Second and Third Blast of Retrait from Plaies and Theaters* (1580) prominently displays the arms of the Corporation of London suggests that at least one anti-theatricalist received encouragement from the City authorities.[56] Other critics have discerned broader and more complex motivations for early modern writings against the theatre, such as anxieties over gender identity or social mobility or even an 'antitheatrical prejudice' that transcends specific historical moments.[57] Whether preaching, patronage or prejudice is assumed to lie behind anti-theatrical writing, however, it must be emphasised that for early examples of it at least, 'antitheatrical' is something of a misnomer: several frequently cited texts from the years immediately following 1576 do not focus primarily upon the theatre, and their criticisms of it should be seen in the context of their wider concerns.

It is evident from the title of John Northbrooke's *A Treatise Wherein Dicing, Dauncing, Vaine Playes or Enterluds with Other Idle Pastimes &c. Commonly Vsed on the Sabboth Day, Are Reproued by the Authoritie of the Word of God and Auntient Writers*, first published in 1577, that his field of interest extends beyond stage plays alone. Broadly speaking, his argument concerns itself with the proper use of time. The main text begins with Age asking Youth why he has not attended church; it transpires that Youth spent the Sabbath asleep after gambling through Saturday night. Age insists that all time, not merely the Sabbath, should be spent in the service of God and concludes from the parable of the vineyard in Matthew 20, and the parables of the talents in Matthew 25 and Luke 19, 'that wee oughte to waste and spende no time, nay, no houre in ydlenesse, but in some good exercise. &c. as it maye onelye redounde to the glorie of the immortall name of God, and profite of our neyghboures'. Naturally, this creates a dualism between time used properly and time used improperly. Examples of the misuse of time are the excessive enjoyment of things we need in moderation, such as food, sleep and recreation. The last of these is permissible in so far as after it one may 'more chearefully returne to his ordinarie labour and vocation'. Excessive recreation, however, constitutes idleness:

> Idlenesse is a wicked will giuen to rest and slouthfulnesse, from all right, necessarie, godly, and profitable workes. &c. Also ydlenesse is not onely of the body or mynde to cease from labour, but especially an omission or letting passe negligentlye all honest exercises: for no day ought to be passed ouer without some good profitable exercises, to the prayse of Gods glorious name, to our brethrens profite, & to our selues commoditie and learning.

Idleness, too, leads on to other sins. But Northbrooke, above all, insists that it is an evil in itself, a failure to use time for its allotted purpose. When he comes to criticise plays, he takes this argument a stage further. Playgoing is one of the many activities Northbrooke attacks as a waste of time that should be put to better use; similarly, it is a prodigal use of money that should be given to the poor or 'to the mariage of poore Maydens, high wayes, or poore schollers'. As well as being idle, however, the theatre is actively corrupt: the buildings are no better than brothels, and the gestures of the players are lewd and filthy.[58]

As with Northbrooke's work, the full title of Stephen Gosson's *The Schoole of Abuse* (1579) indicates the breadth of his concerns: it contains 'a plesaunt inuectiue against Poets, Pipers, Plaiers, Iesters, and such like Caterpillers of a Commonwelth'. Whereas Northbrooke deals with the proper use of time, however, Gosson is concerned with art. His anti-theatricalism is part of a wider questioning of the value of poetry, which 'dwelleth longest in those pointes, that profite least'. Like Northbrooke's theatre, poetry for Gosson is not only idle but also actively corrupt; no wonder Plato banished poets, those 'effeminate writers, vnprofitable members, and vtter enimies to vertue' from his Republic. Poetry once had a noble function: 'too haue the notable exploytes of woorthy Captaines, the holesome councels of good fathers, and vertuous liues of predecessors set downe in numbers' – this both distracted its feasting listeners from their drinking and filled them with the desire for emulation. However, it is now abused, serving only hedonistic purposes and thereby encouraging wanton behaviour; its allurement 'drawes the mind from vertue, and confoundeth wit'. As with Northbrooke, specific criticisms are made against the stage. Its fictions are spectacular and, therefore, all the more alluring; theatres allow the sexes to mingle and prostitutes to ply their trade; players by over-dressing defy sumptuary law. Gosson's central criticism of plays, however, is one to which poetry is also subject: they are idle, and they corrupt by seducing the reason with vanities.[59] As with Northbrooke, an attack on the theatre has a wider context. This fact is confirmed by the scope of Thomas Lodge's *A Reply to Stephen Gosson's Schoole of Abuse* (1579–80), which, like Sidney's contemporaneous *A Defence of Poesie*, devotes most space to answering the general criticism of poetic fiction per se rather than that of the theatre in particular, which takes up only about a quarter of its pages.[60]

In their different ways, the tracts of Northbrooke and Gosson can both be seen as illustrating the cultural trend towards utilitarianism identified by Russell Fraser in *The War Against Poetry*, whereby artistic fictions are condemned for their 'lack of utility'.[61] Theatregoing is condemned as a waste of time, stage plays as an abuse of art. Although Philip Stubbes's *The Anatomie of Abuses* (1583) is a third tract in which anti-theatricalism is not the main thread but rather only one element of a more wide-ranging argument, it differs from its fellows in this respect. Stubbes reprehends a vast range of contemporary wrongdoing, his representative interlocutor in the tract's dialogue convinced by the overwhelming prevalence of all types of sin that 'the fearfull daie of the Lord cannot be farre of'.[62] Stage plays are only one of a huge number of abuses against which, in the light of impending apocalypse, Stubbes launches his invective, including excess in apparel (upon which he treats at great length), whoredom, gluttony, drunkenness, covetousness, usury and swearing.

By the time of Stubbes's treatise, however, the nature and status of literary attacks upon the theatre were changing. Works had begun to appear which did indeed take the stage as the principal object of their criticism: the first of these seems to have been Anglo-Phile Eutheo's *A Second and Third Blast of Retrait from Plaies and Theaters*, of 1580. In some respects, Eutheo can be credited with inventing anti-theatrical literature as a genre. Although, as we have seen, *The Schoole of Abuse* is not primarily concerned with the stage, Eutheo enlists it as the 'first blast'; his own work provides two more such blasts, in the form of a translation of an anti-theatrical section of Salvianus's *De gubernatione Dei*, followed by a 'third blast', apparently by Eutheo himself. Some of his arguments against the theatre recall Northbrooke and Gosson: plays are 'publike enimies to virtue, & religion; allurements vnto sinne; corrupters of good manners; the cause of securitie and carelesnes; meere brothel houses of Bauderie; and bring both the Gospel into slander; the Sabboth into contempt; mens soules into danger; and finalie the whole Commonweale into disorder'. He also shares their tendency to categorise as idle time not spent in the service of God: 'I would to God you would bestowe the time you consume in those vanities in seeking after virtue, and glorie'. More than either Gosson's or Northbrooke's, however, Eutheo's tract is informed by economic arguments against the theatre on the grounds of idleness. He criticises noblemen for retaining players as their servants:

since the reteining of these Caterpillers, the credite of Noble men hath decaied, & they are thought to be couetous by permitting their seruants, which cannot liue of the*m*selues, and whome for neerenes they wil not maintaine, to liue at the deuotion or almes of other men.

By such infamous persons much time is lost; and manie daies of honest trauel are turned into vaine exercises. Wherein is learned nothing but abuse; poore men liuing on their handie labor, are by them trained vnto vnthriftines; scholers by their gaudes are allured from their studies.

It is not entirely clear whether the poor men and scholars referred to in the final sentence are understood to be led into idleness by attending plays or by acting and writing them, but the essential point is plain: actors both follow an idle means of living that is no more than beggary and encourage others away from their proper work with their vain shows. More than in Gosson or Northbrooke, the actors themselves come in for criticism: 'are they not commonlie such kind of men in their conuersation, as they are in profession? Are they not as variable in hart, as they are in their partes?'. Eutheo emphasises the idleness as well as the scurrillity of their occupation, lamenting at the spectacle of 'yong boies, inclining of themselues vnto wickednes, trained vp in filthie speeches, vnnatural and vnseemelie gestures, to be brought vp by these Schoole-masters in bawdrie, and in idlenes'. Notwithstanding the players' plea of the antiquity of their profession,

they are of the most part of men either of auctoritie, or learning held for vagabondes, & infamous persons; they maie aptlie be likened vnto droanes, which wil not labor to bring in, but liue of the labors of the paineful gatherers. They are therefor to be thrust out of the Bee-hiue of a Christian Common-weale.

This vnhonest trade of gaine, hath driuen manie from their occupations, in hope of easier thrift. What success they haue had, some of them haue reported, finding the Prouerbe true, that *Il gotten goodes are il spent.*[63]

The argument that men of authority or learning hold players to be vagabonds and infamous persons recalls Woodrofe's letter, also written in 1580, calling them 'a very superfluous sort of men, and of suche facultie as the lawes haue disalowed'; and the fact that the Lord Mayor and Corporation began to use this argument in the year that *A Second and Third Blast* was published may reflect the relationship implied by the appearance of the arms of the Corporation on the tract's first verso page.

Two works from the 1580s, Stephen Gosson's *Playes Confuted in Fiue Actions* and William Rankins' *A Mirrovr of Monsters*, demonstrate similar tendencies to Eutheo's. The first of these, as its title suggests, concentrates upon plays in particular rather than poetry in general; it is also more extreme than is *The Schoole of Abuse*, advocating (as Arthur F. Kinney puts it) 'not the amendment and regulation but the abolition of plays'.[64] In addition, it demonstrates a greater concern with the actor in particular as well as with the theatre. The player's 'idle occupation' is branded as God's enemy; its practitioners should be expelled from the commonwealth. Like Eutheo, Gosson attacks the conduct of players: though they insist that their productions can have a morally beneficial effect, 'the dayly experie*n*ce of their behauiour, sheweth, that they reape no profit by the discipline them selues'. They do not earn their livelihood by legitimate means, being either 'men of occupations, which they haue forsaken to lyue by playing, or common minstrels, or trayned vp from theire childehoode to this abhominable exercise & haue now no other way to gete theire liuinge'. Gosson hopes accordingly that 'such as haue lefte theire occupations, eyther be turned to the same againe, or cut of from the body as putrefied me*m*bers for infecting the rest'.[65] Rankins similarly criticises players, calling them 'consuming caterpillars', 'serpents', 'sent from their great captaine Sathan ... to deceiue the world'. He portrays the Theatre in Shoreditch as the venue for a marriage between Pride and Lust, attended by more abstract nouns which he believes to be applicable to players: Flattery, Ingratitude, Dissention, Blasphemy, and (the 'cheefe masker') Idleness. The last of these is 'the roote of mischiefe, and originall of vices'; players 'doo not onelie exercise themselues in all kind of Idlenesse, but minister occasion to manie to incurre the like'.[66]

Other than Stubbes's *Anatomie*, which is something of a throwback, works of the 1580s that criticise the theatre tend to differ from those of the previous decade in several important respects. They are concerned solely with the theatre, rather than with wider issues of which the stage is only one aspect. Their focus has widened, or shifted altogether, from playgoing to play-acting. Finally, they employ economic arguments against the stage, representing actors as unproductive drones who entice workers from their labours. One might expect actors to have used the stage to defend themselves from these accusations; however, while the actor and dramatist Thomas Heywood wrote *An Apology for Actors*, published in 1612, I have found only one instance where such a defence was explicitly articulated in the theatre, a (now-lost) 'playe of playes' which Gosson refers to as having attempted to answer the criticisms he made in *The Schoole of Abuse*.[67] Instead, I would suggest that it is in onstage representations of actors in the 1590s – though they are usually peripheral to the main action of the plays in which they appear – that we find reactions to the criticisms of Gosson, Northbrooke and their fellows. Initially, the representations are negative, depicting a histrionic incompetence against which the 'real' actors can define themselves. Over the course of the decade, however, the relationship between the fictional and actual actors becomes more complex, and, increasing, play is made on the ideological framework which enables the entertainment purveyed by the actors to be designated the product of work.

ACTING AS WORK IN THE 1590S

I want to begin by looking at three plays that, in their different ways, assert the status of acting as work by means of contrast. The first of these is *The Taming of a Shrew* (*c.* 1588–93), which, like Shakespeare's *The Taming of the Shrew*, uses the framing device of a trick played on a drunkard whereby he is persuaded that he is a lord recovering from illness. To accomplish the deception, the actual Lord uses players in his service (they are explicitly referred to as 'your plaiers' in line 61) who have felicitously arrived, presumably from touring. The players are represented as buffoons, mistaking their words:

SANDER Marrie my lord you maie haue a Tragicall
Or a comoditie, or what you will.
THE OTHER A Comedie thou shouldst say, souns thout shame vs all. (70–4)

Their Lord does not bother to explain the nature of the deception he intends to perpetrate, merely telling the players that they must not be distracted by their auditor, who is 'something foolish'. His simplification is happily accepted:

SANDER Oh braue, sirha Tom, we must play before
A foolish Lord, come lets go make vs ready,
Go get a dishclout to make cleane your shooes,
And Ile speake for the properties, My Lord, we must
Haue a shoulder of mutton for a propertie,
And a little vinegre to make our Diuell rore. (95–100)[68]

The dirty shoes remind us of the actors' lowly status; the shoulder of mutton may be a subterfuge to add to their presumably meagre diet, as well as being an additional homely detail. Finally, the roaring devil is a medieval hangover that makes the players' repertoire sound dated. However, the play seen by Sly and by us subverts the expectations set up in the Induction, being a modern, romantic comedy set in Athens (although the shoulder of mutton does make an appearance). There is nothing in the text to suggest that it should be badly acted. A gap is thus created between the actors performing the 'real' *Taming of a Shrew* and those who are imagined as performing it within the fiction set up by the Induction. The modernity, competence and professionalism of the real-life actors are magnified by means of contrast with the fictional ones.

This claim of greater aptitude must have had some validity. An urban environment where several companies were competing for the attentions of a finite audience and where playing was increasingly becoming a daily event almost certainly fostered a superior technique to that of earlier actors. It would also have necessitated hard work. Peter Thomson concludes from some instances where the Henslowe papers reveal both the date when the manuscript of a play was delivered and the date when its run of performances began that actors in the 1590s had to pack a great deal of rehearsal into a short time; a total of twenty-four hours might be all the time available to rehearse an entire play.[69] Tiffany Stern has noted the 'extraordinary' number of plays actors had to master: 'The Admiral's Company in their 1594–5 season performed six days a week, and offered thirty-eight plays in all, of which twenty-one were new; few plays remained in the repertory for more than a year.'[70] The articles of agreement made between Robert Dawes and Lady Elizabeth's Men when he joined them in 1614 are a slightly later testimony to the growing need for personal work discipline: they prescribe financial penalties if he should 'at any time fail to come at the hour appointed' to rehearsals, fail to arrive promptly for performances 'ready apparelled', or if he should 'happen to be overcome with drink' at the time of performance.[71] It is the sense of acting as a skill acquired through careful practice and diligent training that lies behind the gentle mockery of the clownish troupe in *The Taming of a Shrew*. By implication, the labour and craftsmanship that have gone into the 'real' play are emphasised.

A similar process is at work in Anthony Munday's *John a Kent and John a Cumber*, a play preserved in a manuscript apparently dated 1590 but which may be, or relate to, the play performed on numerous occasions by the Admiral's Men between 1594 and 1597 as *The Wise Man of Westchester*.[72] Munday's engagement in debate about the status of actors is intriguing in the light of a contemporary's testimony in 1582 that he 'set forth a balet against playes', and the fact that he may also have been the pseudonymous 'setter forth' of *A Second and Third Blast of Retrait from Plaies and Theaters*; it might be seen as another example of what Tracey Hill tactfully refers to as Munday's 'versatility'.[73] As in *The Taming of a*

Shrew, the actors in *John a Kent* are peripheral to the main plot; and they, too, seem intended to magnify the professionalism of the players performing the piece as a whole. 'Turnop *wi*th his crewe of Clownes, & a Minstrell' (334) are rustic amateurs, the servants of Ranulph Earl of Chester, Turnop himself being 'my Lordes man, his hogheard, his familiarity seruaunt' (347–8).[74] As such, they recall the legitimate players invoked by the Corporation of London in 1584, the men who 'for their lyuings vsing other honest and lawfull artes, or reteyned in honest seruices, haue by companies learned some enterludes for some encreasce to their profit by other mens pleasures in vacant time of recreation'. In Munday's play, however, the obtaining of increase to their profits takes the form of waylaying passing aristocrats with unsolicited and shambolic entertainments and expecting payment in return. We see Turnop and his crew stage a brief pageant for the lords Morton and Pembrook, in which the former is signified by a moor holding 'a Tun painted with yellow oker' and the latter by 'a Porrenger full of water [and] a pen in it' (369–71). Morton and Pembrook are told by the Earl of Chester's son,

> My Lordes, my fathers tennants after their homely guise,
> welcom ye with their countrey merriment,
> How bad so ere, yet must ye needes accept it. (389–91)

One function of these clowns is to contrast with the two magicians of the play's title, whose more sophisticated trickery is also depicted in terms of theatre. In their battle to obtain the hands of Marian and Sydanen for two rival pairs of would-be bridegrooms, a masque and a play are used. John a Kent laments early on the fact that his victory has been too easy and determines to make things more difficult for himself: 'Must the first Scene make absolute a play? / no crosse? no chaunge? what? no variety?' (530–1). At the same time, I would suggest, a contrast is being implied here between these fictional actors and the real ones playing them. Turnop and company are incompetent amateurs whose performance is a way of rendering feudal dues and, therefore, need not be a quality product. It is apparently unrehearsed, since we see the actors squabbling over who shall deliver the speech, and the writing is nonsensical:

> Lyke to the Cedar in the loftie Sea,
> or milke white mast vppon the humble mount:
> So hearing that your honors came this way,
> Of our rare wittes we came to giue account. (372–5)

The performers of *John a Kent and John a Cumber*, by contrast, are professionals competing in a theatrical marketplace, whose livelihoods depend on their ability to attract audiences with well-written, well-acted plays. The complaint of the theatre's enemies, that actors are idle caterpillars pursuing an improper vocation and living off begging, is turned on its head: it is those actors who do have other, more legitimate forms of employment that are shown fleecing passers-by with their lacklustre performances.

As in *John a Kent*, where the eponymous wise man compares his magic to that of the theatre, there is a thematic significance to the representation of players in *The Book of Sir Thomas More*, the majority of which is thought to be have been written by Munday around the same time.[75] The historical More likened politics to 'Kynges games, as it were stage playes, and for the more part plaied vpon scafoldes', and, in the play, More's talents have a decidedly theatrical aspect, whether he is using his rhetorical gifts to calm the rioting Londoners or stage-managing miniature dramas like that in which he has his servant dress up as him to deceive Erasmus.[76] Towards the end, the condemned More explicitly compares himself to an actor: 'I confesse his maiestie hath bin euer good to me, and my offence to his highnesse, makes me of a state pleader, a stage player, (though I am olde, and haue a bad voyce) to act this last Sceane of my tragedie' (1931–4). It is, therefore, very appropriate that in one scene we should see More extemporise a part in a play alongside the Lord Cardinal's Men, an itinerant acting troupe who turn up unannounced when More is about to entertain the Lord Mayor of London and various other notables with a feast. They offer to put on a play, 'The Marriage of Wit and Wisdom', before dinner, but when the actor Luggins, who has gone to fetch a false beard, fails to return in time, More himself steps into the breach to improvise the part of Good Counsel. When More and his guests have gone in to dinner, one of the actors says,

> doo ye heare fellowes? would not my Lord make a rare player? Oh, he would vpholde a companie beyond all hoe, better then Mason among the Kings players: did ye marke how extemprically he fell to the matter, and spake Lugginses parte, almoste as it is in the very booke set downe. (1150–3)

As Charles R. Forker and Joseph Candido point out, the role More takes on is particularly apt: 'More *does* play the part of Good Counsel, both in the interlude and in the actual world.'[77] Munday may also have had in mind the story that the young More, as a henchman in Cardinal Morton's household, would 'at Christmas-tide suddenly sometimes step in among the players, and never studying for the matter, make a part of his own there presently among them, which made the lookers-on more sport than all the players beside'.[78] However, I would suggest that the manner in which the actors themselves are depicted is also of interest here. Rather than giving an advertised performance in a public theatre, they turn up unexpectedly to offer their services in a private household. The play they perform is a morality in keeping with *Sir Thomas More*'s early Tudor setting, largely derived by Munday from Thomas Ingelend's *Disobedient Child* and R. Wever's *Lusty Juventus*.[79] When Munday adds material apparently of his own composition, the intention seems to be to stress the old-fashioned character of the interlude, as in the following speech by the Vice Inclination:

> Back with those boyes, and saucie great knaues, /florishing his dagger
> what, stand ye heere so bigge in your braues?
> my dagger about your coxecombes shall walke,
> if I may but so much as heare ye chat or talke. (1068–71)

More himself, before the play commences, manifests an attitude to the players that is not so far from that of Chester's son in *John a Kent*. The performance is not a product to be judged good or bad but an offering to be welcomed in the spirit in which it was meant. To his wife's pessimistic prediction as to the play's quality, More replies, 'I am sure theyle doo their best, / they that would better, comes not at their feaste. ... if Arte faile, weele inche it out with looue' (992–3, 999). The fact that he is able to improvise the character of Good Counsel serves not only to underline his virtuosity but also to indicate the rather formulaic nature of 'The Marriage of Wit and Wisdom', something that is also highlighted when More comments from the sidelines upon Vanity's entrance, 'This is Lady *Vanitie* Ile holde my life: / beware good *witt*, you take not her to wife' (1083–4). At the same time, More's success implicitly undermines the actors' professional expertise: rather than being a specialised skill, their work is something that lies within the capabilities of the gifted amateur.

I would suggest that, as in the other plays I have examined so far, one effect of the way the players are characterised in *Sir Thomas More* is to set up a contrast between the fictional actors and the real ones playing them. By depicting actors who lack technical skills and who purvey an inferior product that is more feudal offering than commodity, the plays conversely imply that the Elizabethan actor is a craftsman who has acquired his proficiency through application and who is offering up his skills within a competitive marketplace. As such, they intervene in the debate about the legitimacy of recreation, arguing that the actor is not an idle rogue or vagabond, whose plays are a deceit to inveigle money out of honest citizens, but rather a trained professional earning money through legitimate work.[80]

Two of Shakespeare's plays from the 1590s, *The Taming of the Shrew* (*c.* 1594–*c.* 1598) and *A Midsummer Night's Dream* (1594–8), appear to convey a similar message but in slightly different ways. The relationship between the first of these and the play *The Taming of a Shrew* already discussed has attracted a good deal of controversy and is a matter that is outside the scope of this book.[81] However, one significant variation between them is in the way in which the fictional players are depicted in their respective inductions. Shakespeare's treatment is more consistent, in that rather than having clownish actors with an old-fashioned repertoire perform a modern and sophisticated romantic comedy he depicts actors whose demeanour is in keeping with the play they perform. The Lord treats them with a respectfulness that anticipates Hamlet's:

LORD Do you intend to stay with me to-night?
2. PLAYER So please your lordship to accept our duty.
LORD With all my heart. This fellow I remember
Since once he play'd a farmer's eldest son.
'Twas where you woo'd the gentlewoman so well.
I have forgot your name; but sure that part
Was aptly fitted and naturally perform'd.
1. PLAYER I think 'twas Soto that your honor means.
LORD 'Tis very true; thou didst it excellent. (Ind. 1. 81–9)

The presentation of the players is much more low-key than in *The Taming of a Shrew*; it is also more confident, showing no need to ridicule them in order to magnify their real-life equivalents. Their work is an accomplishment that, when well carried out, is memorable and praiseworthy. Shakespeare's play creates an overlap between the real and fictional players, such that praise for the one is implicitly praise for the other.

A similar overlap between the two sets of actors exists in *A Midsummer Night's Dream*. In one sense, of course, they are set up in clear contrast to each other: the bumbling amateurs who follow conventional trades by day and whose hilariously bad performance is an offering rather than a commodity against the professionals of the Lord Chamberlain's Men.[82] Puck's closing speech, however, emphasises the parallels between them. 'If we shadows have offended' (V. 1. 423) – 'we' presumably meaning the Lord Chamberlain's Men, since Puck has now taken on the role of Epilogue – recalls both Peter Quince's prologue ('If we offend, it is with our good will', V. 1. 108) and Theseus's excusing of the play ('The best in this kind are but shadows; and the worst are no worse, if imagination amend them', V. I. 211–12). The relationship between the two groups of actors is thus more complicated than in any of the other plays mentioned so far: at the same time, the mechanicals both aggrandise their real-life equivalents by means of contrast (as in *The Taming of a Shrew*, *John a Kent* and *Sir Thomas More*) and, in a curious sense, stand for them.[83] Accordingly, the scenes that show the rehearsals for the play, as well as giving occasion for the mechanicals to be in the wood so that Titania can fall in love with Bottom, emphasise to the audience the labour that has gone into the performance they are watching. Indeed, Philostrate, when telling Theseus why he should not let *Pyramus and Thisbe* be performed, focuses to a striking extent on the work their rehearsal has entailed. The players, he says, are

> Hard-handed men that work in Athens here,
> Which never labor'd in their minds till now;
> And now have toiled their unbreathed memories
> With this same play, against your nuptial ...
> It is not for you. I have heard it over,
> And it is nothing, nothing in the world;
> Unless you can find sport in their intents,
> Extremely stretch'd, and conn'd with cruel pain,
> To do you service. (V. I. 72–5, 77–81)

The mental labour – memorising lines and rehearsing their delivery – that goes into even the worst of plays is made evident. At the same time, however, the very fact that rehearsal is depicted onstage has a further significance, one which is connected with the terms in which patrons of the drama advocated its performance in the face of civic objection.

In the first chapter of *The Queen's Men and their Plays*, Scott McMillin and Sally-Beth MacLean take issue with what they see as the shared assumption of E. K. Chambers and W. W. Greg that the principal reason for the Privy Council's support for playing in the London area, inconsistent and non-unanimous though it may have been, was the need to provide the Queen with seasonal entertainment: in Chambers' words, 'if her majesty's "solace" at Christmas was to be provided upon economical terms, it was necessary that the players should be allowed facilities for "exercise", and incidentally for earning their living, through public performances".[84] McMillin and MacLean suggest that, in fact, the grounds for the Privy Council's support were more political than aesthetic. Puritans on the Council in the 1570s and 1580s, such as Walsingham, Leicester and Knollys, would have been well aware of the theatre's potential as a propaganda tool; they opposed the arguments of the stage's detractors because:

> From their perspective, the danger was not so much that zealous reformers would harm a form of entertainment in which the queen took special pleasure, but that the radical reformers would drive the reform movement apart from a developing English culture and create a division which the government would find unbridgeable.[85]

Whatever the real motives behind the Privy Council's support for plays, however, the fact remains that its stated reason was the Queen's taste for dramatic entertainment. In the patent dated 10 May 1574 authorising Leicester's Men to play in London and throughout the realm, Elizabeth announces that they are licensed to play 'aswell for the recreacion of oure loving subiectes as for oure solace and pleasure when we shall thincke good to see them'.[86] In subsequent documents, the reference to the recreation of Elizabeth's subjects is dropped, however, and only the Queen's own 'solace' is still used as a justification, perhaps in order to evade arguments about the legitimacy of recreation: writers and preachers might fulminate against the idleness of commoners, but they could hardly deny the Queen her entertainment. A letter to the Lord Mayor recorded in a Privy Council minute of 24 December 1578 requires him to allow various companies to play on the basis that 'the companies aforenamed are appointed to playe this tyme of Christmas before her Majestie'.[87] Another letter of November 1581 requests that a ban on playing be lifted now that the plague has abated, on the grounds of 'the releife of theis poore men the players and their redinesse with conuenient matters for her highnes solace this next Christmas, w*hi*ch cannot be without their vsuall exercise therein'. The same justification is used in letters of 11 April 1582 and 26 November 1583.[88] Convenient fiction though it may have been, this gave a peculiar status to plays acted in the London playhouses, such that they were to be seen not as performances in their own right but as rehearsals for a more important performance over the holiday season. Rather than giving their audiences a finished product, the playing companies were, in effect, allowing them (for a price) to watch them at work, practising for the all-important Court performance. In this light, the fact that *A Midsummer Night's Dream* lets us see the process of rehearsal acquires a new significance. The audience's vision of Bottom and company at work rehearsing foregrounds the notion that the play as a whole is, in effect, a rehearsal by the Lord Chamberlain's Men and not a final performance. We are watching the labour that goes into the product, not the product itself. In this sense, the rehearsal scenes in *A Midsummer Night's Dream* are a staging of one of the fictions that permit the public performance of drama by designating it work, not recreation.[89]

A further twist is given to this notion of drama as rehearsal in Munday's *The Downfall of Robert, Earl of Huntingdon* (1598), the first of that dramatist's two Robin Hood plays. Like *Sir Thomas More, The Downfall of Robert, Earl of Huntingdon* is set in the reign of Henry VIII; but this time the intention is not to demean the actors who are represented within it. Rather, the play begins with the courtier Sir John Eltham knocking at the door of the poet Skelton, having just given Henry 'my seruice in suruaying Mappes' (10).[90] Skelton is concerned:

> Then twill trouble you, after your great affairs,
> To take the paine that I intended to intreat you to,
> About rehearsall of your promis'd play. (14–16)

Eltham reassures him: the King himself has asked him to make sure the play be performed as requested. The cast, socially, is extremely mixed, containing not only Skelton, Eltham and Sir Thomas Mantle but also a clown and other commoners. The actors rehearse the dumb show, which Skelton (as Friar Tuck) interprets, concluding:

> The manner and escape you all shall see.
> ELTHAM Which all, good *Skelton?*
> SKELTON Why all these lookers on:
> Whom if wee please, the king will sure be pleas'd. (108–11)

The players then go on to complete their rehearsal, which consists of the whole of the Robin Hood play with occasional interruptions. In its depiction of a rehearsal, and the insistence that such an activity involves labour, or 'paine', *The Downfall of Robert, Earl of Huntingdon* resembles *A Midsummer Night's Dream*; but, clearly, Munday has gone a step further as far as the complexity of the relation between real and fictional actors is concerned. Here, almost the whole of the play purports to be a rehearsal, before a dimly imagined audience, of a drama that will be performed before Henry, much as the public performance of Munday's play is supposedly a rehearsal for a future performance at Court. Tiffany Stern has argued that the play is meant to be imagined as a rehearsal before the Master of the Revels, into whom 'by sleight-of-hand we, the audience, have been transformed'; however, there is no basis for this in the text, and the fact that the rehearsal is a dress rehearsal at Skelton's house makes it seem decidedly unlikely (21, 1).[91] Rather, I would suggest that by turning the whole play into a rehearsal, Munday makes *The Downfall of Robert, Earl of Huntingdon* formally embody one of the arguments for the public theatre's existence.

Such a reading of the play needs to acknowledge the possibility that the Induction may not have appeared in the play's public performance at all, as Celeste Turner argues on the basis of Henslowe's ten-shilling loan to Henry Chettle in earnest for a comedy and 'for mendinge of Roben hood. for the corte'.[92] While the idea of a performance at Court advertising itself as a rehearsal for a performance at Court has its attractions, John C. Meagher has argued that the 'unsettled and unfinished' nature of the printed text 'makes it improbable that Chettle's additions, composed some nine months after the settled and finished version of the play had been presented to the Admiral's Men, are in any way represented here'.[93] Although the assumption that Munday would necessarily have presented the Admiral's Men with a 'settled and finished version of the play' may be disputed, it does seem unlikely that an inconsistent text would represent the play as it was performed at Court. Furthermore, there are aesthetic grounds for assuming that the Induction was a feature of the play as Munday conceived it for the public stage. There is a running joke whereby Friar Tuck's speech repeatedly lapses into Skeltonics; this only makes sense if we imagine that Skelton himself is playing Tuck and has slipped out of character, an interpretation confirmed by Sir John Eltham's complaint that 'you fall into your vaine, / Of ribble rabble rimes, *Skeltonicall*, / So oft, and stand so long, that yon [*sic*] offend' (2234–6; cf. 845–92).[94] These moments, fostering the conceit that we are watching a rehearsal of the Robin Hood play rather than the real thing, do not detach easily from *The Downfall of Robert, Earl of Huntingdon* as a whole, suggesting that they were in the play from the start. Clearly, their function is partly comic, as well as being entirely in keeping with the 'extensive metatheatricality' that Tracey Hill finds throughout both this play and its sequel, *The Death of Robert, Earl of Huntingdon*; however, Munday's blurring of the performance of the Admiral's Men and that of Skelton and his fellows should be seen in the context of his earlier interest in the legitimising of acting as work.[95] The presence of Henry's courtiers within the performance realises the idea of actors as servants of royalty: by taking Elizabethan justifications of the public actor's status and placing them in the Henrician period, Munday gives them both publicity and pedigree.

The Downfall of Robert Earl of Huntingdon is my final example of a tendency in plays of the 1590s, when representing actors, to do so with a view towards defining contemporary theatrical performance as work. Several methods were used to achieve this end. Some plays depicted the actors of the past as amateurish, inept and old-fashioned in order to contrast them with the skilful professionals by whom they were portrayed. Shakespeare, in *The Taming of the Shrew* (and later in *Hamlet*), has one of his characters explicitly praise the fictional actors, and, by extension, the real actors playing them. In plays such as *A Midsummer Night's Dream* and *The Downfall of Robert, Earl of Huntingdon*, a more complex relationship between real and fictional actors obtains, one that plays on the idea of public drama as a rehearsal for a performance at Court. Common to all these instances is an underlying theme that acting is not play but work: this can be seen both in the insistence that the actor is a skilled professional and in the emphasis on rehearsal (and, by implication, public performance, which was another kind of rehearsal) as difficult and laborious. This redefinition of playing as work is something that I should like to place as a kind of backdrop to the remaining chapters. I will suggest that it had repercussions that went beyond the relatively small class of professional actors who had tried to bring it about; in fact, it had profound implications for the whole manner in which the relationship between work and play was represented on the early modern stage.

CHAPTER 3

'Though he be a king, yet he must labour': work and nobility in Shakespeare's histories

In the last chapter, I argued that the relationship between acting and work changed fundamentally over the course of the sixteenth century. On the one hand, financial and doctrinal imperatives drove out of existence the amateur religious drama that had flourished in the English towns during the Middle Ages. On the other, an increase in the number of touring companies and the growth of a secular theatre industry in London meant that more and more people were gaining an income from playing. These developments, I suggest, drew actors into a wider debate about work and idleness, such that they were charged both with following an illegitimate occupation and with enticing other groups in society away from their own work. In response, theatrical depictions of actors in the public theatre of the 1590s attempted to present acting as work, whether by contrasting the performers with fictional amateur actors, by asserting the dignity of the actor's profession or by invoking the notion that public playing was, in fact, a rehearsal for appearances at Court.

The criticisms made of plays and actors, and the methods those working in the theatre used to answer them, both support the argument I put forward in Chapter 1: that in the sixteenth century, it became increasingly common for the activities of groups in society to be understood in terms of work. Actors were condemned for pursuing a mode of life that was not work; in return, their supporters presented acting as a form of legitimate labour. In the current chapter, I shall discuss a parallel instance of a social group being criticised for idleness and parasitism and defending itself, once again, by invoking the idea of work. The implications of certain Protestant teachings, as well as its own changing character, made the social elite of nobles and gentlemen vulnerable to the accusation that it lived without labour; as I shall argue, their apologists responded by presenting these classes as labourers in the vocations of government, public office and the provision of counsel.

I have chosen to focus on the social elite primarily because its relationship with the idea of work was so complex and conflicted. As I have already argued, in the dominant medieval conception of society its identity was predicated on being a class of non-workers, whose role was to make war; I shall suggest that for various reasons, this understanding of its role was modified in the early modern period to incorporate the notion of work. And yet, as I shall emphasise in Chapter 4, the idea that to be a gentleman was to be exempt from labour persisted during the period; indeed, it is arguable that the pressures of social mobility and status anxiety caused it to be proclaimed even more loudly. Not only that: it was an assumption that proved to be of crucial importance for the development of London's theatrical culture at the beginning of the seventeenth century.

The first part of the current chapter focuses on the new conception of nobility that, I argue, evolved during the sixteenth century, one in which the idea of work could be accommodated. In the remainder of the chapter, I discuss a group of plays from the 1590s that provide a particularly useful demonstration of how this emergent discourse could be incorporated in the drama, namely Shakespeare's histories. David Riggs has argued that one feature distinguishing Shakespeare's from earlier historical plays is their greater interest in the social and ideological settings out of which his characters arise: the plays preserve 'the theatrically viable stage business and rhetoric of heroical-historical drama while placing it in a richer context of ethical and political values'.[1] In my reading of the plays, I shall try to show how Shakespeare draws on a number of rival discourses concerning the relationship between nobility and work in order to provide this ideological context, adding depth to his characters and creating dramatic interest and tension. In his depiction of Prince Hal, however, Shakespeare goes beyond this, presenting his audience with a character who actively manipulates concepts of work and idleness in his construction of a public identity. In doing so, he makes use of the same set of arguments concerning acting and work that Shakespeare and other writers were deploying in the stage representations of players I discussed in Chapter 2.

My decision to treat gentlemen and the nobility as a single group might be criticised in so far as, to quote Lawrence Stone, those 'who profess to be unable to distinguish between a gentleman and a baronet a baronet and an earl, betray their insensitivity to the basic presuppositions of Stuart society', not to mention Elizabethan.[2] However, the distinctions between gentleman, baronet and earl in early modern England were arguably much less significant than that between all three groups and the remainder of the population. As Keith Wrightson puts it, 'Gentlemen stood apart, and the possession of gentility constituted one of the most fundamental dividing lines in society.'[3] Although social taxonomists commonly subdivided both those above and below the line into further categories, they also placed great emphasis on the principal division, as Richard Mulcaster does here:

> All the people which be in our countrie be either *gentlemen* or of the *commonalty*. The common is deuided into *marchauntes* and *manuaries* generally, what partition soeuer is the subdiuident. *Marchandize* containeth vnder it all those which liue any way by buying or selling: *Manuarie* those whose handy worke is their ware, and labour their liuing.[4]

Mulcaster subsumes under the term 'gentlemen' all the higher ranks of society; the 'commonalty', significantly for this book, consists of those who work with their hands and those who buy or sell for a living. This division of the commonwealth into common workers and gentle non-workers was commonplace: as William Harrison put it in a passage I shall examine in more detail later on, a gentleman had to be able to 'live without manual labor'.[5] The class of non-workers, which comprised 5 per cent or less of the population, 'owned most of the wealth, wielded the power and made all the decisions, political, economic and social for the national whole'.[6]

Given the extent of its financial and political power, it may seem odd to draw a parallel between this privileged class and the more socially marginal players whose situation I examined in the last chapter. Exceptional individuals such as Shakespeare managed to be members of both groups; even so, contemporary orthodoxy seems to have been that 'the *stage* doth staine pure gentle *bloud*', as John Davies of Hereford put it.[7] What gentlemen shared with players, however, was a vulnerability to the accusation that they lived without labour in defiance of God's commandment; and in the sixteenth century this vulnerability was exacerbated by a development that I discussed in Chapter 1, namely the increased wealth and influence of yeomen, merchants and tradesmen. As Christopher Hill writes, while the idea that every Christian must earn a living through work had been 'the lower-class heresy throughout the centuries', 'The propertied class had always been able to suppress it until the sixteenth century; but then it won its way to respectability, thanks in part at least to the growing social importance of the industrious sort of people.'[8] Partly, perhaps, because of this shift in the balance of power, and partly as an anti-Catholic criticism of idle monks and friars, senior prelates increasingly emphasised the duty of every member of the commonwealth to labour in his or her vocation, citing in their support texts such as St Paul's dictum in 2 Thess. 3: 10 that, 'if there were anie, which wolde not worke, that he shulde not eat'.[9] In some instances, they evidently felt able to stress that this injunction applied even to the highest ranks of society: Hugh Latimer commented on Paul's words in a 1549 sermon, 'It were a good ordinance in a commonweal, that every man should be set on work, every man in his vocation', and went on to conclude, 'Every man must labour; yea, though he be a king, yet he must labour.'[10] Later in the century, William Perkins not only attacked monastics and vagabonds for their idleness but also insisted that 'miserable and damnable is the state of those that being enriched with great liuings and reuenewes, doe spend their daies in eating and drinking, in sports and pastimes, not imploying themselues in seruice for Church or Commonwealth'.[11] The most radical reformers seem to have taken a more extreme view, as Laurence Humphrey testified in 1563 when he addressed the question of

> Whether Nobles oughte to be borne in a wel ordred, and Christianlike gouerned state. For I heare it at this present muche doubted, and cald in question of many. And truly, all in vayne should I weare my while in framing Nobilitye, if (as some thinke) it ought not be suffered. For some impugne it with wordes, some with weapons. Either parte thinkes it ought be abolished. With wordes fighte not onelye the *Anabaptystes* and *Lybertines*: but euen some learned hold opinion: that they deserue as vnprofitable members to be cutte of. With weapons both ofte and sharpely haue the commens inuaded them.[12]

Although Humphrey himself favours the continued existence of the nobility, the terms he uses to convey others' opposition to it anticipate strikingly the invectives against actors I discussed in the last chapter. The view of the nobility as 'vnprofitable members' brings to mind Stephen Gosson's call for players either to go back to legitimate occupations or to be 'cut of from the body as putrefied me*m*bers for infecting the rest'; Anglo-Phile Eutheo said they should be 'thrust out of the Bee-hiue of a Christian Common-weale'. In the section that follows, I want to outline some of the ways in which apologists for the privileged classes of society seem to have responded to such complaints.

TUDOR JUSTIFICATIONS OF NOBILITY

Elsewhere in his treatise *The Nobles; or, Of Nobilitye*, Humphrey writes that the reason why 'our forefathers dischargd the Nobles of baser craftes, was not for they shoulde walowe and freese in ydlenes: but to practise warlike feates.and employe good artes'.[13] He was referring to the medieval notion that gentlemen's freedom from manual labour was based on their duty to defend the realm. I quoted some examples of this in my Introduction: Thomas Wimbledon's statement that 'To knighthode it falleth to letten wrongs and thefftes to ben done, and to maintain Goddes law and them that ben techers thereof, and also to kepe the londe from enemies of other londes' and a Dominican preacher's image of the Church as a body, with 'knights to defend it in the manner of hands'.[14] Edmund Dudley, the grandfather of the Elizabethan Earls of Warwick and Leicester, wrote, around 1510, that, whereas 'the good lyf of all the commynaltie in substance standith in trew labor and lawfull busynes', the purpose of the nobility is 'to defend the poore people from all wronges and Iniuries' and 'euer to be reddy to defend your prince, the churche and the realme'.[15] As Humphrey's remarks suggest, this conception of nobility was to some extent still current well into the sixteenth century. Although humanist writers had stressed to a novel extent the importance of learning in fashioning a gentleman, it was still taken as axiomatic that (as Lodovico da Canossa puts it in Hoby's 1561 translation of Castiglione) 'the principall and true profession of a Courtyer ought to be in feates of armes'.[16] It is this assumption that underlies Elyot's recommendation of physical exercise in *The Boke Named the Gouernour* (1531): 'it maketh the spirites of a man more stronge and valiant, so that by the hardinesse of the membres, all labours be more tollerable'.[17] The words 'stronge and valiant' indicate that the labours Elyot means are on the battlefield; the exploits of Leicester, Sidney and Essex suggest that many of the elite associated their status with martial endeavours at least until the end of Elizabeth's reign.

However, as historians such as Mervyn James and Lawrence Stone have argued, the nobility's status and sense of identity at this time were in the midst of a change which had begun at the start of the Tudor period; and this made the traditional justification of their privilege on the grounds of military service less easy to maintain. In 'English Politics and the Concept of Honour, 1485–1642', James argues that whereas the nobility's martial code of honour had in the medieval period often placed them in conflict with their rulers, Tudor monarchs succeeded in making themselves the fount of honour, using the heraldic order to control access to the nobility. Many of the 'new men' they created were ennobled for their political rather than their military service, and members of the existing nobility increasingly felt that honour precluded their rising up against the monarch. At the same time, a growing number of books such as Lydgate's

The Fall of Princes (1494) and Baldwin's *The Mirror for Magistrates* (1559) promoted what James calls the 'moralisation of politics', placing limits on the circumstances in which gentlemen could use violence.[18] In *The Crisis of the Aristocracy, 1558–1641*, Stone similarly argues that Tudor monarchs were keenly aware of the threat a militarised aristocracy posed to their own security. Elizabeth deliberately undermined the power base of northern earls, such as Derby, Shrewsbury, Northumberland, Westmoreland and Cumberland, whom she feared might be won over to the Catholic Queen of Scots: Northumberland was deprived of the Wardenship of the Middle March, and the loyal southerner Hunsdon was put in charge of Berwick and the East Marches. In the wake of the 1569 rebellion, the Earls of Northumberland were confined to Sussex, away from their traditional power base; the Earls of Westmoreland were exiled and lost their estates; and other nobles likewise moved south or had their lands sequestered. Furthermore, 'During the long period of peace from 1562 to 1588 the nobility lost the habit of military service, and even during the war years of the 1590's only a minority took an active part in military campaigns.' Finally, the nature of war itself was changing: as it became more professionalised, it became less appealing to a gentleman. 'A military commander had now to be an expert in logistics, in transport and victualling, in engineering and administration.'[19]

In the circumstances identified by James and Stone, the use of gentlemen's involvement in war as a justification for their exemption from work was clearly less tenable. This may be one reason why Elyot's *Governour*, while still identifying a military role for the privileged class also stresses an ethos of public service derived from classical texts such as Cicero's *De officiis*. Unlike medieval writers on knighthood, Elyot uses the idea of work when describing this ethos, as in his discussion of the origins of nobility:

> in the begynnyng, whan priuate possessions and dignitie were gyuen by the consent of the people, who than had all thinge in commune, and equalitie in degree and condition, undoubtedly they gaue the one and the other to him at whose vertue they meruailed, and by whose labour and industrie they received a commune benefite, as of a commune father that with equall affection loued them.[20]

Following the social and religious upheavals of the Reformation, however, the imperative to redefine the function of the nobility in terms of labour seems to have become more pressing. This is particularly evident in Humphrey's *The Nobles*, a work that claims, as we have seen, to be a response to the calls of radical reformers for the abolition of that estate; its qualified defence of nobility also reflects the Protestant convictions of its author, who wrote the original Latin version as a Marian exile. For Humphrey, nobility is a 'callyng', not simply an inherited rank; accordingly, it is both legitimate for commoners to attain nobility 'by theyr owne vertue and commendacion of wisedome' and possible for hereditary nobles to lose it through failure to labour in their vocation. Humphrey allows 'not so much as one ynche of Nobility' to the hereditary nobleman who, though otherwise morally unblemished, 'neither knowes nor coueytes learning, nor in trauaile of his body, or exercise of mind, passeth the course of his weary life: but spendeth his yeares in pleasure ease & rest: haunteth plaies, feastes, bathes & bankettings'. He thus turns on its head the assumption that noblemen are, by definition, exempt from work: 'rather the better and Nobler they are, the more ought they vpraise their courage therto. As stronger beastes beare greater burthens.' Quite explicitly, he responds to the accusation that nobles are idle drones by emphasising their duty of public service, which he defines as a form of work: using the same image as Menenius Agrippa in *Coriolanus*, he wants to 'perswade the people not to thinke all Nobles grosse paunches, liuing on others sweates, theym selues labourlesse: but with their labour, counsayle, and seruice, to minister to the other limmes what they want'.[21]

Humphrey's defence of the nobility against the charge of idleness on the grounds that the nobleman is a labouring public servant is one that is duplicated in a number of works from the mid-sixteenth century onward. This phenomenon is perhaps unsurprising: the revolutionary potential of St Paul's injunction to labour at a period when increasing numbers of commoners had access to an English Bible must have presented the privileged classes with cause for concern. When the Book of Homilies first printed under Edward VI was reprinted in 1562, one addition to the text was 'An Homilie against Idlenesse', which repeats the Pauline injunction that all must work only in order to qualify it. The homily insists that 'when it is said, all men should labour, it is not so straitly meant, that all men should should [*sic*] vse handy labour'. Instead,

> whosoeuer doeth good to the common weale and societie of men with his industrie and labour, whether it be gouerning the common weale publikely, or by bearing publike office or ministery, or by doing any common necessary affaires of his countrey, or by giuing counsell, or by teaching and instructing others, or by what other meanes soeuer hee bee occupyed, so that a profit and benefit redound thereof vnto others, the same person is not to be accounted idle, though he worke no bodily labour, nor is to be denyed his liuing (if hee attend his vocation) though hee worke not with his hands.[22]

Work is no longer defined in terms of the readily identifiable outward sign of manual labour. Instead, its meaning has been extended to cover any activity that benefits the common weal; this is an elastic definition, as phrases such as 'any common necessary affaires' and 'what meanes soeuer' testify. In *An Exposition upon the Two Epistles of the Apostle St. Paul to the Thessalonians* (1583), John Jewell, possibly the author of the Homily against Idleness, goes a stage further.[23] He takes to task those who believe 'Kings and counsellors, bishops, preachers, and all other sorts of learned men' disobey Paul's commandment by living idly; in fact, their mental work is harder than the physical work of other men. 'The toil which princes take, and the great cares wherewith they are occupied, pass all other cares in the world.'[24] In a 1586 exposition on the same text, Thomas Tymme directs the accusation of idleness against Catholic monks and priests and goes on to follow the Homily in arguing that,

> whatsoeuer he be that doth any manner of way seeke to benefite the society of men by his industrie, whether it be in gouerning a familie, or in dealing in publique or priuate affayres, eyther in counsayling, or in teaching, or by any other manner, of way, the same is not to be reckoned among idle persons.[25]

This notion that the exercise of public duties is a form of work achieved expression in Elizabeth's descriptions of her own relationship with the commonwealth she governed: at the dissolution of Parliament in April 1593, she assured the Lords and Commons

> that the care you have taken for myself, yourselves, and the commonweal, that you do it for a prince that neither careth for any particular – no, not for life – but so to live that you may flourish. For before God and in my conscience, I protest (whereunto many that know me can witness) that the greatest expense of my time, the labor of my studies, and the travail of my thoughts chiefly tendeth to God's service and the government of you, to live and continue in a flourishing and happy estate.[26]

GOVERNMENT AS WORK IN *2 HENRY VI*

In texts such as homilies and religious commentaries, which were made available to the masses in oral or written form, the privileged classes of early modern England overtly defended themselves against accusations of idleness by characterising their activities as work. In the remainder of this chapter, I want to explore the question of whether Shakespeare's plays can be seen as another medium in which this conception of nobility was promulgated. So far as the critical background to this debate is concerned, a useful starting point might be Alfred Hart's 1934 investigation of Shakespeare's use of the homilies, which found that certain notions propounded by the Homilies on Obedience and on Disobedience and Wilful Rebellion – 'the divine right of the reigning monarch, the duty of passive obedience, enjoined on subjects by God, and the misery and chaos resulting from civil war and rebellion' – are persistently alluded to in Shakespeare's plays. Hart assumes that Shakespeare himself subscribed to these notions, partly out of conviction, partly out of a pragmatic awareness that '[t]he London companies of actors owed their legal existence, and every actor his livelihood, to the favour of the sovereign and the court', but mainly because from childhood he would have been indoctrinated through their repetition at Holy Trinity Church: 'on nine Sundays or holydays in each year the congregation would hear a portion of the homily on Obedience or a sixth of that on Disobedience and Wilful Rebellion'.[27] Hart's argument has some affinities with that put forward a decade later in *Shakespeare's History Plays* by E. M. W. Tillyard, who, like Hart, assumes that Shakespeare shared the intellectual convictions of the Elizabethan ruling class; Shakespeare's awareness of a governing 'principle of order' informs his treatment of English history. Perhaps most notoriously, Tillyard depicts Shakespeare as an exponent of the 'Tudor myth', 'a universally held and still comprehensible scheme of history: a scheme fundamentally religious, by which events evolve under a law of justice and under the ruling of God's Providence, and of which Elizabeth's England was the acknowledged outcome'.[28] More recently, critics have returned to such arguments in order to articulate their own contrasting beliefs about the ideological implications of Shakespeare's drama. Commenting on Tillyard's 'Tudor myth', Jonathan Dollimore writes that not only do 'most of Shakespeare's history plays fail to substantiate this (non-existent) unitary myth'; 'some of them have precisely the opposite effect of revealing how myth is exploited ideologically'. Rather than attacking such mystifications outright, however, 'Jacobean tragedy discloses ideology as misrepresentation; it interrogates ideology from within, seizing on and exposing its contradictions and inconsistencies and offering alternative ways of understanding social and political process.'[29] Stephen Greenblatt takes a more pessimistic view of the early modern drama's radical potential, arguing that it derives much of its theatrical power from the power displays of the State; and, as in manifestations of political authority, subversion is invoked only to be contained or dispersed. The 'apparent production of subversion is ... the very condition of power'.[30] The tension between these two positions appears irreconcilable: one argues that what appears to be state propaganda is, in fact, revelation of the conditions of propaganda's production; the other, that what appears to be subversion is, in fact, the containment of subversion. A neat way of resolving it, however, is offered by Phyllis Rackin, who suggests that the stand-off between views of the drama as subversive and as reactionary reiterates a conflict already inherent in Shakespeare's histories between a secular historiography that emphasises human agency and chance and one that insists on the inescapable nature of divine providence. 'The ideological conflict between providential and Machiavellian notions of historical causation was built into the plays from the beginning, generating theatrical energy and engaging the audience in the problematic process of historical interpretation.' Although this conflict to some extent reflects the transitional period in which the history plays were written, it is also one that Shakespeare deliberately fosters for dramatic purposes: 'Drama thrives on every form of conflict, on conflicts between ideas as well as conflicts between persons.'[31] It is a question dealt with overtly in the plays and parodied after the trial by combat between Peter and Horner in *2 Henry VI*, when York tells the victorious apprentice to 'thank God, and the good wine in thy master's way' (II. 3. 95–6): York cynically invokes both providential and Machiavellian readings of the outcome. I think Rackin's strategy is a helpful one, as it offers a way of situating the drama within early modern social and ideological struggles while avoiding any simplistic identification of it either with subversive or with reactionary forces. This is an issue I touched on in the last chapter, when I argued against aligning the stage straightforwardly with the Court against the City: although acting companies had noble patrons, and were supported by the Privy Council against the Corporation of London in the battle for control over playing, the theatres themselves were the product of City money – as well, of course, as being attended by playgoers of diverse classes. As John Cocke wrote of a 'common Player' in 1615, 'howsoeuer hee pretends to haue a royall Master or Mistresse, his wages and dependance proue him to be the seruant of the people'.[32] The multiplicity of groups with an interest in theatrical production, whether as playgoers, patrons or entrepreneurs, as well as plays' frequent multiple authorship, their use of diverse source material and their basis in dialogue, all militated against ideological unity. Rackin argues that much of the theatrical energy of Shakespeare's histories comes precisely from their ideological disunity; I shall suggest in the following paragraphs that rather than being straightforwardly promulgated in the histories as Hart's or Tillyard's model might have it, the emergent notion that government constitutes work is placed by Shakespeare in opposition to other conceptions of nobility, giving rise to a creative tension that heightens the plays' dramatic and intellectual interest.

2 Henry VI (*c.* 1590–2) is an appropriate place to begin, partly because of its relative chronological priority but also because it is a play whose political bias has been keenly debated, particularly with respect to the scenes depicting Jack Cade's insurrection. On the one hand, the scenes can be seen as subversive, offering commoners in the audience 'a vicarious expression' of their discontent.[33] On the other, Shakespeare can be seen as demonising the rebels, for instance in his emphasis upon their bloody and apparently motiveless anti-literacy: Cade has the Clerk of Chartham hanged 'with his pen and inkhorn about his neck' purely for being able to sign his name (IV. 2. 109–10). The sheer excess of the scenes seems to generate an antipathy that closes down their subversive potential, as Rackin points out, and they have been interpreted by some as an attempt to distance the theatre from the riot and disorder with which its opponents associated it.[34] More recently, however, critics have identified a festive dimension to Cade's rising, created through the use of carnivalesque language, Cade's depiction as anarchic mock-king and the fact that he may well have been played by Will Kemp, the resident clown of Lord Strange's and then the Lord Chamberlain's Men.[35] For Ronald Knowles, Cade represents a parodic inversion of the 'absolutist aspirations' of his master, York: 'The depiction of Cade and his followers here is not simply the expression of anti-egalitarianism, the anarchic many-headed monster run wild, but rather the recognition that such rebellions become a grotesque mimicry of the barbarism of feudal hierarchy.' This notion of carnival offers a useful way of conceptualising Cade's rising in the play, as it allows a consideration of how the scenes might work as theatre that goes beyond the question of whether an audience is supposed to sympathise or be horrified. Not only does the clown playing Cade have 'an unwritten compact with the audience to make them laugh' simultaneously with him and at Cade; the insurrection scenes provide an ironic commentary on the play's story of dynastic struggle.[36] Furthermore, as I now want to suggest, they also provide one of several perspectives on the relationship between work and class offered in the play.

In *2 Henry VI*, the assumption inherent in the medieval division of society into *bellatores*, *oratores* and *laboratores*, namely that labour is restricted to one class and something from which the others are exempt, is repeatedly given expression in the class-based insults used by the Duke of Suffolk against commoners, which invariably draw attention to their status as workers. In III. 2 he dismisses the commons of Bury as 'hinds', or rural labourers (271), 'a sort of tinkers' (277). In the scene that culminates in his death, he calls his captors 'paltry, servile, abject drudges' (IV. i. 105); 'drones' contrasted to 'eagles' like himself (109). Particular venom is reserved for the Lieutenant, 'Obscure and lousy swain' (50), 'a jaded groom' (52). This character is evidently a former servant of Suffolk, who dwells on the drudgery his captor once performed for him:

> Hast thou not kiss'd thy hand and held my stirrup?
> Bare-headed plodded by my foot-cloth mule
> And thought thee happy when I shook my head?
> How often hast thou waited at my cup,
> Fed from my trencher, kneel'd down at the board,
> When I have feasted with Queen Margaret? ...
> How in our voiding lobby hast thou stood
> And duly waited for my coming forth? (53–8, 61–2)

However, as David Riggs has pointed out, the chivalric Suffolk is 'drastically reduced in stature' in the play, as is the dynastic contender York, who displays a 'valor that has ceased to find expression in the open trial of warfare'. Instead, Shakespeare's most impressive aristocratic character is Humphrey, Duke of Gloucester, who 'suggests a new type of ideal ruler, the Ciceronian governor'.[37] While Suffolk is contemptuous towards the idea of work, using it as a means of degrading those he despises, Gloucester has a very different notion of the relationship between class and labour, as in his complaint in the play's opening scene regarding the loss of Henry's French territories. In recounting the exertions that went into their acquisition, Gloucester invokes the traditional militaristic conception of the role of the aristocratic class: did Henry V 'so often lodge in open field, / In winter's cold and summer's parching heat, / To conquer France, his true inheritance?' (I. i. 80–2). 'Have you yourselves, Somerset, Buckingham, / Brave York, Salisbury, and victorious Warwick, / Receiv'd deep scars in France and Normandy?' (85–7). But he also asks, 'And did my brother Bedford toil his wits, / To keep by policy what Henry got?' (83–4);

> Or hath mine uncle Beauford and myself,
> With all the learned Council of the realm,
> Studied so long, sat in the Council-house
> Early and late, debating to and fro
> How France and Frenchmen might be kept in awe,
> And hath his Highness in his infancy
> Crowned in Paris in despite of foes?
> And shall these labors and these honors die? (88–95)

As well as remembering hardships on the battlefield, Gloucester refers to Bedford's intellectual labours and to study and debate in the council house by himself, Beauford and the rest. 'Early and late' is an interesting touch, as it is one example of an image that recurs in Shakespeare's histories of the noble or princely governor working on into the night. Later in the play, for example, when Gloucester defends himself against the charge that he misappropriated soldiers' pay, he protests, 'So help me God, as I have watch'd the night, / Ay, night by night, in studying good for England' (III. 1. 110–11). His ability to provide wise counsel is demonstrated in II. 1, where he unmasks the fraudulent beggar Simpcox; his eloquence is testified to even by his enemies, when his long denunciation of their plots is greeted with sneering comments on the verbal dexterity of 'smooth Duke Humphrey' (III. 1. 65). Suffolk says he has 'twit our sovereign lady here / With ignominious words, though clerkly couch'd'; when Gloucester quibbles on a remark of the Queen's, Buckingham says 'He'll wrest the sense and hold us here all day' (178–9, 186). We also see eloquence deployed for the common good in III. 2, when the Earl of Warwick succeeds in calming the 'spleenful mutiny' of the 'rude multitude' in the wake of Gloucester's death (128, 135); later in the scene, Salisbury's successful articulation to the King of their grievances against Suffolk deters them from having to 'by violence tear him from your palace, / And torture him with grievous ling'ring death' (246–7). In IV. 8 it is the speeches of Buckingham and Clifford that ultimately quell the rebellion by persuading the masses to desert Cade.

While *2 Henry VI* reflects the familiar idea that a nobleman's role is one of 'trew defence', as Dudley calls it, it is also informed by the emergent notion of the governor, serving the realm through the mental labour of counsel or eloquence.[38] However, aristocratic industry is not always presented so favourably. At the end of the first scene, when the other characters have left the stage, York soliloquises on the loss of the French territories, his belief in his own title to the throne, and his decision to temporise by siding for the moment with the Nevills and Duke Humphrey:

> Then, York, be still awhile, till time do serve.
> Watch thou, and wake when others be asleep,
> To pry into the secrets of the state,
> Till Henry, surfeiting in joys of love
> With his new bride and England's dear-bought queen,
> And Humphrey with the peers be fall'n at jars:
> Then will I raise aloft the milk-white rose. (248–54)

Once again, the image of the nobleman studying into the night is deployed; but here the speaker's business is more sinister, as he determines to plot and plan while others sleep. Shakespeare may here be recollecting the Homily against Idleness: 'In verye deede the best tyme that the deuyll can haue to worke his feate, is when men be a sleepe, that is to say, idle. Then is he moste busie in his worke.'[39] A similar sense of malign restlessness is created in his soliloquy at the end of III. 1, after York has been charged with putting down the Irish rebellion: 'My brain, more busy than the laboring spider, / Weaves tedious snares to trap mine enemies' (339–40). For York, labour does not have the positive valuation it carries with Gloucester; his industriousness is that of the ever-busy Machiavellian villain. The two sorts of activity are contrasted by Salisbury in the first scene when he says of Beauford, Buckingham and Somerset, 'While these do labor for their own preferment, / Behooves it us to labor for the realm' (181–2); Salisbury here gives us another instance of what Helgerson calls the play's 'vision of an aristocracy committed to the service of the commons'.[40]

If the example of York indicates that for a nobleman to be busy through the night is not necessarily a good thing, a different interrogation of the humanist ideal typified by Gloucester comes during the insurrection scenes. Knowles provides an apt discussion of the ways the following lines parody the Homily against Idleness:

HOLLAND Well, I say, it was never merry world in England since gentlemen came up.
BEVIS O miserable age! virtue is not regarded in handicrafts-men.
HOLLAND The nobility think scorn to go in leather aprons.
BEVIS Nay more, the King's Council are no good workmen.
HOLLAND True; and yet it is said, labor in thy vocation; which is as much to say as, let the magistrates be laboring men; and therefore should we be magistrates.
BEVIS Thou hast hit it; for there's no better sign of a brave mind than a hard hand. (IV. 2. 7–20)

As Knowles writes, Holland inverts the homily's insistence that those who govern are labouring in their vocation, 'restricting the meaning of "labour" to what the homily distinguishes as "handy labour" ', with the mock-logical conclusion that government should be restricted to those who labour with their hands.[41] Knowles does not note, however, the way in which the claim that government is a form of work is also travestied in the following exchange between the rebels and Lord Say:

SAY This tongue hath parley'd unto foreign kings
For your behoof —
CADE Tut, when struck'st thou one blow in the field?
SAY Great men have reaching hands; oft have I struck
Those that I never saw, and struck them dead.
BEVIS O monstrous coward! What, to come behind folks?
SAY These cheeks are pale for watching for your good.
CADE Give him a box o'th'ear, and that will make 'em red again.
SAY Long sitting to determine poor men's causes
Hath made me full of sickness and diseases.
CADE Ye shall have a hempen caudle then, and the help of hatchet.
(IV. 7. 77–91)

In trying to persuade the rebels that he has done them service, Say invokes various types of governmental labour, such as diplomacy, presiding as a justice and (once again) 'watching' into the night. His listeners, however, are unconvinced of the value of these activities, apparently retaining the assumption that a nobleman's proper place is 'in the field'; indeed, this might sit alongside the many other ways identified by Knowles and by Riggs in which Cade resembles (or parodies) the militaristic York, who laments Henry's 'bookish rule' (I. 1. 259) and derides Somerset for the absence of scars on his skin (III. 1. 300–1).[42]

The rejection by the rebels of Say's arguments represents a fourth position in the play with regard to the question of work and class. Suffolk's disparagement of the commons as workers reveals a conception of his identity as a nobleman that is entirely in keeping with Queen Margaret's memory of his chivalrous demeanour: how 'in the city Tours / Thou ran'st a-tilt in honor of my love / And stol'st away the ladies' hearts of France' (I. 3. 50–2). Gloucester, by contrast, regards himself as a humanist governor in a way that anticipates sixteenth-century arguments but may also allude to the historical Duke Humphrey's importance as a patron of Renaissance learning.[43] The idea of government as a form of work is both travestied by the rebels in their garbling of the Homily against Idleness, and explicitly rejected in the dialogue with Say. Finally, York is portrayed as a restless Machiavel, his energy anticipating the 'bustle' of his son in *Richard III* (I. 1. 152).

RICHARD AND BULLINGBROOK

I have chosen to focus upon *2 Henry VI* in the first tetralogy of histories because it seems to me to be far more concerned than the other plays with the questions of work and status that interest me in this chapter; this may well be because the play's depiction of an uprising by members of the labouring class gives these questions a particular urgency that they do not possess elsewhere. Shakespeare, I have argued, makes use of a variety of discourses concerning work and nobility, and the conflict between them is both intellectually engaging – what is the true social role of the elite? – and dramatically exciting, as in Suffolk's death scene or in the dialogue between Cade and Say. In the second tetralogy, competing ideas about work are again brought into play, although Shakespeare's focus narrows from the nobility in general to concentrate on the single figure of the King. As I shall argue, they are used in the first three plays, especially *Richard II*, as a means of contrasting Richard and Bullingbrook.

The idea that Shakespeare sets Richard and Bullingbrook up as contrasting figures in *Richard II* (1594–5) is a familiar one. In his 2002 edition of the play, Charles R. Forker takes the contrast as read when he summarises the action as 'the dethronement of an unsuitable anointed monarch by an illegitimate but more able one'; 'Richard, the man of words, postures and ceremonial dignity, is defeated by Bolingbroke, the man of actions and pragmatic realism.'[44] Richard's legitimacy, verbosity, ceremoniousness and incompetence are set against the practical ability of the usurping Bullingbrook. I want to concentrate on a different, but related, element of this opposition, one that is suggested by a comment made by Graham Holderness when commenting on the 'garden scene', III. 4. Holderness argues that the gardeners' extended comparison of their garden to the troubled kingdom 'expresses a melancholy but resigned secular understanding of political change. A king rules not by divine right but by hard work and a respect for the mutuality and reciprocal obligations of the "commonwealth" '.[45] This conceptualising of kingship in terms of work rather than, or as well as, ceremony is, I will argue, a product of the discourse that I have tried to isolate in this chapter and is an important element of Shakespeare's characterisation of his principal antagonists.

As Rackin puts it, 'Richard II lives in a providential world where authority alone is sufficient to maintain him in office'.[46] He exercises power in a manner that does not recognise the right of external rules or agents to limit it, for example in his interruption of the ritual of trial by combat in I. 3 and in his sequestering of Bullingbrook's inheritance in II. 1. Bullingbrook's later comment, 'If that my cousin king be King in England, / It must be granted I am Duke of Lancaster' (II. 3. 123–4) highlights the fact that the same hereditary principle that gives Richard his royal authority should guarantee Bullingbrook his title; Richard, however, evidently does not see himself as bound by any need to be consistent. As his fortunes worsen, the terms in which he describes his authority become increasingly mystical: on his return from Ireland, he salutes his 'Dear earth' and asks it not to feed Bullingbrook but to place spiders, nettles and adders in the rebels' way (III. 2. 6–26). He asserts the unshakeable nature of his divinely derived authority, insisting that 'Not all the water in the rough rude sea / Can wash the balm off from an anointed king' (III. 2. 54–5), although his lack of material support is evident from the statement that for each of Bullingbrook's soldiers, 'God for his Richard hath in heavenly pay / A glorious angel' (III. 2. 60–1). Only God's hand, as Richard tells Bullingbrook at Flint Castle, can dismiss him from his stewardship: 'For well we know no hand of blood and bone / Can gripe the sacred handle of our sceptre, / Unless he do profane, steal, or usurp' (III. 3. 79–81).

This sense of unlimited authority and divine right, however, is placed in conflict with the idea identified by Holderness that a monarch has a duty to labour for the realm. This is most clearly articulated in the garden scene, where the Gardener portrays the garden in which he and his men work as a state in miniature:

> Go thou, and like an executioner
> Cut off the heads of too fast growing sprays,
> That look too lofty in our commonwealth:
> All must be even in our government.
> You thus employed, I will go root away
> The noisome weeds which without profit suck
> The soil's fertility from wholesome flowers. (III. 4. 33–9)

The premonition of the eavesdropping Queen, that the gardeners 'will talk of state' (27), is initially proved wrong: the Gardener talks of gardening, not of politics, albeit in metaphors drawn from statecraft. However, the First Man is quick to apply his master's speech to the current situation, asking why their garden should be ordered when the land as a whole

> Is full of weeds, her fairest flowers chok'd up,
> Her fruit-trees all unprun'd, her hedges ruin'd,
> Her knots disordered, and her wholesome herbs
> Swarming with caterpillars? (44–7)

While the Gardener began by comparing the garden to an ordered commonwealth, his Man reverses the terms of the comparison, comparing the commonwealth of England to a garden in which fair flowers are choked and pests are rife – implying, it seems, that the flower of nobility cannot flourish and that parasites are endemic. This prompts what, to me, seems a surprising image from the Gardener. Given his earlier reference to 'government', we might expect him to attribute the disorder in the realm to the King's bad husbandry; but while he does this later on, initially he compares Richard, not to a gardener, but to a plant or tree:

> The weeds which his broad-spreading leaves did shelter,
> That seem'd in eating him to hold him up,
> Are pluck'd up root and all by Bullingbrook,
> I mean the Earl of Wiltshire, Bushy, Green. (50–3)

It is the usurper Bullingbrook, not Richard, who deals with these parasitic flatterers, whom we might now identify with the 'noisome weeds which without profit suck / The soil's fertility from wholesome flowers' in the Gardener's earlier speech. While Bullingbrook's harsh treatment of them is imagined as energetic manual labour, Richard is reduced to vegetable passivity. Only now does the Gardener invoke Richard's failures of government, describing them, like Bullingbrook's purge, in horticultural terms: 'O, what pity is it / That he had not so trimm'd and dress'd his land / As we this garden!' (55–7). Richard ought to have checked the growth of his nobles, as the gardeners do the bark of a fruit-tree, 'Lest being over-proud in sap and blood, / With too much riches it confound itself' (59–60); likewise,

> Superfluous branches
> We lop away, that bearing boughs may live;
> Had he done so, himself had borne the crown,
> Which waste of idle hours hath quite thrown down. (63–6)

The misfortune of the 'wasteful King' (55) is seen as the result of his failure to lop off excess foliage, or, to put it another way, of being too idle to be bothered to manage his nobles properly. Richard acknowledges something like this when, imprisoned at Pomfret, he laments, 'I wasted time, and now doth time waste me' (V. 5. 49). Bullingbrook's success, by contrast, is associated with a willingness to work.

There is, however, a significant further dimension to the horticultural metaphors deployed by the Gardener and his Man. The recurrent images of pests and superfluous elements and their destruction – weeds, caterpillars, weeding, the cutting off of excess foliage – link these passages to a discourse that, as I have already shown, was applied in the sixteenth century to classes within society that were accused of idleness and non-productivity, such as the actors who, Gosson argued, should be 'cut of from the body as putrefied me*m*bers'. Indeed, this discourse is employed earlier in *Richard II* by Bullingbrook, in his invective against 'Bushy, Bagot, and their complices, / The caterpillars of the commonwealth, / Which I have sworn to weed and pluck away' (II. 3. 165–7). As Andrew Gurr notes in his edition of the play, the phrase 'caterpillars of the commonwealth' appears also in William Harrison's *Description of England*, which was published as part of Holinshed's *Chronicles* (one of Shakespeare's sources for *Richard II*) in 1577.[47] Harrison applies it to able-bodied beggars who counterfeit illness: 'they are all thieves and caterpillars in the commonwealth and by the word of God not permitted to eat, sith they do but lick the sweat from the true laborer's brows and bereave the godly poor of that which is due unto them to maintain their excess'.[48] As I noted in Chapter 2, the image of the caterpillar, consuming but not producing, was applied to actors by William Rankins, who called them 'consuming caterpillars'; the full title of Stephen Gosson's *The Schoole of Abuse* refers to them as 'Caterpillers of a Commonwelth'. The difference between these examples and the words of Bullingbrook and the gardeners, however, is the social status of the people to whom the epithets are applied. Bushy, Bagot and the others are neither common players nor counterfeit beggars, but noblemen. The inescapable implication is that despite their high rank, they are not exempt from St Paul's injunction that those who will not work shall not eat, or, to use an anachronistically Elizabethan text, from the judgement of the Homily against Idleness:

> But yf we geue our selues to idlenesse & slouth, to lurking and loitering, to wylful wandering, and wastefull spending, neuer setling our selues to honest labour, but liuing like drone bees by the labours of other men, then do we breake the Lordes co*m*maundement, we go astray from our vocation, and incur the danger of GODS wrath and heauy displeasure, to our endlesse destruction, except by repentance we turne againe vnfaignedly vnto GOD.[49]

In using against noblemen language and concepts more usually deployed against poor and marginal members of society, Bullingbrook and the gardeners are following the example of Laurence Humphrey, who rejected an idle 'counterfayte Nobilitie': 'For droanes we prise not, that awayte to spoyle the laboures and hony of bees. Who of others sweat and bloud, purchase their commodities, & feede their pleasures.'[50] Bullingbrook, however, is also making an oblique challenge against the authority of Richard. As Forker notes, he never explicitly rejects Richard's claims to absolute power derived from God, being 'too shrewd politically to contest a concept of divine viceregency so important for his own authority and security in the next reign'.[51] However, Bullingbrook's use of Pauline arguments against Bushy and Bagot entails a willingness to hold noblemen to the standards expected of less fortunate classes and may be meant to imply that Richard's idleness, profligacy and riot lay him open to the charge of failing to labour in the vocation of kingship. Richard freely admits that the reason why he needs to 'farm our royal realm' to fund the Irish wars is because 'our coffers, with too great a court / And liberal largess, are grown somewhat light' (I. 4. 45, 43–4). York complains to the sick Gaunt that Richard's ears are stopped with flattery, with '[l]ascivious metres' (II. 1. 19) and news of Italianate fashions: 'Where doth the world thrust forth a vanity – / So it be new, there's no respect how vile – / That is not quickly buzz'd into his ears?' (24–6). Gaunt, responding, foretells an end to Richard's 'rash fierce blaze of riot' (33) and accuses the King to his face of having 'tapp'd out and drunkenly carous'd' the blood royal (127). Even the sympathetic York explains the burgeoning rebellion as 'the sick hour that his surfeit made' (II. 2. 84). As a surfeiting, indolent and spendthrift aristocrat, Richard is represented in similar terms to the idle noblemen attacked by Humphrey and Perkins; according to the terms of their arguments, he too should be cut off from the commonwealth as an unprofitable member, although the logic of absolutism forbids such a conclusion.

The garden scene's depiction of kingship in terms derived from manual labour, and the implied notion that it is a vocation in which Richard is failing, are two ways in which Shakespeare draws upon Elizabethan ideas concerning government and work in order to accentuate the difference between Richard and Bullingbrook. A third is in his repeated use of the word 'care' to describe the duties of kingship, in this play as in the second tetralogy as a whole. As I noted earlier, John Jewell wrote that the 'toil which princes take, and the great cares wherewith they are occupied, pass all other cares in the world'; Elizabeth portrayed herself as a prince that 'careth' only 'so to live that you may flourish', and would emphasise, in the Golden Speech of 1601, the 'cares and troubles of a crown'.[52] Not only does Richard's behaviour as King imply a lack of care, however: languishing in Wales, he expresses relief at the news that the cares of princes are to be lifted from him. 'Say, is my kingdom lost? Why, 'twas my care, / And what loss is it to be rid of care?' (III. 2. 95–6). A similar disdain for his responsibilities is implied in the subsequent scene when, descending from Flint castle, he compares himself to 'glist'ring Phaëton, / Wanting the manage of unruly jades' (III. 3. 178–9): he represents effective government not as a skill in which he is shamefully wanting but as one that is beneath his notice, like the control of inferior horses. Finally, in IV. 1,

York alludes to this sense that Richard is simply no longer able to manage the cares of state when he reminds him that resignation of the kingship to Bullingbrook was initially motivated by 'tired majesty' (178). Forker draws a parallel with Hall's account, where Richard privately admits to Bullingbrook 'that he had euel gouerned his dominion and kingdome, and therfore he desyred to be disburdoned of so greate a charge and so heauy a burdein'.[53] In the play, however, Richard goes on to argue that his passing on the cares of kingship to Bullingbrook is itself the cause of care: 'My care is loss of care, by old care done, / Your care is gain of care, by new care won' (196–7). A distinction is created between the care experienced by Richard, which derives from his current misfortune, and that taken on by Bullingbrook, which the latter sees as inherent in kingship: 'Part of your cares you give me with your crown' (194).

In the two parts of *Henry IV* (*c.* 1596–8; *c.* 1597–*c.* 1598), Shakespeare develops the line of characterisation that is initiated here, as Henry, unlike Richard, is depicted as continually labouring under the cares of rule. In the very first line of Part 1 he is 'wan with care', 'shaken' by war, anticipating further 'broils' (I. 1. 3) in the Holy Land, and disheartened at the 'riot and dishonour' he sees in the heir to the throne (84). It is in Part 2, however, that 'Th' incessant care and labor' of Henry's mind, as his son Clarence puts it at IV. 4. 118, are particularly emphasised. In III. 1, we see the ailing Henry working on into the night, like Gloucester in *2 Henry VI*, writing letters for a page to take to Warwick and Surrey. Contrasting himself with the 'many thousand of my poorest subjects' who 'Are at this hour asleep' (4–5), he goes on to consider sleep's failure to observe social distinctions, willing to reside 'in smoky cribs, / Upon uneasy pallets' (9–10), or 'with the vile / In loathsome beds' (15–16), or even with the ship-boy 'upon the high and giddy mast' (18), while denying repose to a king. Giorgio Melchiori has argued that while this scene is 'irrelevant to the development of the action', it is of thematic importance in 'identifying the country's sickness with the king's'.[54] I would suggest, however, that Henry's preoccupation with the cares of government is just as important as his unhealthy condition. Shakespeare draws upon a familiar topos whereby the continual wakefulness of a responsible monarch is contrasted with the peaceful slumber enjoyed by his subjects: Humphrey, for example, writes of princes, 'Who be they good, care, bowe, counsayle, watche, commen with theym selues, their counsaile, while others chiefely theyr subiectes, careles snorte at home'.[55] Shakespeare uses the contrast between sleeping subject and sleepless King again in Henry V's nocturnal soliloquy before Agincourt, which culminates in the complaint that the subject 'little wots / What watch the King keeps to maintain the peace, / Whose hours the peasant best advantages' (IV. 1. 282–4); here, at the bedside of the dying King, Hal identifies the source of his father's cares in the crown on his pillow:

> O polish'd perturbation! golden care!
> That keep'st the ports of slumber open wide
> To many a watchful night, sleep with it now!
> Yet not so sound, and half so deeply sweet,
> As he whose brow with homely biggen bound
> Snores out the watch of night. (IV. 5. 23–8)

Again, the insomnia of the great is contrasted with the sweet sleep of the humble. Ironically, however, when Henry wakes to find the crown gone, in his speech to his sons he identifies his cares as deriving not from his unique role as King but from the role as father that he shares with other men who 'Have broke their sleep with thoughts, their brains with care, / Their bones with industry' (68–9) – a striking declaration of affinity with the manual labourers he previously envied. Crossing status barriers again, he compares himself to bourgeois merchants who 'have engrossed and pil'd up / The cank'red heaps of strange-achieved gold' (70–1) for their sons' upbringing, like bees bringing wax and honey back to the hive, only to be 'murd'red for our pains' (78). Henry's sense of kinship with commoners is short-lived, however: in his dialogue with the Prince, he refers to his son's hunger 'for mine empty chair' (94), relocating his anxieties in terms of the royal succession. The effect is compounded by the shades of *Richard II* that can be discerned here. Henry's invitation to the Prince to 'Pluck down my officers, break my decrees' (117) recalls Richard's 'My acts, decrees, and statutes I deny; / God pardon all oaths that are broke to me!' (*Richard II*, IV. 1. 213–14), and he creates an image of his son's rule that echoes that of Richard:

> Harry the Fift is crown'd! Up, vanity!
> Down, royal state! All you sage counsellors, hence!
> And to the English court assemble now,
> From every region, apes of idleness! (119–22)

His speech culminates in an apostrophe to 'my poor kingdom' (133) that also seems addressed to Hal: 'When that my care could not withhold thy riots, / What wilt thou do when riot is thy care?' (135–6). The quibble on different types of care recalls Richard's conceit, 'My care is loss of care, by old care done, / Your care is gain of care, by new care won'. Shakespeare seems to be creating a parallel between Henry's deposition of Richard and his own sense that he is being deposed by his son, who, ironically, has more in common with the idle and frivolous Richard than with himself. The similarity was made explicit in Part 1: 'As thou art to this hour was Richard then / When I from France set foot at Ravenspurgh' (III. 2. 94–5). This scene concludes the pattern I have traced over this section of the current chapter, whereby Henry and Richard are counterpointed in terms of their relation to the concept of work. Repeatedly, Henry is associated with care and with labour; the association of Richard with irresponsibility and idleness continues after Richard's death, when he becomes an example of incompetent rule that Henry fears his son will emulate.

PRINCE HAL/HENRY V

So far in this chapter, I have examined the creative uses to which Shakespeare puts the notion, emergent in the sixteenth century, that the social elite was a class of workers, whether that work was manifested in government, in provision of wise counsel or in eloquence. In *2 Henry VI*, it informs the characterisation of Gloucester but is parodied by the rebels, as well as playing off against Suffolk's aristocratic disdain for labour and York's Machiavellian industry. In *Richard II* and the two parts of *Henry IV*, it is used to develop the contrast between Richard and Bullingbrook. Shakespeare is, I think, unusual in his willingness to make use of this particular discourse; it is one point of contrast between his *Richard II* and Marlowe's *Edward II* (1591–3), two plays which, in other respects, have a great deal in common. As Charles Forker writes, 'Each presents a weak and youthfully wilful monarch dominated by self-serving, upstart favourites and opposed by senior nobles who represent tradition, stability, and mostly, wise counsel'; in both plays, strife and rebellion result from the protagonist's failures and folly.[56] However, the suggestion that Richard is deficient in his monarchical vocation, that he has failed not just to govern himself but also to govern the realm, is strikingly absent from *Edward II*. For the discontented peers of that play, the problem lies not in Edward's shortcomings as a king but in the upstart Frenchman he heaps with offices and dignities. In the first scene, the Earl of Lancaster insists that they 'naturally would love and honour you / But for that base and obscure Gaveston' (I. 1. 99–100).[57] In the second, the peers' combination against the King is stimulated by the creation of Gaveston as Lord Chamberlain, Chief Secretary, Earl of Cornwall and King of Man and the expropriation for him of the Bishop of Coventry's goods and rents;

Mortimer calls him a 'peasant' 'Who, swol'n with venom of ambitious pride, / Will be the ruin of our realm and us' (I. 2. 30, 31–2). While Mortimer complains that 'The idle triumphs, masques, lascivious shows, / And prodigal gifts bestowed on Gaveston / ... The murmuring commons overstretchèd hath' (II. 2. 156–7, 159), as well as draining the treasury, these matters seem to be of secondary importance to the peers: their main complaint is Edward's elevation of Gaveston, and it is far from clear that the social consequences would, by themselves, prompt an upper-class rebellion. The play as a whole explores monarchy and nobility in terms of status and prerogative; the language of labour that Shakespeare uses is quite alien to it.

In this final section, I will concentrate on the figure of Hal or, as he later becomes, Henry V, arguing that he too is characterised with reference to the dichotomy of work and idleness. What sets Hal apart from the other characters I have discussed, however, is that rather than being defined by this dichotomy, he is represented by Shakespeare as consciously manipulating it. He makes concepts of labour and idleness work for him, whether in his artful construction of a profligate youth or in his redefinition of war as popular festivity. In the process, he implies that they are, indeed, no more than concepts and have no inherent basis in particular forms of human activity. Rather, they are ambivalent terms that can be mobilised by the powerful – specifically, by the monarch – to legitimise, or to condemn, the behaviour of subjects within a kingdom.

As J. Dover Wilson and E. M. W. Tillyard both noted in the first half of the last century, Hal's trajectory in the two parts of *Henry IV* has some affinities with that of the protagonist of a medieval morality play. As Tillyard puts it, in Part 1, Hal must 'choose, Morality-fashion, between Sloth or Vanity, to which he is drawn by his bad companions, and Chivalry, to which he is drawn by his father and his brothers'. In Part 2, he must similarly choose 'between disorder or misrule, to which he is drawn by his bad companions, and Order or Justice (the supreme kingly virtue) to which he is drawn by his father and by his father's deputy the Lord Chief Justice'.[58] One might quibble with Tillyard's precision in identifying the abstract qualities that confront Hal, but the broader perception that these two plays are structured around Hal's moral regeneration is hard to dispute. To put it with crude simplicity, Hal consorts for a time with 'that reverent Vice, that grey Iniquity', Falstaff, and his companions (*1 Henry IV*, II. 4. 453–4), before banishing 'plump Jack' (479) on his accession to the throne with the moralistic direction, 'I know thee not, old man, fall to thy prayers' (*2 Henry IV*, V. 5. 47). This reading of Hal's development is retrospectively confirmed by the Archbishop of Canterbury in the first scene of *Henry V* (1599): 'The breath no sooner left his father's body, / But that his wildness, mortified in him, / Seem'd to die too' (25–7). Canterbury's use of religious terminology intimates the miraculous suddenness of the change: it is a 'reformation' (33), a purging of 'th' offending Adam' as if by angelic agency (28–9).

Of course, if we have heard or read Hal's soliloquy from *1 Henry IV*, I. 2, which I shall discuss in detail later, we will know that Hal's youthful wildness has been deliberately assumed in order to make this reformation more impressive. As Robert Ornstein puts it, 'it is not Shakespeare who casts Hal as a hero of a Morality drama of temptation and redemption. It is Hal who casts himself in the role even as he casts Falstaff, in the role of reverend Vice and gray Iniquity.'[59] When we first see Hal and Falstaff, the former is, in a sense, constructing the latter as a representative of the idleness and dissipation that he will go on to reject. Hal responds to an enquiry as to the time of day with the following riotous fantasia:

> What a devil hast thou to do with the time of the day? unless hours were cups of sack, and minutes capons, and clocks the tongues of bawds, and dials the signs of leaping-houses, and the blessed sun himself a fair hot wench in flame-color'd taffeta; I see no reason why thou shouldst be so superfluous to demand the time of the day. (I. 2. 6–12)

As Holderness says of Hal's incredulous reply, the conversion of measurements of time to symbols of physical pleasure is a carnivalesque 'inversion of the existing world-order' that 'produces an exhilarating sense of liberation: those ideologies implied by the concept of time (moral seriousness, civic duty, work) are interrogated by this practice of inversion'.[60] From the outset, Hal portrays Falstaff in terms of a reversal of the values of the everyday, labouring world – as David Ruiter puts it, creating 'a metaphorical "Feast of Falstaff" '.[61] In fairness, however, this role is one that Falstaff, for his part, seems entirely happy to take on. He asks of Hal,

> Marry then, sweet wag, when thou art king, let not us that are squires of the night's body be call'd thieves of the day's beauty. Let us be Diana's foresters, gentlemen of the shade, minions of the moon, and let men say we be men of good government, being govern'd, as the sea is, by our noble and chaste mistress the moon, under whose countenance we steal. (23–9)

As with Hal's description of Falstaff's way of life, conventional categories of behaviour are reversed here. One who goes by night is not a thief of the day's beauty, with the implications of time-wasting that the phrase carries (David Scott Kastan glosses the phrase, 'those who waste the daylight in sloth'); rather, he is a forester of Diana, a gentleman of the shade.[62] This inversion of the concepts of idleness and work is, in fact, a favourite rhetorical trick of Falstaff's. When Hal ironically compliments his 'good amendment of life ... from praying to purse-taking', Falstaff parodies the language of St Paul and of the Homily against Idleness: 'Why, Hal, 'tis my vocation, Hal, 'tis no sin for a man to labor in his vocation' (102–5). Even more absurd is the moment when Falstaff robs the travellers, crying, 'Ah, whoreson caterpillars! bacon-fed knaves! they hate us youth' (II. 2. 84–5): he adopts the language of parasitism familiar from *Richard II* and deploys insults that could more appropriately be used against himself.

The irony of Falstaff's inversionary language lies not only in its ridiculousness, however. In portraying his idleness and criminality as honest work, Falstaff does in jest what Hal does in earnest, as the Prince's revelatory 'I know you all' soliloquy at the end of I. 2 indicates. Critics have tended to interpret Hal's use in this speech of terms such as 'idleness' (196), 'holidays' (204), 'sport' and 'work' (205) as an indication that his youthful behaviour should be thought of as a period of idleness which will come to an end when he begins the work of kingship: C. L. Barber, for instance, sees Hal as confiding in us that 'Falstaff is merely a pastime, to be dismissed in due course'. He takes the lines, 'If all the year were playing holidays, / To sport would be as tedious as to work' (204–5) as meaning that for Hal's holiday to intrude upon the time of his kingship would be tedious and inappropriate.[63] For Graham Holderness, Hal sets up holiday as a temporary subversiveness designed to be contained by work, while, most recently, David Ruiter argues that Hal 'clearly expresses his desire to highlight for the public his change from youthful rogue to glorious king' – 'from Hal as holiday youth to Henry V as everyday ruler.'[64] However, I would argue that to see Hal's youth simply in terms of idleness or holiday and his future kingship in terms of work or the everyday is to ignore some of the complexities of this speech, as David Riggs partially recognises:

> As a professional politician, Bolingbroke will try to convince his truant son that pleasing the populace is a full-time job; but unrelieved 'work' of any sort, Hal decides, is as 'tedious' for the performer as it is for his onlookers ... If, however, one reserves youth for play, then work, when the time comes for it, will share in the attractiveness of sport. His reformation will 'show more goodly' not because its theatrical effect has been calculated in advance, but because it will possess the 'rare' spontaneity of 'play'.[65]

Riggs, here, is evidently responding to the fact that in the speech, it is not the riotous behaviour of Hal's youth that is compared to holiday, but rather his repudiation of that behaviour:

> If all the year were playing holidays,
> To sport would be as tedious as to work;
> But when they seldom come, they wish'd for come,
> And nothing pleaseth but rare accidents.
> So when this loose behavior I throw off
> And pay the debt I never promised,
> By how much better than my word I am,
> By so much shall I falsify men's hopes. (204–11)

The reformation will be all the more pleasing because of the contrast to his earlier self, just as holidays please because they are a break from everyday working life. I would go further than Riggs, however: if Hal's future kingship is going to be a holiday, then his present activities are to be understood not as play but as work. This reading is borne out by other aspects of the speech. Hal begins by promising to 'a while uphold / The unyok'd humor of your idleness' (195–6), apparently characterising his companions' attitude as unrestrained in the manner of a man or beast who has stopped working, has 'unyok'd'. In this context, 'uphold' must mean something like 'consent to', 'participate in' or even 'finance'. The word 'unyok'd', however, can also be taken to mean that the idleness of Falstaff and his fellows is itself a burden that lacks a yoke to attach it to a carrier. In upholding this unyoked humour, Hal is not participating in it but is literally holding it up from beneath: what is idleness for his companions is labour for him. This alternative reading of the phrase receives some confirmation a few lines later in Hal's anticipation of a time 'when this loose behavior I throw off': ostensible idleness is not a pleasure but a weight to be discarded. And at the end of the passage, Hal tells us that he will 'so offend, to make offense a skill' (216); he talks of his assumed behaviour as if it were a trade, rather like Hamlet when he assures his mother that he is only 'mad in craft' (*Hamlet*, III. 4. 188).

What is it that makes Hal's apparent idleness a form of work? One answer could be drawn from the Earl of Warwick's explanation of his behaviour to the sick King in *2 Henry IV*:

> The Prince but studies his companions
> Like a strange tongue, wherein, to gain the language,
> 'Tis needful that the most immodest word
> Be look'd upon and learnt, which once attain'd,
> Your Highness knows, comes to no further use
> But to be known and hated. (IV. 4. 68–73)

According to this reading, Hal's behaviour is work because it is a studious 'search for proficiency' in subversiveness with the ultimate goal of its repudiation and containment.[66] Another interpretation is provided in the first scene of *Henry V*, where the Bishop of Ely responds to Canterbury's account of Hal's miraculous reformation by suggesting that just as berries grow best when shaded by weeds,

> so the Prince obscured his contemplation
> Under the veil of wildness, which (no doubt)
> Grew like the summer grass, fastest by night,
> Unseen, yet crescive in his faculty. (I. 1. 63–66)

Again, the 'veil of wildness' conceals the fact of work, although here the work resides in the cultivation of kingly virtues rather than the acquisition of knowledge. However, a third way of interpreting Hal's speech in *1 Henry IV*, I. 2 is to see his work not as lying beneath his idle façade but as consisting in the creation of the façade itself. Ornstein's contention that the role of morality hero is one that Hal deliberately and consciously adopts seems to be confirmed here: Hal announces that he will play the role of prodigal for a time so that his reformation will 'show more goodly and attract more eyes / Than that which hath no foil to set it off' (214–15). This strategy is fundamentally theatrical, not only in its reliance on an assumed role but also in the effect Hal wants to produce. He imagines himself as drawing towards him the admiring gazes of his subjects, as a spectacle to be 'wond'red at'; his promise to throw off his 'loose behavior', which I earlier read as implying a disburdening, can also be read in this context as a theatrical disrobing, the removal of a baggy disguise to reveal the true form beneath. In Chapter 2, I argued that dramatists of the 1590s represented acting as a form of work; by the time of *Henry IV*, Shakespeare had already emphasised in *A Midsummer Night's Dream* the mental labour and 'cruel pain' that go into acting, even the bad acting of Bottom and his confederates. This might explain why Hal refers to his offence as a skill and why his use of the work/holiday dichotomy appears to suggest that he is currently working in anticipation of a festive kingship. It might also explain why critics have tended (in my view at least) to misread Hal's soliloquy: by talking about his behaviour in terms suggestive of theatricality, he locates it in an area where the relationship between work and play is inherently problematic, not least in its terminology. To be an actor is to work at playing; for the actor, all the year really is playing holidays, and to sport is the same thing as to work.

The idea that Hal's youth was more productive than it appeared is one to which he returns in *Henry V* when confronted with the Dauphin's contemptuous gift of tennis balls: 'we understand him well, / How he comes o'er us with our wilder days, / Not measuring what use we made of them' (I. 2. 266–8). However, whereas in *1 Henry IV* he implied that his laborious youth would be followed by a festive kingship, here he portrays himself as still toiling, in that he will not fully assume his regal majesty until he contends for the throne of France: 'For that I have laid by my majesty, / And plodded like a man for working-days' (276–7). This modified version of his earlier promise is borne out at Agincourt, where Henry redefines the labour and hardship of the English soldiers in terms derived from popular festivity.

On the morning of the battle, the Earl of Westmorland wishes 'that we now had here / But one ten thousand of those men in England / That do no work to-day!' (IV. 3. 16–18). The speech is derived from Holinshed, who records one soldier's utterance, 'I would to God there were with vs now, so manie good soldiers as are at this houre within England!'[67] Shakespeare, however, both makes Westmorland the speaker and adds the detail of the men of England being idle. The reason for their idleness, of course, is the fact that today is the feast of Saints Crispin and Crispinian, a coincidence out of which Henry makes notorious rhetorical capital in the speech that follows: 'He that outlives this day, and comes safe home, / Will stand a' tiptoe when this day is named, / And rouse him at the name of Crispian' (41–3). Henry imagines a future in which celebration of the religious festival of Crispin and Crispinian will collapse into commemoration of the secular anniversary of Agincourt: veterans will feast their neighbours, show off their scars,

> And Crispin Crispian shall ne'er go by,
> From this day to the ending of the world,
> But we in it shall be remembered –
> We few, we happy few, we band of brothers. (57–60)

James Shapiro writes of these lines, 'It's hard to imagine a better example of the displacement of the religious by the nationalist' and makes a comparison with Elizabeth's inauguration of an Accession Day festival on what had been the Catholic feast of St Hugh of Lincoln.[68] What Henry is doing here, however, is not only a proto-Protestant colonisation of a saint's day for political purposes. He also draws from 'Crispin Crispian' a festive atmosphere that changes the nature of the battle that is about to take place:

> For he to-day that sheds his blood with me
> Shall be my brother; be he ne'er so vile,
> This day shall gentle his condition. (61–3)

Henry invests Agincourt with the spirit of Carnival, levelling the boundary between gentle and vile in a brotherhood of bloodshed: Agincourt's occurrence on a day when men in England 'do no work' erodes the workaday distinction between the classes who have to labour and the classes who do not. He creates a sense that, contrary to what we may have been led to believe by his conversation with Bates, Court and Williams in IV. 1, the battle is something more than a conflict between unwilling common soldiers and a superior foe in an uncertain cause. This culminates in the moment of religious awe with which Henry greets news of the miraculously low English casualties: 'O God, thy arm was here; / And not to us, but to thy arm alone, / Ascribe we all!' (IV. 8. 106–8).

The festive atmosphere, however, is by no means consistent or sustained. Only thirty lines after the 'Crispin Crispian' speech, Henry abruptly changes tack when addressing the French herald, talking of 'this day's work' (IV. 3. 97) and describing his host as 'but warriors for the working-day' (109), 'besmirch'd / With rainy marching in the painful field' (110–11). Of course, it would hardly be appropriate for Henry to talk about the coming battle in the same way to Mountjoy as to his own soldiers; the lines also serve to remind us that Henry's army are the underdogs, thereby making their eventual victory all the more impressive. But the fact that they come so soon after so striking an appropriation of popular festivity suggests that there is a certain arbitrariness to Henry's definitions of war. War can be a day's work, an exhausting and painful labour, or it can be a holiday. Its status as one or the other seems to be a matter of monarchical will.

If this seems to ascribe altogether too much power to the monarch in determining whether an action is work or not, it may be useful to return to the lengthy speech in I. 2 in which Canterbury explains why the men Henry is leaving at home will be adequate to defend England against the Scot:

> Therefore doth heaven divide
> The state of man in divers functions,
> Setting endeavor in continual motion;
> To which is fixed, as an aim or butt,
> Obedience; for so work the honey-bees,
> Creatures that by a rule in nature teach
> The act of order to a peopled kingdom. (183–9)

In a passage heavily indebted to Virgil's *Georgics*, IV. 158–68 and *Aeneid*, I. 430–6, Canterbury goes on to describe the bees' commonwealth, in which the various estates work harmoniously under the watchful eye of the monarch:

> Who busied in his majesty surveys
> The singing masons building roofs of gold,
> The civil citizens kneading up the honey,
> The poor mechanic porters crowding in
> Their heavy burthens at his narrow gate,
> The sad-ey'd justice, with his surly hum,
> Delivering o'er to executors pale
> The lazy yawning drone. I this infer,
> That many things, having full reference
> To one consent, may work contrariously,
> As many arrows loosed several ways
> Come to one mark. (197–208)

The idea that the monarch is carrying out surveillance and that idle traitors (in this polity, to be the former is to be the latter) may be delivered to 'executors pale', seems to anticipate Henry's uncanny awareness of the treason that is revealed in II. 2: 'The King hath note of all that they intend, / By interception which they dream not of' (II. 2. 6–7). But the king bee seems also to have a role as the object of the work done by his subjects. It is to his tent that the soldier bees bring their 'pillage' (195); furthermore, it is in reference to his 'consent' that the bees do their contrarious work. 'Obedience' to a monarch should be the mark that men aim at in their 'continual motion'. In other words, activity in the commonwealth is defined as productive in so far as it is directed towards the figure of the king. Canterbury seems to be articulating a more explicitly monarchist version of the argument of the Homily against Idleness that 'whosoeuer doeth good to the common weale and societie of men with his industrie and labour ... is not to be accounted idle'. The difference is that he locates the good of the common weal in the person of the monarch: it is the king's consent that legitimises human behaviour as a form of work.

Canterbury, of course, tactfully glosses over the problems inherent in vesting this sort of authority in an individual who is human and, therefore, fallible, problems that are made explicit by Williams in IV. 1 when arguing over the monarch's responsibility for his subjects: 'if the cause be not good, the King himself hath a heavy reckoning to make, when all those legs, and arms, and heads, chopp'd off in a battle, shall join together at the latter day and cry all, "We died at such a place"' (134–8). While not questioning the authority of the King to mobilise his subjects in war,

Williams does raise the possibility that the cause in which he does so may not be good; if we apply this notion to Canterbury's social model, the implication is that the monarch's legitimisation of activities as work is fallible and potentially arbitrary rather than necessarily just. Subversive as it is, however, this is an idea entirely in keeping with the way Hal has been represented in the three plays in which he appears. Rather than taking definitions of work as given, he artfully and actively manipulates them in his own public self-definition. He invents Falstaff as the personification of idleness in order ultimately to reject him; yet his own period of ostensible idleness in Falstaff's company is imagined, both in *Henry IV* and retrospectively in *Henry V*, as a period of work, whether because it is a cover for the acquisition of kingly attributes or because the role-playing itself, like that of Elizabethan actors, is a form of labour. Furthermore, the paradoxical notion that in his idle youth he 'plodded like a man for working-days' allows him to set up his eventual military triumphs as, by contrast, a form of festivity: hardship and labour on the battlefield are reimagined in advance in terms of holiday and carnival. The ultimate effect of Hal's creative approach to ideas of work and idleness is that we, too, come to see them as arbitrary rather than fixed; and this subversion is facilitated by the material context in which *Henry IV* and *Henry V* are realised, namely, a professional theatrical environment where the status of working and playing as discrete and separate activities is unavoidably called into doubt.

CHAPTER 4

'We may shut vp our shops, and make holiday': workers and playhouses, 1599–1601

When the Lord Chamberlain's Men first performed *Henry V*, in or around 1599, who, if anyone, was working in the playhouse?

On the basis of the Chorus's opening speech, it seems to be the actors themselves:

> O, pardon since a crooked figure may
> Attest in little place a million,
> And let us, ciphers to this great accompt,
> On your imaginary forces work. (Pro. 15–18)

Elsewhere, however, it seems to be the audience who are asked to work:

> Work, work your thoughts, and therein see a siege. (III. Cho. 25)
> But now behold,
> In the quick forge and working-house of thought,
> How London doth pour out her citizens! (V. Cho. 22–4)

Earlier on in the speech before Act III, though, the audience is told not to work but to 'Play with your fancies: and in them behold / Upon the hempen tackle ship-boys climbing' (III. Cho. 7–8). Yet, before the final act, the Chorus insists on his own status as a player: 'myself have play'd / The interim, by rememb'ring you 'tis past' (V. Cho. 42–3).

As this selection of quotations demonstrates, the speeches of the Chorus in *Henry V* have frequent recourse to the language of work and of play when describing how dramatic illusion is created. However, they are also noticeably inconsistent about whether the playhouse is a place of work and, if so, who is doing the working. The actors are described as working on the audience's imaginations to produce the drama, but so, later, are the audience members themselves, whose mind's eye is figured as a forge – anticipating Hamlet's comparison of his 'imaginations' to 'Vulcan's stithy' (*Hamlet*, III. 2. 83–4). At the same time, both are described as playing: the audience play with their fancies, either recreationally as with a toy, or in a sort of mental theatre in which they can behold Henry's fleet; the Chorus plays the interim, representing not one of the dramatis personae but an abstraction, a period of time.

One way of reconciling these contradictions might be through referring to Lukas Erne's suggestion that the Chorus's speeches were intended not for spectators but for readers 'imaginatively creating a playhouse performance'.[1] This theory draws on Andrew Gurr's view that the 1600 Quarto of *Henry V*, which omits the Choruses, is closer than the Folio text to 'the version of the play that Shakespeare's company first put on the stage in 1599'.[2] However, as James P. Bednarz has pointed out, the fact that Ben Jonson appears to parody the Act III Chorus in *Every Man Out of His Humour* (printed 1600) at the end of Act IV would seem to indicate that the *Henry V* Choruses must have been performed on stage on at least some occasions, otherwise Jonson's audiences (or readers) would have failed to get the joke.[3] Rather, I would suggest that the contradictions can, to some extent, be seen as another instance of the terminological complexity that, as I have argued already in this book, beset the early modern stage. Actors, or players, were individuals who made playing their work; the paradox is not merely an etymological coincidence but reflects a wider phenomenon whereby acting, an activity that had been predominantly amateur and occasional, had assumed the controversial status of an ongoing livelihood, and the play, in the purpose-built theatres of Elizabethan London, had become a commodity that could be bought and sold. However, the Chorus's uncertainty about who was working in the playhouse can also be seen as reflecting a more specific debate that was at its height around 1599–1601, as I shall argue in this chapter. The debate was twofold: it revisited the controversy of whether actors themselves should be seen as workers or non-workers, but it also engaged with the question of whether certain groups of workers should be present in theatre audiences and, more generally, with what the social space occupied by the stage ought to be. My exploration of that debate begins with a discussion of three plays from 1599 that all engage with the question of the right of manual workers to enjoy recreation on their own terms.

SHOEMAKERS' HOLIDAYS IN *HENRY V*, *THE SHOEMAKERS' HOLIDAY* AND *JULIUS CAESAR*

In the last chapter, I discussed Henry V's reference, in his speech before the battle of Agincourt, to the feast of Saints Crispin and Crispinian and noted the parallel between his creation of a secular anniversary on what had been a religious holiday and Elizabeth's establishment of the Accession Day festival on 17 November, formerly the feast of St Hugh of Lincoln. Some recent critics have found a similar overlap of monarchist and religious holidays in Thomas Dekker's play *The Shoemakers' Holiday*, performed by the Admiral's Men at the Rose theatre a few months after *Henry V*.[4] The play culminates in a Shrovetide feast to which the shoemaker-turned-Lord Mayor Simon Eyre invites all the apprentices of London in satisfaction of a promise made in his youth. As the pancake bell rings, Eyre's journeyman and foreman rename the festival in honour of St Hugh, the patron saint of shoemakers:

FIRKE Nay more my hearts, euery Shrouetuesday is our yeere of Iubile: and when the pancake bel rings, we are as free as my lord Maior, we may shut vp our shops, and make holiday: Ile haue it calld, Saint *Hughes* Holiday.
ALL Agreed, agreed, *Saint Hughes Holiday*.
HODGE And this shal continue for euer. (V. 2. 202–7)

When, in the final scene, Eyre thanks the King for allowing the illicit wedding of Rose and Lacy to stand, he gratefully associates him with St Hugh as patron of the feast: '*Sim Eyre* and my brethren the gentlemen shoomakers shal set your sweete maiesties image, cheeke by iowle by Saint *Hugh*, for this honour you haue done poore *Simon Eyre*' (V. 5. 6–8). L. D. Timms has argued that the image of the monarch cheek by jowl with St Hugh is meant to imply not just Henry VI, who was monarch at the time of Eyre's mayoralty, but Elizabeth: her Accession Day, like Eyre's feast, was 'a national celebration of peace and plenty' and occurred on a date that some still associated with St Hugh.[5] Marta Straznicky notes that Dekker appears to make a further allusion to that saint in his play: the full name of Rowland Lacy's obstructive uncle is Hugh Lacy, Earl of Lincoln.[6] Neither Timms nor Straznicky seems aware, however, that Hugh of Lincoln was a different St Hugh from that referred to by the shoemakers. The former was born in Burgundy around 1140 and ultimately made Bishop of Lincoln by Henry II; the latter is an apocryphal figure mentioned neither in *The Oxford Dictionary of Saints* nor in *The Golden Legend*.[7] The earliest reference I have been able to find to this St Hugh is in the opening narrative of the work from which Dekker also took the story of Simon Eyre, namely the first part of *The Gentle Craft* (entered Stationers' Register 1597), by Thomas Deloney. This Hugh is 'sonne vnto the remowned King of *Powis*, a noble Britaine borne, who in the prime of his yeares loued the faire Virgin *Winifred*, who was the onely daughter of

Donwallo, which was the last King that euer reigned in *Tegina*, which is now called Flint-shire'.[8] The chaste Winifred refusing his love, he travels Europe before returning penniless and becoming a shoemaker. He and Winifred are eventually martyred under Diocletian; he bequeaths his bones to his shoemaker colleagues, who make tools from them. Dekker's blurring of the distinction between the two St Hughs seems to have been conscious: the fact that he names one character Hugh, Earl of Lincoln looks like a clear allusion to the canonical saint, but he evidently also read the story of the other St Hugh, as well as that of Simon Eyre, in *The Gentle Craft*. The history of the younger Lacy in *The Shoemakers' Holiday* bears obvious similarities with it: Lacy, too, travelled on Continental Europe and was forced to learn shoemaking after squandering his allowance (I. i. 16–31).

Besides the confusion of Hughs, another oddity of Dekker's choice of patron saint for his shoemakers is the fact that there was another more canonical saint, or pair of saints, with whom that group of workers was associated; indeed, their narrative appears in Deloney between those of St Hugh and Simon Eyre. They are Crispin and Crispinian, located by Deloney in Roman Britain like St Hugh, although their cult was actually centred in Soissons in northern France. As David Farmer explains,

> French hagiographers made them noble Romans and brothers who preached in Gaul and exercised their trade of shoemaking so as to avoid living from the alms of the faithful ... An unlikely English tradition claimed that they fled to Faversham during the persecutions and plied their trade at a house on the site of the Swan Inn in Preston Street, visited by English and foreign pilgrims as late as the 17th century.[9]

Dekker had apparently read Deloney's version of the story, since an episode where Crispin woos Ursula, the Emperor's daughter, while ostensibly fitting her for a pair of shoes is echoed in *The Shoemakers' Holiday*, IV. 3; interestingly, the Swan is the name Dekker gives to the inn where Eyre is to meet the Dutch sailor from whom he buys a shipload of commodities at a knock-down price. However, in his play, there is no reference to Crispin and Crispinian – just as in *Henry V* there is no reference to the association of these saints with the craft of shoemaking. This striking lack of overlap between *The Shoemakers' Holiday* and *Henry V* is all the more notable given the other intertextual relationships that seem to exist between the two plays. As R. L. Smallwood and Stanley Wells point out, they share a background of wars in France; Dekker's genial king has affinities with Henry V; and 'the sense of comradeship and cheerful harmony that Dekker establishes around Eyre in the final scenes' recalls the patriotic mood that surrounds Henry's victories.[10] Dekker seems to make a more specific allusion to Shakespeare in having Eyre offer to shave off his beard 'and stuffe tennis balls with it to please my bully king' (V. 5. 23–4), while Dodger's account to Lincoln of the numbers of war dead echoes that produced after Agincourt:

> Twelue thousand of the Frenchmen that day dide,
> Foure thousand English, and no man of name,
> But Captaine *Hyam*, and young *Ardington*. (II. 4. 8–10)

> Edward the Duke of York, the Earl of Suffolk,
> Sir Richard Ketly, Davy Gam, esquire;
> None else of name; and of all other men
> But five and twenty. (*Henry V*, IV. 8. 103–6)

As these last quotations indicate, however, Dekker's use of Shakespeare goes beyond a shared atmosphere of cheerful nationalism. By reversing the order in which common casualties and 'men of name' are referred to, Dekker places greater emphasis on the unnamed private soldiers; furthermore, Dodger's figures for the English dead are noticeably less fantastic than those passed to Henry. This coupling of grim realism with a greater interest in the plight of ordinary soldiers pervades the play: it begins with a scene in which the gentleman Lacy buys his way out of military service but refuses to let the newly married shoemaker Rafe do the same. Rafe is forced to leave his wife to earn her own living and eventually returns crippled from the wars to find that she has vanished; his story echoes, perhaps, Williams's vision in *Henry V* IV. 1. 135–40 of severed arms and legs, and of dying men crying upon 'their wives left poor behind them'. More graphically than Shakespeare, however, Dekker dramatises what conscription means for the poor and their families, bringing the lamed shoemaker on stage and showing us his wife working as a seamstress, vulnerable to the unwanted attentions of men like Hammon. If there is an intertextual relationship between the two plays, then, it seems to be accompanied by a marked change of social standpoint; and this may help explain the absence of Crispin and Crispinian from Dekker's play. When Henry V links the battle of Agincourt with their feast, he fails to mention that it is, quite literally, a shoemakers' holiday; conversely, Dekker refuses to associate his own shoemakers' holiday with the feast that Shakespeare shows being colonised by militarist royalty.[11]

The differences between the holidays celebrated in the two plays seem to revolve around the question of who is in control of the holiday, and why. Henry takes the holy day of a pair of saints and empties it of its association with a particular artisan group, reinventing it as the anniversary of a hoped-for military victory: 'And Crispin Crispian shall ne'er go by, / From this day to the ending of the world, / But we in it shall be remembered' (IV. 3. 57–9). The question of whether this elision of artisan culture reflects a broader tendency on the part of Shakespeare's company is one that I shall address later when discussing *Julius Caesar*; however, it certainly contrasts with Dekker's insistence on the right of workers, not monarchs, to determine the auspices and meaning of their festival. As we saw earlier, it is Firke who consecrates Shrove Tuesday as St Hugh's Holiday; and it is Eyre himself who makes it a feast for apprentices:

> I promised the mad Cappidosians, when we all serued at the Conduit together, that if euer I came to be Mayor of *London*, I woould feast them al, and Ile doot, Ile doot by the life of *Pharaoh*, by this beard *Sim Eire* wil be no flincher. Besides, I haue procurd, that vpon euery Shrouetuesday, at the sound of the pancake bell: my fine dapper Assyrian lads, shall clap vp their shop windows, and away, this is the day, and this day they shall doot, they shall doot:
> Boyes, that day are you free, let masters care,
> And prentises shal pray for *Simon Eyre*. (V. 1. 43–52)

Disagreement over whether young people have the right to a holiday on Shrove Tuesday seems to be a persistent element of the day's meaning: as a schoolboy in north-east England in the 1920s, my grandfather knew the rhyme, 'Pancake Tuesday's a very happy day / If we don't get a holiday we'll all run away.' However, the more specific motif of the shoemaker creating his own holiday is one that Alison A. Chapman has found to be recurrent in early modern English literature, and she suggests that 'the trade had become symbolically associated in the sixteenth and seventeenth centuries with questions of calendrical and ritual order'. The figure of the holiday-making shoemaker, she argues, served as a focus for popular resistance to monarchical interference with the calendar in the abrogation of saints' days and the inauguration of new holidays such as Accession Day.[12] Chapman is surely right to locate *The Shoemakers' Holiday* in relation to a broad social and religious context in which holiday had become a controversial issue: both in England and on the Continent, Protestant reformers attacked the abundance of religious festivals that had existed under Catholicism, with Edward VI's parliament in 1552 limiting the number of holy days to twenty-seven.[13] However, Dekker's apparent advocacy of feast days does not align him as straightforwardly against the establishment as Chapman implies: by the 1590s, as Christopher Hill explains, a split had developed in England between a church hierarchy keen to preserve some religious holidays as days free of labour and a

Puritan opposition that 'insisted on the right to work every day except Sunday'. In this climate, even the status of Accession Day as a national holiday was sufficiently controversial to require the defence of Thomas Holland in a sermon of 1601; Dekker's upholding of the right of apprentices to their Shrovetide holiday associates him with the hierarchy rather than with more ardent reformers.[14] I would also suggest, though, that to locate the holiday theme in his play simply in relation to the controversy over saints' days is to omit an important element of its application. As I shall argue over the following paragraphs, *The Shoemakers' Holiday* should also be understood in the light of an Elizabethan debate over workers' rights in which the theatres themselves were inextricably implicated.

While the Shrovetide feast in which Dekker's play culminates is the most obvious shoemakers' holiday in *The Shoemakers' Holiday*, it is not the only one. In II. 3, after Hodge has explained to Firke that the Dutch skipper is offering to sell Eyre the entire contents of his ship on credit, Firke spies Eyre and his wife approaching: 'Mum, here comes my dame and my maister, sheele scold on my life, for loytering this Monday, but al's one, let them al say what they can, Monday's our holyday' (23–5).[15] Firke and Hodge threaten to leave if they are not allowed their day off, just as they did earlier if Eyre did not employ Hans. After Eyre becomes Sheriff of London, they are treated once again: 'Come *Madge*, away, / Shutte vp the shop knaues, and make holiday' (III. 2. 148–9). These two holidays besides Shrove Tuesday are, as it were, non-canonical, in that they are not associated with any saint's day or official feast; but they are no less controversial for that, since the right of workers to time off on an ad-hoc basis was one that gave both London's and England's rulers cause for anxiety. As I argued in Chapter 1, Elizabethan legislation that imposed work on the poor, such as the 1563 Statute of Artificers and the 1576 Act for the Setting of the Poor on Work, seems to have been inspired in part by anxiety over the problem of masterlessness; and the civic authorities in Dekker's London, too, frequently expressed concern over the behaviour of servants, apprentices and journeymen when not under their masters' control. Charles Whitney has brought together several guild ordinances from the 1580s and 1590s banning freemen from allowing those under their supervision to enjoy illicit recreations: for example, an ordinance of the Plasterers' Company from January 1586–7, renewed in 1597, notes the 'great disorder and abuse aswell emongest the prentices as Jorneymen ... in haunting and frequentinge taverns alehouses and plaies' and ascribes this to there being 'verie fewe that gouerne their servauntes as they ought to be gouerned'. A failure on the part of citizens to oversee adequately the apprentices, journeymen and servants in their care is presented as the cause of disorder and of abuses such as playgoing. Accordingly, every householder of the Company is exhorted to 'see his apprentices and jorneymen to goe to the churche to heare devine seruice or to some other place where godes woorde is and shalbe preached at due tymes of the daie and also to spend the reste of same Sondaie and hollidaies in some honest and lawfull exercises', under pain of a 2 shilling and 6 pence fine (the offending apprentices are to receive corporal punishment). Nor was it only on Sundays and holidays that masters were criticised for failing to supervise their servants: records from the Bakers' Court books of 1589 and 1591–2 show that freemen of that company allowed their charges to go to plays on working days.[16] The free time that Eyre allows his employees in *The Shoemakers' Holiday*, not to mention the day off that he guarantees all the apprentices of London, might therefore be seen in relation to an environment where workers' entitlement to non-religious recreation, and the right of their masters to give it to them, had long been under threat. Furthermore, in choosing to highlight these issues, Dekker was engaging in a debate in which he had a personal interest: as the quotations above indicate, one of the recreations which gave mayors and aldermen particular concern was playgoing itself. In upholding the idea of time off for employees, Dekker was insisting on the right of a significant proportion of his audience actually to be in the theatre at all.

My reading of Dekker's play as intervening in a specific controversy in late-Elizabethan London allies me with several recent commentators who have rejected the traditional view of *The Shoemakers' Holiday* as essentially a 'noble description of the gentle craft' offering a 'vivid characterization of Simon Eyre, the jolly shoemaker, whose virtues made him lord mayor of London'.[17] David Scott Kastan has focused on the various conflicts of the play – between classes, between native and immigrant workers, between the French and English nations – which are artificially resolved in the play's comic ending, where 'Rafe and Jane are reunited, Lacy and Rose are wed, and class conflicts dissolve in the harmonies celebrated and confirmed in the Shrove Tuesday banquet in Leadenhall'.[18] Marta Straznicky has questioned whether the ending eliminates discord between artisans and commercial capitalists such as Otley, who is Mayor at the beginning of the play, or in fact embodies it.[19] Finally, Charles Whitney has investigated the real-life mayor John Spencer (1594–5), whose unsuccessful attempts to prevent his daughter Elizabeth from seeing the profligate Lord

Compton Dekker appears to satirise in Otley's determination that his daughter will not marry Lacy. As I briefly noted in Chapter 2, Whitney finds Spencer to have been one of the more ardently anti-theatrical mayors of Elizabethan London: he wrote a letter to Burghley in November 1594 attacking plays for their profanity, their corruption of audiences and their distraction of workers, challenging the argument that they constituted a legitimate form of recreation. As an alderman in 1587, he also seems to have helped to draft the ordinance against time off for apprentices and servants that was adopted by the Plasterers as well as by other companies. Whitney argues that in defiance of Spencer, Dekker 'locates the source of theatrical power in ordinary London workers, including apprentices'; I would make the more specific suggestion that the play's mockery of Spencer is consistent with its interest in the question of recreation.[20] In modelling the unsympathetic and ultimately unsuccessful Otley on Spencer, Dekker pokes fun at an individual who had tried to curb workers' rights to free time in general and who was opposed to playgoing in particular.

I have tried to argue in the preceding paragraphs that the theme of holiday in *The Shoemakers' Holiday* is not simply a natural concomitant of its cheerful, festive atmosphere but actually situates the play in a late-Elizabethan debate over how much freedom groups such as servants, apprentices and journeymen should be allowed in their recreation – recreation that often took the form of playgoing. Even if this reading of the play is inaccurate, it is difficult to dispute that Dekker chooses to associate the theatre for which he writes with these groups in society; and this phenomenon is rather striking in view of the arguments about the social position of the theatre in the early 1590s put forward by critics such as Richard Wilson and Richard Helgerson. They find that an atmosphere of public unrest, which manifested itself in disturbances such as the feltmakers' riot of June 1592, impelled dramatists and playing companies to distance themselves from the phenomenon of civil disorder and from the classes who were assumed to be responsible for it. Rebels were demonised in plays such as *2 Henry VI*, *Jack Straw* and *The Massacre at Paris*, while advocates of the theatre explicitly disowned the apprentice contingent in audiences: Thomas Nashe wrote in 1592 that the players 'heartily wishe they might bee troubled with none of their youth nor their prentises; for some of them (I meane the ruder handicrafts seruants) neuer come abroade, but they are in danger of vndoing'.[21] By 1599, however, Dekker appears to assume the presence at least of apprentices and journeymen in his audience, in so far as members of those groups are positively characterised. He even goes so far as to stage a near riot between apprentices and servingmen when 'Hodge, Firke, Rafe, *and fiue or sixe shoomakers, all with cudgels, or such weapons*' (V. 2. 0 s.d.) disrupt Hammon's wedding to Jane, the presumed widow of Rafe: their invocation 'cry clubs for apprentises' (28) calls up what would have been for many of London's inhabitants the alarming possibility of an armed apprentice mob.

If *The Shoemakers' Holiday* appears actively to embrace the apprentices and journeymen in its audience, it is rather harder to gauge the position of a third play of 1599 in which the motif of the shoemaker's holiday appears, namely *Julius Caesar*. Chapman wonders whether the recurrence of this topos may reflect 'a specific (although as yet undiscovered) occurrence or person that piqued the playwrights' interest'; I prefer to see *Henry V*, *The Shoemakers' Holiday* and *Julius Caesar* as engaged in some sort of dialogue over the question of audience composition.[22] As I suggested earlier, one influence upon Dekker's treatment of 'Saint Hughes Holiday' in *The Shoemakers' Holiday* may have been the erasure of the artisan dimension from the feast of Crispin and Crispinian in *Henry V*; the question of workers' rights to a holiday (and by implication to be in the theatre) is one that Shakespeare addresses in *Julius Caesar*, which begins with a confrontation between the tribunes Flavius and Murellus and 'certain Commoners':

FLAVIUS Hence home, you idle creatures, get you home
Is this a holiday? What, know you not,
Being mechanical, you ought not walk
Upon a laboring day without the sign
Of your profession? Speak, what trade art thou?
CARPENTER Why, sir, a carpenter.
MURELLUS Where is thy leather apron and thy rule?
What dost thou with thy best apparel on?
You, sir, what trade are you?
COBBLER Truly, sir, in respect of a fine workman, I am but, as you would say, a cobbler.
MURELLUS But what trade art thou? Answer me directly.
COBBLER A trade, sir, that I hope I may use with a safe conscience, which is indeed, sir, a mender of bad soles. (I. 1. 1–13)

After more quibbling from the cobbler, Flavius is eventually enlightened, and asks:

FLAVIUS But wherefore art not in thy shop today?
COBBLER Truly, sir, to wear out their shoes, to get myself into more work. But indeed, sir, we make holiday to see Caesar, and to rejoice in his triumph. (27–31)

Murellus chastises the commoners for their inconstancy: in the past, they made the same show to welcome Pompey into Rome and now they 'cull out a holiday' for one who 'comes in triumph over Pompey's blood' (49, 51). When they have left the stage, Flavius tells Murellus to go towards the Capitol and 'Disrobe the images' (64), brushing aside the protest, 'You know it is the feast of Lupercal': 'It is no matter, let no images / Be hung with Caesar's trophies' (67–9). The source of his concern – that the statues may have been hung with Caesar's trophies under the aegis of Lupercalia – returns the opening of *Julius Caesar* to the territory of festive politics explored in the two plays already discussed: as in *Henry V*, Shakespeare shows a popular festival being turned to political ends. Not only are the republican-minded tribunes unnerved at such a possibility; they reject the right of the plebeians to create their own holiday like Dekker's shoemakers.

Alexander Leggatt has suggested that the opening lines of *Julius Caesar* may be another 'theatrical in-joke' twitting the likes of Spencer: Flavius 'might be one of the city fathers of London, lecturing the playgoers'.[23] Richard Wilson, however, takes a different line, relating the scene to his broader argument that the English stage was consciously trying to distance itself from its popular origins. Flavius's lines, the 'first words uttered on the stage of the Globe', 'seem to know themselves ... as a conscious declaration of company policy towards the Elizabethan theatre public': artisans in the theatre audience are told that, on a normal working day, they have no business making holiday by coming to the playhouse.[24] There are some obvious problems with this argument: for one thing, the position taken by the play in relation to Flavius and Murellus is perhaps more difficult to isolate than Wilson allows. It is far from clear that the peremptory and dull tribunes are in any way speaking for Shakespeare or for the Lord Chamberlain's Men: the Cobbler, whose wit makes them look foolish, is a much more sympathetic figure. Second, Wilson assumes that 'theatre-owners such as Philip Henslowe' excluded workers by not playing on the Sabbath, when in fact Henslowe records numerous Sunday performances; these are not necessarily mere errors on Henslowe's part.[25] Finally, if my own argument about *The Shoemakers' Holiday* is correct then Wilson's comments about a 'campaign to legitimise the Shakespearean stage and dissociate it from the subversiveness of London's artisanal subculture' apply only to Shakespeare's company, and not to the Admiral's Men.

Despite these strictures, Wilson's argument is worth considering, since it appears to be borne out by some details of the history of the Lord

Chamberlain's Men. Mindful that his company's lease on the Theatre at Shoreditch was due to expire in April 1597, in February 1596, James Burbage spent 600 pounds on a property in the Blackfriars, going on to spend additional funds refurbishing it as an indoor playhouse. His plan was thwarted in November by a petition to the Privy Council from leading residents of Blackfriars (including the company's patron George Carey himself) objecting to the siting of a theatre in the district, and the company appears to have spent the next two years playing at the Curtain. The attempt to move to the Blackfriars, however, implies a significant shift of priorities on the part of the Lord Chamberlain's Men. Being smaller than amphitheatres like the Theatre and the Curtain, an indoor theatre would have had to charge higher prices in order to make a profit; this was, indeed, the case when the Blackfriars came to be used by the Children of the Chapel in 1600, as I shall explain later. These higher prices correlated to the more socially exclusive area in which the playhouse was situated, as Andrew Gurr points out, making the intended move to the Blackfriars potentially 'an ingenious solution for the problem of replacing the Theatre, and an emphatic shift up-market, from the amphitheatre serving primarily the penny-paying standers in the yard to the "private" or "select" kind of audience which expected seats and a roof over their heads'.[26] Gurr reads Burbage's attempt to move to a smaller, indoor playing space nearer the homes of the wealthy as an indication that, even in 1596, the Lord Chamberlain's Men were thinking about trying to attract a more elite class of playgoers.[27] Their eventual relocation to the Globe, an amphitheatre playhouse in Southwark, can be seen as a halfway move in the same direction: as David Farley-Hills points out, the Globe was 'ideally situated not only for attracting city clientele over London Bridge, but also for the "wiser" and freer spending sort from the West End of London and Westminster who had easy and comfortable access by water across the Thames'.[28] Wealthier playgoers and students from the Inns of Court could get to the Globe directly across the river, rather than having to traverse the City as they had to the Theatre or Curtain.

Another phenomenon that may indicate an attempt on the part of Shakespeare's company to target a more elite class of playgoers is the departure of its clown Will Kemp, also in 1599. He appears to have represented a style of comedy that was associated with the lower social strata: almost forty years later, a character in Richard Brome's *The Antipodes* (1638) would describe improvisatory clowning as having been 'allowed' only 'in the days of Tarlton and Kemp, / Before the stage was purg'd from barbarism, / And brought to the perfection it now shines with'.[29] Kemp's barbarism seems to have consisted in features of his clowning which he shared with his predecessor Tarlton: unscriptedness, bawdy and complicity with the audience, elements which were combined in the jigs for which Kemp was famed. Kemp's replacement Robert Armin, however, seems to have represented an altogether different sort of comedy. David Wiles describes him as 'an intellectual, a Londoner, and as well attuned to Renaissance notions of folly as to the English folk tradition'; the roles Shakespeare wrote for him involve less complicity with the audience and a higher social status and linguistic register.[30] Whether or not Kemp left voluntarily – and the reference to slanderous 'Ballad-makers and their coherents' as 'Shakerags' in *Kemps Nine Daies Wonder* (1600) may indicate some animosity – the fact that he was not replaced with a clown of a similar sort to himself implies that his departure allowed the Lord Chamberlain's Men to move away from a style of humour that had lower-class associations to one perhaps more in keeping with a gentle audience.[31]

While Wilson perhaps overstates his argument that the sending home of the plebeians at the start of *Julius Caesar* should be read as a banishing of artisans from the new Globe theatre, the attempt by the Lord Chamberlain's Men to move to the Blackfriars in 1596, their actual move to the Globe in 1599 and the departure of Kemp do provide some indication as to why the presence of workers in his audience might have been a question that interested Shakespeare at the time when he wrote that play. Another, perhaps even more important factor that affected the way different playing companies located themselves in relation to the idea of work is one that I shall discuss in the next section of this chapter: this is the revival of the companies of child players at St Paul's and Blackfriars.

ACTING AND IDLENESS, III: THE CHILDREN'S COMPANIES

One of the most important and influential developments in the London theatre in the years 1599 and 1600 was the resumption of playing by groups of boy actors, associated with the choirs of St Paul's Cathedral and of the Chapel Royal at Windsor, for the first time since the 1580s. The Children of Paul's performed, as they had done previously, in the precincts of the cathedral; the Children of the Chapel began playing in 1600 at the indoor theatre James Burbage had built in the Blackfriars, the same neighbourhood where an earlier group of Chapel Children had performed in the 1580s.[32] The fact that they apparently did not meet with the same problems Burbage had encountered implies that the Blackfriars' inhabitants considered the boys a less objectionable proposition, and a possible explanation for this will be ventured later; at any rate, the Blackfriars enterprise had been anticipated by the Children of Paul's, who began performing again towards the end of 1599. Reavley Gair has suggested that the first play staged at the reopened Paul's was John Marston's *Antonio and Mellida*, since it contains elements that seem designed to provide an introductory showcase for the company: 'the first act opens with a military parade of the principals', while the second allows the boys to show off their skills in singing and dancing, as does the singing contest of the final act. Furthermore, the drama opens with a metadramatic discussion by the boys of the parts they have to play and the problems they are having in preparing their performances: as Gair suggests, the point of this may be that 'Paul's has not operated as a dramatic company for some nine years, so there is no reserve of theatrical experience to draw upon'.[33] I find this a convincing reading of the play, but it should be emphasised that many early plays by both revived companies have a similarly self-conscious quality about them, often featuring inductions and other metatheatrical paraphernalia. Michael Shapiro has related this to what he sees as the inherently artificial nature of the children's performance, where boys played the part of mature men (and indeed women).[34] However, I would draw upon Gair's comments on *Antonio and Mellida* to suggest that these metadramatic commentaries also function as a kind of advertisement for the child companies themselves, placing them as a distinctive offering within the commercial theatre around 1600; and, as I shall argue in the following paragraphs, that distinctiveness is often imagined in terms of a particular relationship to the linked concepts of work and social status.

As several critics have remarked, a recurrent feature of inductions and prologues written for both child companies, particularly in the years immediately following their revival, is an insistence on the socially privileged nature of their audiences.[35] The Prologue to *Antonio and Mellida* addresses the 'Select, and most respected Auditors' (Vol. I, p. 11), while the Introduction to *Jack Drum's Entertainment* (1600) refers to 'this choise selected influence' (Vol. III, p. 179). In Act V of the latter play, Sir Edward Fortune provides a more graphic description of the audience at Paul's:

SIR EDWARD Now by my troth and I had thought ont too,
I would have had a play: Ifaith I would.
I sawe the Children of *Powles* last night,
And troth they pleasde mee prettie, prettie well,
The Apes in time will do it hansomely.

PLANET Ifaith I like the Audience that frequenteth there
With much applause: A man shall not be choakte
With the stench of Garlike, nor be pasted
To the barmy Jacket of a Beer-brewer.
BRABANT JUNIOR Tis a good gentle Audience. (Vol. III, p. 234)

Such passages are not limited to Marston or to the Children of Paul's. *Cynthia's Revels* (1600–1), written by Ben Jonson for the Children of the Chapel, begins with another metadramatic Induction in which some of the boy actors argue over who will deliver the Prologue, summarise the plot and take it in turn to parody first 'one of your gentile auditors' (116–17) and then 'a more sober, or better-gather'd gallant' (134–5) taking his seat in the theatre. When the Prologue is finally spoken, it expresses the author's hope that the audience's critical judgement will match its social distinction:

If gracious silence, sweet attention,
Quicke sight, and quicker apprehension,
(The lights of iudgement's throne) shine any where;
Our doubtfull authour hopes this is their sphere.
And therefore opens he himselfe to those;
To other weaker beames, his labours close:
As loth to prostitute their virgin straine
To eu'rie vulgar and adult'rate braine. (1–8)

The question of whether such passages reflect a genuine difference in social status between audiences at St Paul's and Blackfriars and those who attended the theatres of the adult companies is one that has attracted considerable critical debate. In 1952, Alfred Harbage characterised the children's theatre as a 'theatre of a coterie', performing less frequently and to smaller, higher-paying audiences than did the adults in their 'theatre of a nation'.[36] In 1981, however, Ann Jennalie Cook questioned Harbage's identification of two 'rival traditions', instead arguing that, in all of London's theatres, 'the spectators came chiefly from the upper levels of the social order'. Thus, when the child companies resumed playing in 1599, they attempted to attract an elite audience away from the adult companies.[37] Writing in 1987, Andrew Gurr accepted Cook's argument that the adult and child companies were competing for an elite audience after 1599; however, he disputed her assumption that this elite formed the majority of the playgoing population. 'Given the number of citizens in London, their relative affluence, and their proximity to all the playhouse venues, it may not be wildly wrong to think of them and their lesser neighbours the prosperous artisan class as a kind of silent majority in the playhouses.'[38] The current consensus appears to be that while citizens and apprentices, as well as gentlemen, went to plays, theatregoing habits were less stratified by class than Harbage assumed in that even after 1599 socially elite playgoers continued to attend the adult theatres.[39] However, it does seem safe to say that the higher prices charged at the indoor theatres would have narrowed the social range of their audiences: Gurr puts the basic cost of a seat in one of the amphitheatres at one penny, rising to sixpence for a room in the gallery, whereas prices in the halls began somewhere between three and six pence and rose to two shillings and sixpence.[40] It is unclear whether these higher prices reflect a deliberate policy of exclusivity on the part of the child companies or whether, as Munro suggests, they are simply the inevitable result of the fact that they performed less frequently and in smaller theatres.[41] Either way, they do seem to have produced an atmosphere of social privilege on which both Jonson and Marston were able to capitalise, as the passages quoted above indicate. They portrayed their respective theatres as environments where playgoers would not have to put up with the presence of manual workers such as Marston's beer-brewer; in having his 'more sober' gallant express the wish that dramatists 'would not so penuriously gleane wit, from euerie laundresse, or hackney-man, or deriue their best grace (with seruile imitation) from common stages' (Ind. 180–2), Jonson similarly implies a link between the public playhouses and people who laboured for a living. As I suggested earlier, if, in *Julius Caesar*, Shakespeare raises the question of whether cobblers, carpenters and the like should be present at the Globe, he does so obliquely and ambivalently; here, by contrast, the notion that such people ought not to be at Paul's or the Blackfriars is unmistakable.

It is not only from the audiences at the private theatres that workers are supposed to be absent, however: the early plays written by both Marston and Jonson for the child companies seem to suggest that they are absent from the stage as well. The Induction to *Antonio and Mellida* may be read as portraying the boy actors as inexperienced, as Gair argues, but the statement of the boy playing Piero that, 'we can say our parts: but wee are ignorant in what mould we must cast our Actors' (Vol. I, p. 5) apparently requires us to accept the more specific conceit that the play has not been rehearsed: if it had, the children would surely have an idea of what acting style to adopt. The (presumably fictional) notion that the play being performed has been rehearsed little or not at all recurs in several of the early child company plays. *Jack Drum's Entertainment* starts with an Introduction in which the Tire-man apologises to the audience for the fact that the play has not begun: the playwright has snatched his book from the actors and is preventing them from coming on stage. One of the children then enters to explain that the author was

loth,
Wanting a Prologue, & our selves not perfect,
To rush upon your eyes without respect:
Yet if youle pardon his defects and ours,
Heele give us passage, & you pleasing sceanes. (Vol. III, p. 179)

Once again, the actors are 'not perfect' in that they have not adequately rehearsed the play. The boy goes on to promise that they will work harder, but not in the sense we might expect:

And for our parts to gratifie your favour,
Weele studie till our cheekes looke wan with care,
That you our pleasures, we your loves may share. (Vol. III, p. 179)

The boy does not envisage the actors practising their performance like the mechanicals in *A Midsummer Night's Dream* but rather pledges to 'studie', to learn his lines, in a manner that recalls the children's status as schoolboys. The squabble in *Cynthia's Revels* over who will read the Prologue similarly implies that the lines have been 'studied' but not actually performed before:

1. Pray you away; why fellowes? Gods so? what doe you meane?
2. Mary that you shall not speake the Prologue, sir.
3. Why? doe you hope to speake it?
2. I, and I thinke I haue most right to it: I am sure I studied it first.
3. That's all one, if the Authour thinke I can speake it better.
1. I pleade possession of the cloake: Gentles, your suffrages I pray you.
(Ind. 1–10)

Clearly, while the children know their lines, there has been no rehearsal of them – not of the Prologue, at any rate. A final intimation that the company has not prepared adequately for performance is expressed in *Antonio's Revenge* (1599–1601). In II. 1, Balurdo enters 'with a beard, halfe of, halfe on' and attempts to give an explanation of his condition while staying in character but is eventually forced to admit that the 'tyring man hath not glewd on my beard halfe fast enough' (Vol. I, p. 85).

Tiffany Stern has suggested that the fiction of unrehearsedness created in these plays alludes to their supposed function as rehearsals for performances at Court: by emphasising this notion and 'by performing only two or three times a week (separating themselves from adult players who needed to perform daily to support themselves), the boys gave themselves the mystique of court players. And their "rehearsal" is shown to be so near to performance as to be, literally, indistinguishable from it.'[42] The performances of the child companies in 1570s London do, indeed, seem to have been rehearsals which audiences paid to attend, although, as Munro puts it, 'their late Elizabethan and early Jacobean counterparts were increasingly commercialised'.[43] I suggested in Chapter 2 that the notion of performance as rehearsal was one on which the adult companies drew in the 1590s in order to give themselves greater legitimacy; however, I am not sure that it entirely accounts for the studied amateurism of the child companies after 1599. Jonson and Marston imply that their plays are unrehearsed, but, unlike the characters in *The Downfall of Robert, Earl of Huntingdon*, they never explicitly state that what is being performed is a rehearsal. This, indeed, would make a nonsense of the fact that the speaker in *Jack Drum's Entertainment* apologises for the play's unrehearsedness, something that, if it were meant to be a rehearsal, would go without saying. When Stern talks of the boys' separateness from 'adult players who needed to perform daily to support themselves', however, I think she is closer to the mark: I would suggest that the ethos of unpreparedness was intended by the writers for the child companies as a means of distinguishing them from the adults. As I argued in Chapter 2, the adults emphasised the importance of rehearsal, depicting it onstage in *A Midsummer Night's Dream* and *The Downfall of Robert, Earl of Huntingdon*, and used various means to present themselves as professionally competent purveyors of a superior product. The drama of the children, however, is playfully depicted as unrehearsed and incompetent. While the adults' performances are the product of work, theirs are given up to the 'authentick censure' of the audience as 'The woorthlesse present of slight idlenesse' (*Antonio's Revenge*, The Prologue; Vol. I, p. 11).

The Prologue's choice of words in this last instance is rather ambiguous. Is the idleness that of the actors who have not rehearsed the play properly, of the playwright who ought to have been doing something more worthwhile when he wrote it, or of the audience, who are enjoying the pleasurable experience of being idle at the present time? The triplicate of meanings is significant, because it unites actors, playwright and audience in a common ethos. There is a similar moment in the Induction of Marston's *What You Will* (1601), where the author's confidant Phylomuse explains that the play is 'even *What You Will*, a slight toye, lightly composed, to swiftly finisht, ill plotted, worse written, I feare me worst acted, and indeed *What You Will*' (Vol. II, p. 233). The play is a toy for the audience's idle consumption, and neither playwright nor actors have put much effort into its production. These plays seem to indicate a link between the private theatres' self-advertisement as places for non-workers and the fiction of unrehearsedness repeatedly created on stage. In the same way that the private halls are contrasted with the amphitheatres in terms of their supposed audience demographic, so the child companies are contrasted with the adults in terms of the status of their acting as work or non-work. This may be the point of the lines in the Prologue to *Antonio's Revenge* that refer to the tragedy about to be performed:

> May we be happie in our weake devoyer,
> And all parte pleas'd in most wisht content:
> But sweate of *Hercules* can nere beget
> So blest an issue. (Vol. I, p. 69)

The task before the children is only a weak one, but, nevertheless, a successful performance would be beyond the means even of sweating Hercules. The allusion seems to be to the Globe, which is supposed to have adopted the image of Hercules bearing the Earth as its emblem; in *Antonio and Mellida*, the boy playing Alberto had criticised the fashion for strutting roles whose actors stalk as proudly 'as if *Hercules* / Or burly *Atlas* shouldred up their state' (Vol. I, p. 5).[44] Here, the Prologue goes on to lament the disparity between the company's desire for excellence and its ability to achieve it:

> Yet heere's the prop that doth support our hopes;
> When our Sceanes falter, or invention halts,
> Your favour will give crutches to our faults. (Vol. I, p. 70)

I think the sense is that whereas performances at the Globe are borne up by the labour of the actors, implicit in the perspiring Hercules, the deficiencies of the actors at Paul's are compensated for in a less undignified way, by the freely given favour of the audiences. Once again, a private theatre is represented not as a place where workers come to watch other workers but where non-labouring audiences and amateur actors unite in a shared ethos of idleness. An explanation for the failure of the Children of the Chapel to excite the same opposition that the Lord Chamberlain's Men did on moving to Burbage's playhouse in the Blackfriars may lie in the way the children's companies were thus able to capitalise on the amateur status of their actors: they could distance themselves from their adult equivalents both as offering a different and less professional form of acting and as attracting a more socially elevated audience.

Over the last few paragraphs, I have tried to suggest that the references in plays by Marston and Jonson to the nature of the audiences at Paul's and at Blackfriars were more than just an attempt to advertise those theatres as pleasant places to come because of the absence of smelly artisans. Rather, those references should be seen alongside the repeated insistence on amateurism and unpreparedness as means of constructing the private theatres as a particular type of social space: one not just (in theory at least) empty of workers but also conceptually distant from the whole idea of work. In order to explain why playwrights might have wanted to represent their theatres in such terms, however, it will be necessary to address once again a theme I have already discussed in this book: the social meanings of labour in early modern England.

LABOUR AND STATUS IN EARLY MODERN ENGLAND

In Chapter 3, I argued that the crucial social distinction in sixteenth- and seventeenth-century England was between gentlemen and commoners and that this distinction was often imagined as a split between those who did and those who did not perform manual or commercial labour. This partially reflected the conventional medieval division of society into *bellatores, oratores* and *laboratores*, but it also constituted an important revision of it. Due to factors including the Reformation, the growing influence of the commercial classes and the decreasing importance of warfare in the lives of the elite, the social role of the gentle classes was reconceptualised: they served the commonwealth through government, public office and other forms of non-manual work rather than, or as well as, through fighting. Certain varieties of work thus became compatible with the status of gentleman. However, an argument that will underpin the remainder of this book is that the medieval definition of a gentleman as someone exempt from labour continued to influence the way social status was understood in the early modern period. Even as some gentlemen saw and represented themselves as people who worked, albeit with their heads rather than with their hands, the assumption that to be a gentleman was to be idle persisted and, indeed, in some respects, grew more pervasive.

I would attribute this continued influence in large part to the disjuncture between the ostensibly clear-cut dualism of gentleman and commoner and, in Keith Wrightson's analysis, the actual 'complexity of the criteria which, in practice, established a man's rank' in early modern England.[45] In *The*

Description of England, William Harrison outlines the various ways other than heredity through which one can come to be a gentleman:

Whosoever studieth the laws of the realm, whoso abideth in the university giving his mind to his book, or professeth physic and the liberal sciences, or, beside his service in the room of a captain in the wars or good counsel given at home, whereby his commonwealth is benefited, can live without manual labor, and therto is able and will bear the port, charge, and countenance of a gentleman, he shall for money have a coat and arms bestowed upon him by heralds (who in the charter of the same do of custom pretend antiquity and service and many gay things), and thereunto being made so good cheap, be called master, which is the title that men give to esquires and gentlemen, and reputed for a gentleman ever after.[46]

Harrison's words imply a considerable degree of mobility within the society he describes. As well as inheriting gentle status, one can acquire it through a university education, or through the practice of law or medicine, or through military service. However, he seems to say that notwithstanding all these, if a man can live without manual labour and afford to keep up a gentlemanly appearance, he can effectively buy his coat and arms 'for money', 'good cheap'. The observation, or complaint, that it is now possible to buy the status of gentleman can frequently be heard from early modern writers. Laurence Humphrey complains of the 'great or rather to great multitude' of those who have 'by fraude, guile, and deceit, like ill meanes, or princes blinded iudgement, bought or purchased Nobilytie'; Richard Mulcaster that 'of all the meanes to make a gentleman, it is the most vile, to be made for money'.[47]

One reason behind this commoditisation of status was the fact that the Reformation had taken vast tracts of land out of the Church's possession and had placed them in the gift (or sale) of the Crown so that it became possible for wealthy or favoured individuals without hereditary titles to join the landed classes and to live off their rents like gentlemen rather than through commerce or other forms of work. Having attained a gentlemanly lifestyle, many evidently sought the social status that would ratify it: over 2,000 grants of arms were made between 1560 and 1589, and a further 1,180 or more by 1619.[48] The fluidity of the land market and the upward mobility which it facilitated seem to have led to a correspondingly acute status anxiety, both among newly created gentlemen keen to prove themselves worthy of their rank and among gentlemen of longer standing who wanted to distinguish themselves from the *arrivistes*. Accordingly, the external manifestations of gentle status assumed a heightened importance, as Harrison suggests when he stipulates that one must be able to 'bear the port, charge, and countenance of a gentleman'. Stone highlights, as a cause of the decline of some noble families, the phenomenon of 'conspicuous consumption', whereby members of the elite spent vast sums on royal service, attendance at Court, high living in London or provincial hospitality in order to demonstrate their worthiness.[49] However, more complex indicators of gentility were also invoked, as Barnaby Rich suggested in 1609:

> all our strife and contention is, who shall sit aboue the salte, who shall goe next the wall, who shall stand formost in the Herauldes bookes, and who shall goe before, and who shall come behind ... it is growne to a general controuersie, not onely amongst the inferior sorte of those that would faine be reputed to be Gentlemen, but likewise amongst the better sort of those that be knowne to be Gentlemen by birth, and others that by their places and professions are gentelized, and worthy to bee so esteemed.[50]

Of considerable importance among these signifiers of status was the ability to 'live without manual labor', as Harrison put it. Sir Thomas Smith modified the passage when he used it in his *De republica anglorum* (1583), writing that one must be able to 'live idly and without manuall labour', and, indeed, the notion that gentlemen should not work with their hands seems often to have been exaggerated into a virtual cult of idleness.[51] Robert Burton wrote that

> idlenesse is an appendix to nobility, they count it a disgrace to worke, and spend all their daies in sports, recreations, and pastimes, and will therefore takes no paines; be of no vocation: they feed liberally, fare well, want exercise, action, employment, (for to worke, I say they may not abide) and company to their desires.[52]

Maurice Ashley quotes Viscount Conway: 'We eat, and drink and rise up to play and this is to live like a gentleman, for what is a gentleman but his pleasure?'.[53] In this context, certain games and recreations assumed a heightened significance as (in Marcia Vale's words) 'ubiquitous and visible badges of social and physical superiority over the lower orders', or, more specifically, as indications that one did not need to work.[54]

As an activity that required both a disposable income and free time, theatregoing could readily be used as a way of advertising one's gentle status. In *The Gull's Horn-Book* (1609), for example, Thomas Dekker satirically tells his gentleman readers that they ought to criticise loudly when at the theatre: thereby, 'you publish your temperance to the world, in that you seem not to resort thither to taste vain pleasures with a hungry appetite but only as a gentleman to spend a foolish hour or two because you can do nothing else'.[55] One does not go to the theatre for enjoyment's sake but to advertise one's freedom from other obligations. This seems to be the intention of the gentle auditor parodied by one of the children in the Induction to *Cynthia's Revels*:

> By this light, I wonder that any man is so mad, to come to see these rascally *Tits* play here—They doe act like so manie *wrens*, or *pismires*—not the fift part of a good face amongst them all—And then their *musicke* is abominable—able to stretch a mans eares worse then tenne—pillories, and their ditties—most lamentable things, like the pittifull fellowes that make them—Poets. (Ind. 120–7)

Like Dekker's gallant, the speaker attends a performance he affects to despise in order to show that he is free to waste his leisure hours on trifles: theatregoing takes on the status of a conspicuous consumption of time. Even his speech is prolonged, punctuated by draws on his pipe.

These examples from Dekker and Jonson show how some of the accusations that the theatre's opponents made against it – it was a waste of time and was incompatible with productive labour – could be turned to its advantage when trying to appeal to a certain class of playgoer. Undoubtedly, the idle gallants parodied by these writers are meant to be figures of ridicule, but they do serve to demonstrate some of the social meanings that could be attached to theatregoing in the context of an elite culture that thrived on leisure, consumption and display. While the pipe-smoking gentleman is clearly not Jonson's ideal auditor, Jonson and Marston depict both the playhouses and the actors for whom they write in terms designed to attract a social group that made a fetish of idleness.

CRANES AND PIGMIES: *PATIENT GRISSIL* AND THE CHILDREN'S COMPANIES

The opinions of theatre historians as to the effect that the revived children's companies had upon their adult counterparts vary depending on the degree of competition assumed to exist between them. As we have seen, Harbage regards the two as representing quite different theatrical cultures, the adults appealing to a diverse, the children to a coterie audience. Roslyn Knutson hypothesises a cooperative rather than a competitive relationship, analogous to that between the members of livery companies, and also points out that as landlord of the Blackfriars property 'Richard Burbage and all who profited from his financial ventures had an interest in the success' of the Children of the Chapel.[56] Conversely, while

Cook and Gurr disagree on the demographic composition of London's community of playgoers, they both assume that adults and children were trying to attract the same group of elite playgoers into their theatres, an assumption that my analysis of the inductions and other metatheatrical features of the early child-company plays would appear to support. However, Gurr sees the Admiral's and the Lord Chamberlain's Men as reacting in different ways to this threat to their custom. He views the decision of the Admiral's to move north from the Rose theatre to the Fortune, built by Henslowe and Alleyn near Finsbury Fields in 1600, as one symptom of a wider policy to appeal 'more narrowly and explicitly to the city and citizens than to the lawyers and gentry' who were attracted to St Paul's and the Blackfriars. By contrast, while the Chamberlain's continued to perform plays that seem to have been designed to compete with the Admiral's – devil plays such as *The Merry Devil of Edmonton* (1599–1604), domestic dramas such as *A Yorkshire Tragedy* (1605–8), citizen plays like *The London Prodigal* (1603–5) – Gurr believes that they decided also to 'compet[e] with the boys and their new fashions'.[57] At the end of this chapter, I shall discuss *Hamlet* in the context of Gurr's argument that the Chamberlain's sought to maintain a bifold appeal. First, however, I shall address another play of 1599–1600 that I believe supports his view that the Admiral's Men made a conscious decision to appeal to a citizen, rather than an elite, audience.

My earlier discussion of *The Shoemakers' Holiday*, with its obvious interest in the working and recreational lives of London tradesmen, suggests that before playing had resumed at St Paul's, the Admiral's Men may already have been trying to align themselves with the citizen element of the play-going community. *Patient Grissil*, by Dekker, William Haughton and Henry Chettle, identifies itself just as markedly with this group, while displaying, if anything, an even greater consciousness of the symbolic importance of work in the theatrical market-place of 1599–1600. The play is a version of the Griselda story previously told in Boccaccio's *Decameron*, by Petrarch, by Chaucer's Clerk, by John Phillip in *The Commodye of Pacient and Meeke Grissill* (*c.* 1559) and by Thomas Deloney in *The Garland of Good Will* (*c.* 1592–3).[58] The playwrights make numerous additions to the tale, among them the extension of Griselda's family to include the servant Babulo and the heroine's brother Laureo, a student forced to leave the university by lack of funds.[59] Towards the end of the play, these characters engage in a conversation that appears to situate *Patient Grissil* firmly within the commercial context I have tried to delineate in this chapter.

Enter LAUREO *reading and* BABULO *with him.*

BABULO Come I haue left my worke to see what mattens you mumble to your selfe, faith *Laureo* I would you could leaue this lattin, and fal to make baskets, you think tis enough if at dinner you tell vs a tale of Pignies, and then mounch vp our victuals, but that fits not vs: or the historie of the well *Helicon,* and then drinke vp our beare: we cannot liue vpon it.

LAUREO A Scholler doth disdaine to spend his spirits,
Vpon such base imploiments as hand labours.

BABULO Then you should disdaine to eate vs out of house and home: you stand all day peeping into an ambrie there, and talke of monsters and miracles, and countries to no purpose: before I fell to my trade I was a traueller, and found more in one yeare then you can by your poets and paltries in seauen yeares.

LAUREO What wonders hast thou seene, which are not heere?

BABULO Oh God, I pittie thy capacitye good scholler: as a little wind makes a sweet ball smell, so a crumme of learning makes your trade proude: what wonders? wonders not of nine daies, but *1599.* I haue seene vnder *Iohn Prester* and *Tamer Cams,* people with heds like Dogs. (V. I. 1–19)

Babulo's final speech places the scene, not within its ostensible location of Italy, but in theatrical London at the turn of the century. His reference to wonders not of nine days but of 1599 alludes not only to the current date but to Will Kemp's celebrated jig from London to Norwich, begun on 11 February 1599–1600, the story of which Kemp went on to have published as *Kemps Nine Daies VVonder* in 1600. The dog-headed people, like Prester John and like some of the other wonders Babulo goes on to describe, are derived from *The Voyages and Trauailes of Sir John Maundeuile Knight* (*c.* 1583), but they also seem to refer to the current popularity of satire both within the theatre and (until the Bishops' Ban of 1 June 1599) in print.[60] The genre was frequently characterised in canine terms, as in the title of Thomas Middleton's *Micro-cynicon: Sixe Snarling Satyres* (1599), and here, Laureo goes on to criticise 'them that snarle, / And bay and barke at other mens abuse' (20–1). A final allusion to the contemporary scene appears in another of the travellers' tales on which Babulo invites Laureo to comment: 'but let me descend and grow lower and lower, what say you to the litle litle *Pigmies,* no higher then a boyes gig, and yet they tug and fight with the long neckt Cranes' (43–5). Laureo identifies the pigmies as 'poore and wretched people', the cranes as 'rich oppressors' (46–7), but it is hard not to read the lines as a reference to the relationship between the children's companies and their adult counterparts along the lines of Rosencrantz's 'little eyases' speech in *Hamlet* II. 2. 338–44.

In view of the way in which this part of the play seems to announce itself as a commentary on the theatrical environment of 1599–1600, it is worth pondering the possible significance of the antagonism that is set up between the two characters. As his allusion to the nine days' wonder suggests, Babulo is a clown in the tradition of Kemp, the voice of popular morality and (so far as it is compatible with personal safety) subversiveness. Invited by the Marquess Gwalter to come with Grissil to Court, he responds, 'I haue a better trade sir, basketmaking' (I. 2. 311) and goes on to opine that 'beggers are fit for beggers, gentlefolkes for gentlefolkes: I am afraid that this wonder of the rich louing the poor, wil last but nine daies' (317–19). His defiant pride in his origins and his work contrasts with the social attitudes expressed by Laureo, who feels that his (incomplete) university education exempts him from the 'hand labours' carried out by the rest of his family. In dramatising a face-off between a plain-speaking clown who respects manual labour and a pretentious student whose disdain for it expresses his desire for social mobility, Dekker, Haughton and Chettle seem to be allegorising one interpretation of what was happening in the London theatre of 1599–1600: a socially and aesthetically elitist tendency was trying to distance itself from a broader, lower-status tradition in which it had its origins. And, while Laureo is hardly demonised, expressing a brotherly outrage at Grissil's mistreatment by Gwalter with which an audience can readily agree, the play firmly associates itself with the values of Babulo, along with those of his master Janicola and Grissil herself. These include patience (as manifested in Grissil and her father), satisfaction with one's social station and industriousness. In the second scene, we see the trio sit down to their work of basket-making, 'And that our labour may not seeme to long, / Weele cunningly beguile it with a song' (I. 2. 90–1). The song begins:

> Art thou poore yet hast thou golden Slumbers:
> Oh sweet content!
> Art thou rich yet is thy minde perplexed?
> Oh punnishment.
> Dost thou laugh to see how fooles are vexed?
> To ad to golden numbers, golden numbers.
> O sweet content, o sweet &c.
> Foote. Worke apace, apace, apace, apace:
> Honest labour beares a louely face,
> Then hey noney noney: hey noney, noney. (94–103)

The phrase, 'worke apace' also appears in *The Shoemakers' Holiday* (IV. 1. 34) and a similar spectacle of characters singing as they work appears earlier on in that scene:

Enter HODGE *at his shop board,* RAFE, FIRKE, LACIE *as* HANS, *and a boy at work.*

ALL Hey downe, a downe, downe derie.
HODGE Well said my hearts, plie your worke to day, we loytred yesterday, to it pell mell, that we may liue to be Lord Maiors, or Aldermen at least.
FIRKE Hey downe a downe derie. (1–5)

The staging of manual work in *The Shoemakers' Holiday* may be another indication that, even before the revival of the Children of Paul's, the Admiral's Men were keen to align themselves with London's tradesmen. However, the scene in *Patient Grissil* is more significant, as it dates from a time when Jonson and Marston were taking pains to stress the absence of manual labour from their auditoria and the absence of workers from their stages. In this context, the insistence that 'Honest labour beares a louely face' has an air of defiance about it. I wonder whether the actors performing the scene genuinely were weaving baskets, as in the 1960s performance of *The Shoemakers' Holiday* by students from the Department of Boot and Shoe Manufacture at Northampton College of Technology who, in the words of a letter to the *Daily Telegraph*, 'were actually making shoes on the stage'.[61] In that case, they would have been working as actors and as basket-weavers simultaneously, with the finished baskets as material testimonies to the manual labour that had been carried out onstage. A similar overlap occurs in V. 2, when Grissil and her family are made to carry wood and coals at the wedding of Gwalter to his second wife. Presumably the logs and coals were genuine (if not, what were they made of?); the actors would have been *performing* manual work, in both senses of the word.

HAMLET AND OTIATION

While the earliest plays of the revived children's companies overtly lay claim (however accurately) to a socially privileged audience, and *The Shoemakers' Holiday* and *Patient Grissil* invoke a culture of manual labour in a way that may reflect the commercial priorities of the Admiral's Men, *Hamlet* has sometimes been seen by critics as the product of a company unsure of where it was going. Andrew Gurr writes of the Lord Chamberlain's Men in 1600 facing 'a choice, between going the Henslowe way and catering for an increasingly narrow and conservative citizen taste or competing with the boys and their new fashions'.[62] Annabel Patterson has suggested that it was Shakespeare's desire to speak both to the 'judicious few' and the 'underprivileged many' that led him to create a prince who, in his advice to the players, expresses an elitist aesthetic but who makes use elsewhere of a 'language learned from the politically voiceless, who can still be heard elliptically in proverbs, snatches of popular songs, and the upside-down speech that belongs to Bottom and his fellows'.[63] Robert Weimann, too, finds in Hamlet's speech and behaviour a doubleness that reflects a tension between elite and popular styles of acting, 'the difference between a high Renaissance figuration and an antic practice'. This doubleness makes the play socially inclusive, but it also invokes the possibility of exclusion and separation, 'of conflict and tension between elite and popular forms of culture', anticipating the 'separation of upper-class and lower-class cultures' in early modern Europe described by Peter Burke.[64] Just as the play's references to child actors, to 'this goodly frame, the earth' (II. 2. 298) and to improvisational clowning allude to its company's situation at the turn of the century, with new competitors, a new playhouse and a new clown, so the social ambivalence of its hero is held to reflect the divided loyalties of the Lord Chamberlain's Men. The obsessiveness with which the play *Hamlet* refers, repeatedly, to the circumstances of its production – a trait that it shares with the other plays I have discussed in this chapter – loads it with a symbolic weight that makes such an analysis less schematic than it might appear; and in the paragraphs that follow, I want to develop the arguments of Patterson and Weimann in a way that is informed by the picture of the London theatre in 1599–1601 that has been delineated in this chapter. I shall argue that the Prince's split personality, oscillating between courtliness and a subversively 'antic disposition' (I. 5. 172), extends to a contradictory attitude towards work – a concept that, I have suggested, had come to assume central symbolic importance for Shakespeare, his colleagues and his competitors.

In his opening soliloquy, Hamlet laments the marriage of his widowed mother to a man 'no more like my father / Than I to Hercules' (I. 2. 152–3). As well as providing another reference to the mythical hero with whom the Globe theatre was associated, the Prince's contrasting of himself with Hercules seems apt in view of the melancholy desire for annihilation he expresses earlier on in the speech, when he wishes that his flesh would melt or that he were permitted by the Almighty to kill himself. As Brian Vickers has argued, such suicidal despair was regarded in the early modern period as a form of sloth: in the first book of *The Faerie Queene*, Canto IX, Stanza 40, Despair recommends suicide to the Redcross Knight as offering 'eternall rest / And happie ease' and insists that 'Sleepe after toyle, port after stormie seas, / Ease after warre, death after life does greatly please'.[65] Early on in his career, in a scene frequently depicted by Renaissance artists, Hercules encountered the figures of Virtue and Pleasure at a crossroads, and they invited him to choose between them. He chose the former and went on to accomplish the twelve labours.[66] Hamlet, by contrast, goes on to prove sluggish in accomplishing the task offered him by the Ghost, that of avenging his father:

> I find thee apt,
> And duller shouldst thou be than the fat weed
> That roots itself in ease on Lethe wharf,
> Wouldst thou not stir in this. (I. 5. 31–4)

The Ghost's speech invokes a vocabulary of labour and idleness, of aptness and stirring contrasted with dullness and fatness, that Hamlet repeatedly returns to when lamenting his failure to act. In II. 2, he berates himself as a 'rogue', a 'dull and muddy-mettled rascal', 'John-a-dreams' (550, 567), who must 'like a whore unpack my heart with words, / And fall a-cursing like a very drab' (585–6). The strong overtones of idleness in words like 'rogue' and 'rascal' serve to contrast Hamlet with the industrious revenger Pyrrhus from the First Player's speech earlier in the scene:

> A roused vengeance sets him new a-work,
> And never did the Cyclops' hammers fall
> On Mars's armor forg'd for proof eterne
> With less remorse than Pyrrhus' bleeding sword
> Now falls on Priam. (488–92)

As in the Ghost's speech, revenge is imagined as labour, and Pyrrhus's sword falls like the hammers in Vulcan's smithy. Hamlet's failure to carry out this labour seems to affect the way he talks about suicide in his third soliloquy: his question, 'who would fardels bear, / To grunt and sweat under a weary life' (III. 1. 75–6) imagines it as a relief from a life of toil, illustrating Vickers' argument that Shakespeare's contemporaries associated it with sloth. However, after contemplating the possibility of continued existence after death, he goes on to describe suicide in more positive terms, as an 'enterprise' (85) or 'action' (87) prevented only because 'conscience does make cowards of us all' (82). The terms in which he talks of killing himself seem to have become shaped by his sense of cowardice or sloth in failing to kill Claudius; indeed, his complaint that 'the native hue of resolution / Is sicklied o'er with the pale cast of thought' (83–4) would apply equally well to either action.

Hamlet's willingness to imagine revenge as a form of labour, and to regard himself as an idle rogue in failing to carry it out, appears to place him as another instance of the tendency I discussed in the last chapter, whereby the activities of sixteenth-century aristocrats were increasingly conceptualised in terms of work. These elements of his characterisation imply a positive valuation of work that is less obvious than that in the Admiral's Men plays I have discussed but nevertheless contrasts with the ethos of idleness and amateurism cultivated in the children's theatres. However, they are contradicted by other moments in the play where the Prince displays social attitudes that one would associate more readily with plays of the child companies. Offered the chance to kill the praying Claudius, for example, he complains that such an action would be 'hire and salary, not revenge' (III. 3. 79), using the language of wage labour to describe a form of vengeance that would be incompatible with his honour code. He is shocked by the gravedigger's ability to sing as he works but accepts Horatio's explanation that 'Custom' has inured him to it (V. 1. 67): ''Tis e'en so; the hand of little employment hath the daintier sense' (69–70). Hamlet here stresses his own freedom from manual labour and the refined sensibility it brings; more generally, his melancholy disposition may mark him out as a member of the social elite, since one cause of melancholy identified by Robert Burton was 'Idlenesse, (the badge of gentry) or want of Exercise, the base of body and minde, the nurse of naughtinesse, step-mother of discipline, the chiefe author of all mischiefe'.[67] Perhaps the most interesting instance of Hamlet expressing an elitist disdain for work, however, comes when he explains to Horatio how he wrote the death warrant of Rosencrantz and Guildenstern:

> I sat me down,
> Devis'd a new commission, wrote it fair.
> I once did hold it, as our statists do,
> A baseness to write fair, and labor'd much
> How to forget that learning, but, sir, now
> It did me yeman's service. (V. 2. 31–6)

Hamlet evidently possesses the courtly accomplishment of neat hand-writing; however, he describes it as a 'baseness' that he once tried to forget, and the association with social inferiority is reiterated when he says that this skill did him 'yeman's service' when he came to forge the new commission. Jonathan Goldberg has drawn a parallel with the complaint of a writing master in the ninth dialogue of Juan Vives' *Linguae latinae exercitatio* (1538) that the nobility 'think it fine and proper ... not to know how to shape their letters properly'; evidently, some Renaissance noblemen regarded calligraphy as the business of clerks.[68] Hamlet shares this disdain, expressing an attitude that seems at first to be an example not of *sprezzatura*, which would make writing well look easy, but of what Frank Whigham calls 'sprezzatura about the exercise of sprezzatura': 'Substantive inadequacies can be viewed as insignificant, not worth hiding, indicating a position above concern for the possible disapproval of those present, who are thereby revealed as inferiors whose judgement is immaterial.'[69] However, it is undermined by Hamlet's statement that he 'labor'd much' to forget how to write well: he reveals the effort that went into the unlearning of his courtiership. Even the impression of incompetence is shown to be a piece of image-making, the result of laborious artifice. The paradox resembles that of Dekker's gallant, who needs to study *The Gull's Horn-Book* in order to learn how to look idle.

This notion that the appearance of idleness itself requires work is implied several times during the course of the play, especially in the context of Hamlet's assumed madness, for which 'idleness' twice serves as a synonym (or euphemism): when Claudius, Gertrude and the others enter in III. 2, Hamlet says to Horatio, 'They are coming to the play. I must be idle' (90), and his mother rebukes him for his 'idle tongue' at III. 4. 11. The first implication that dissembling may be a form of labour comes at II. 2. 280, when Hamlet tells Rosencrantz and Guildenstern that their modesties 'have not craft enough to color' the fact that they were sent for: the word 'craft' implies both deceit and the skill of a tradesman. In the subsequent scene, Guildenstern recalls Hamlet's words when he tells Claudius of his 'crafty madness' (III. 1. 8); again, the Prince tells his mother at III. 4. 188 that he is only 'mad in craft'. Of course, the appearance of madness is part of Hamlet's method: it allows him space to manoeuvre in Claudius's court while seeming idle and non-threatening. The tactic calls to mind George Puttenham's advice in *The Arte of English Poesie* (1589) that the courtier poet should be constantly dissembling, 'whereby the better to winne his purposes & good aduantages'. The courtier should appear busy when he is actually idle or, by contrast, 'as I haue obserued in many of the Princes Courts of Italie, to seeme idle when they be earnestly occupied & entend to nothing but mischieuous practizes, and do busily negotiat by coulor of otiation'.[70]

'Otiation' is a useful word to apply to Hamlet's behaviour in Elsinore, as it encapsulates the notion of active idleness implied by the repeated puns on 'craft'. More generally, it might serve to denote other instances of assumed inactivity or incompetence that I have mentioned in this chapter: the practice of theatregoing as a means of advertising freedom from work;

the exaggerated amateurism on display in the children's theatres; the studiedly bad handwriting of the noblemen mentioned by Vives. Shakespeare's presentation of Hamlet's idleness as a form of work develops a notion that, as we have seen, he had already explored in Prince Hal; but it also constitutes a response to the child companies of a quite different kind to that represented by *Patient Grissil.* That play was associated by its dramatists with the notion of work from which the child companies had sought to distance themselves. *Hamlet*, however, treats idleness and amateurism as consciously assumed behaviour – as forms of acting and, therefore, as forms of work.

CHAPTER 5

'Work upon that now!': labour and status on the stage, 1599–1610

In the last chapter, I tried to argue that the theatrical environment of London during the years 1599–1601 was one in which the concept of work was made to bear a great deal of symbolic baggage. Several plays engaged with the question of whether workers should be present in the playhouse: with differences of emphasis, *The Shoemakers' Holiday* and *Julius Caesar* show apprentices and citizens insisting on their right to make holiday as they please, a demand that holds a particular significance for being represented in two of the spaces where their real-life London counterparts liked to spend their free time. On the other hand, early plays for the revived children's companies invoke the idea of work negatively, insisting that their theatres are spaces from which workers should be absent. This absence extends to the stage itself: the amateurism of the child actors is stressed, in a manner that contrasts with the representations of adult actors I discussed in Chapter 2. In the final part of the chapter, I discussed two plays that seem to respond in different ways to the use made by the children's companies of ideas of work and idleness: *Patient Grissil* aligns itself with London's workers in its proud depiction of manual work on stage, whereas *Hamlet* suggests that gentlemanly idleness is itself a performance that requires work in order to be successful. It also contains a protagonist whose ideas about work, and about work's social signification, are decidedly ambivalent, and I suggested that this ambivalence might be connected to the situation faced by the Lord Chamberlain's Men at the end of the 1590s.

In this final chapter, I shall examine whether the adoption of different attitudes towards work by different companies at the turn of the century was merely a short-term phenomenon that briefly prevailed after the revival of the children's companies, or whether it indicates a longer-term trend in the London theatre. I divide the chapter into three parts: in the first, I consider the plays of the Admiral's Men and the Earl of Worcester's Men; in the second, those of the children's companies, in particular the company associated with the Blackfriars theatre; and in the third, those of the Lord Chamberlain's Men. I have not attempted anything like a comprehensive account of the companies' output; rather, I have chosen to concentrate on plays that seem especially preoccupied with the interlinked questions of work and social status which have concerned me in the course of this book.

THE ADMIRAL'S/PRINCE HENRY'S MEN AND WORCESTER'S/QUEEN ANNE'S MEN

While the Admiral's Men and the Earl of Worcester's Men (or, as they would become after James's accession, Prince Henry's Men and Queen Anne's Men) were two entirely different companies with different patrons and personnel, there is a case for considering them together. For one thing, they are linked by the figure of Philip Henslowe, the landlord of the Admiral's at the Rose from 1594 to July 1600 and the company's 'banker and financial manager' in the latter half of the 1590s.[1] After the departure of the Admiral's Men for the Fortune, Worcester's Men were among the companies who made use of the Rose, playing there between August 1602 and 12 March 1603; once again, Henslowe seems effectively to have been the company's manager, buying them plays such as Heywood's *A Woman Killed with Kindness* and supplying them with material from the Admiral's Men's repertory such as *Sir John Oldcastle*.[2] Many plays staged by Worcester's Men were written by dramatists who also wrote for the Admiral's, such as Henry Chettle, John Day, Thomas Dekker and Thomas Heywood; there also seem to be strong similarities between the types of play the two companies offered theatregoers. Both staged plays on the lives of illustrious citizens of London: in 1605, for example, Queen Anne's Men had the second part of *If You Know Not Me You Know Nobody*, which depicts Thomas Gresham's building of the Royal Exchange, while Prince Henry's performed the lost *Richard Whittington*. Both staged plays on Protestant heroes and martyrs, such as *Sir John Oldcastle* (Admiral's Men, 1599) and *Sir Thomas Wyatt* (Worcester's/Queen Anne's Men, 1602–7). And both staged plays that seem to recommend wifely patience and obedience, such as *Patient Grissil* and *How a Man May Choose a Good Wife from a Bad* (Worcester's Men, *c.* 1601–2). As I have already noted, Andrew Gurr has suggested that the 'return of the boy players at Paul's and the Blackfriars in 1599 may have sharpened the sense of loyalty to citizen values in the Henslowe writers', and he interprets the presence of such plays in the repertory as an attempt to appeal to London's tradesmen, apprentices and merchants. He also concedes that members of the social elite continued to frequent these companies' plays: according to the lawyer Philip Gawdy, when the Lord Mayor had playhouses and bowling alleys 'beset' to conscript soldiers for the Low Countries in 1602, his officers impressed not only 'gentlemen, and sarvingmen, but Lawyers, Clarkes, country men that had lawe causes, aye the Quenes men, knightes, and as it was credibly reported one Earle'.[3] Nevertheless, as will become evident from my discussion of two Blackfriars plays later on in this chapter, the repertories of both these companies seem to have been widely associated with the values of London's citizenry.

That does not mean, however, that the repertories were dominated by representations of London's citizens; in fact, the willingness to present working life that we see in Dekker's plays of 1599–1600 does not seem to have persisted. Among the extant plays of the two companies we can find, in addition to the plays focusing in marriage and on Protestant heroes referred to above, lurid tragedies such as *The Spanish Moor's Tragedy* and *Hoffman* (Admiral's Men, 1600 and 1602), plays on classical subjects, such as Thomas Heywood's *The Rape of Lucrece* and *The Golden Age* (Queen Anne's Men, 1606–8 and 1609–11) and plays depicting contemporary personalities, such as *The Travels of the Three English Brothers* (Queen Anne's Men, 1607) and *The Roaring Girl* (Prince Henry's Men, 1610 or earlier). Some plays, such as the second part of *If You Know Not Me* and the lost *Richard Whittington*, as well as the plays discussed in this chapter, focus on manual and commercial workers, but they are by no means in a majority. Moreover, it has been argued by Laura Caroline Stevenson and others that such positive depictions as there are of these workers focus not on their commercial or artisanal talents but on their quasi-aristocratic qualities, reflecting the pervasive aesthetic influence of the social elite. A classic example is Thomas Heywood's treatment of the Elizabethan merchant-financier Thomas Gresham in the second part of *If You Know Not Me*: rather than showing the qualities that made Gresham a successful merchant, the play focuses on Gresham's building of the Royal Exchange, which it depicts as an essentially philanthropic gesture. We also see Gresham 'daunce all my care away' when he loses a sugar monopoly for which he paid the King of Barbary sixty thousand pounds and then pay a further sixteen thousand for a pearl to be ground up and added to a cup of wine which he drinks as a toast to Queen Elizabeth.[4] While Barbara

J. Baines has criticised Gresham's drinking of the pearl as both 'downright idiotic' and 'morally problematic', for Stevenson, the foundation of the Exchange and the pearl-drinking are both examples of 'aristocratic conspicuous expenditure'. To show Gresham working to become rich would be to imply that he was motivated by avarice; instead, Heywood 'asks us to admire Gresham's ability to spend, even to lose, money', as well as his devotion to the monarch.[5]

If Stevenson is right, we might expect to find some workers in the plays of the Henslowe companies, but little in the way of work, since that was a practice little valued in the systems of representation that dominated early modern culture. My earlier reading of *The Shoemakers' Holiday* and *Patient Grissil*, however, would seem to indicate that her argument does not hold for all the plays in their repertories; furthermore, even the play that seems to encapsulate it most perfectly, Thomas Heywood's *The Four Prentices of London* (1600 or earlier), proves, on examination, to be less hidebound by the ideological dominance of the aristocracy than Stevenson supposes.[6] The premise of the play is that the Earl of Bullein (i.e., Bouillon, not Boulogne, as some critics have it), dispossessed of his lands, has been forced into exile and now lives in London 'like a Cittizen' (29). Necessity has compelled him to have his sons, Godfrey, Guy, Charles and Eustace, bound as apprentices to urban trades: 'all high borne, / Yet of the Citty-trades they have no scorne' (34–5). This neatly exemplifies Stevenson's comment that 'when an author wishes to assert the dignity of trade, he does not argue that trade is good for the nation; he says that gentlemen think well enough of merchants to apprentice their sons to them'.[7] Her broader argument about merchants and tradesmen being valorised in chivalric terms is supported by the fact that we never see the brothers actually working: instead, they leave their trades almost immediately to fight in the Crusades, thus permitting the displays of heroism that make up the bulk of the play's dramatic incident. The following speech from Eustace provides a good illustration of her case:

> Upon this shield I beare the *Grocers* Armes,
> Unto which Trade I was enrold and bound:
> And like a strange Knight, I will aid the Christians,
> Thou Trade which didst sustaine my poverty,
> Didst helpelesse, helpe me; though I left thee then,
> Yet that the world shall see I am not ingrate,
> Or scorning that, which gave my fortunes breath,
> I will enlarge these Armes, and make their name
> The originall and life of all my fame. (1694–1702)

Though he expresses a desire to make up for having left his trade, Eustace proposes to magnify the glory of the Grocers' Company not by doing business but by making war with their arms emblazoned on his shield. Furthermore, as Stevenson points out, the fact that he and his brothers are of noble descent undercuts the play's ostensible agenda of praising London's citizenry:

> The 'prentices' are in fact no city boys, but the sons of the banished Earl of Boulogne; while their father assures the audience that they 'have no scorn' of civic trades and the boys assure their father that they are obedient and loyal apprentices, they agree in private that they are merely marking time until they can prove their own chivalric talents.[8]

Not only does a positive representation of London's commercial class require it to be presented in chivalric terms; in *The Four Prentices of London*, it is debatable whether that class is being represented at all.

While the four apprentices seem like embodiments of Stevenson's argument that early modern workers could not be positively represented as workers, however, their peculiarly mixed status also alludes to the socially mixed composition of London's apprentice community. As Lisa H. Cooper notes, Heywood wrote in an era of social mobility not just for wealthy merchants who purchased titles (a phenomenon I have already discussed) but, in the other direction, for members of the gentry who 'were apprenticing their sons within the livery companies of London'.[9] The phenomenon of the noble apprentice was not just a tradesman's fantasy but a fact of Elizabethan life: according to Christopher Brooks, the percentage of young men admitted to the freedom of London who called themselves sons of gentlemen more than trebled between 1550 and 1650 from an initial figure of about 5 per cent.[10] Richard Grassby sees it as a by-product of primogeniture: 'Several sons were necessary to guarantee the male succession, but if all survived to maturity [...] the younger were obliged to work.'[11] No doubt, as Brooks suggests, this led to personal conflicts between apprentices of gentle birth and the masters whom they saw themselves as a cut above, and this is something I shall later discuss with regard to *Eastward Ho*.[12] But it also led to a more theoretical debate over whether apprenticeship was compatible with gentility. In *The Blazon of Gentrie* (1586), John Ferne has the speaker Paradine disqualify craftsmen from nobility on the grounds that 'during the time wherein they are bound to seruice, for the apprehending of that craft, they seeme as bound and of seruile state' under their masters' authority.[13] In other words, the experience of subordination inherent in apprenticeship is incompatible with gentle status; Sir Thomas Smith calls it a 'kinde of servitude or bondage'.[14] This view, predictably, was attacked by citizens and their apologists, most fully in Edmund Bolton's work of 1629 (written a decade earlier), *The Cities Aduocate, in this Case or Question of Honor and Armes; Whether Apprentiship Extinguisheth Gentry? Containing a Clear Refutation of the Pernicious Common Errour Affirming it, Swallowed by Erasmus of Roterdam, Sir Thomas Smith in His Common-Weale, Sir Iohn Fern in His Blazon, Raphe Broke Yorke Herald, and Others*, a book whose title needs little further comment. As Cooper points out, the debate over 'whether apprenticeship extinguisheth gentry' is one in which *The Four Prentices of London* clearly intervenes. At the outset, the old Earl ponders the contrast between his current fortunes and former state and puts to Godfrey a question that seems to assume that his sons are finding it equally hard to adapt: 'knowing in thy thoughts what thou hast been, / How canst thou brooke to be as thou art now?' (61–2). Cooper finds varying degrees of ambivalence in the brothers' responses, but Godfrey's is an unambiguous statement of the compatibility of noble blood with apprenticeship: 'I hold it no disparage to my birth, / Though I be borne an Earle, to have the skill / And the full knowledge of the *Mercers* Trade' (73–5). Indeed, as Theodora A. Jankowski notes, Godfrey goes so far as to say that gentlemen ought to be compelled to labour with their hands:

> I praise that City which made Princes Trades-men:
> Where that man, noble or ignoble borne,
> That would not practise some mechanicke skill,
> Which might support his state in penury,
> Should die the death; not sufferd like a drone,
> To sucke the hony from the publicke Hive. (67–72)[15]

Far from presenting the commercial classes in the terms of the aristocracy, as Stevenson argues, in these lines Heywood has a character suggest that the aristocracy ought to be held to the standards of the commercial classes.

While Godfrey's brothers Guy and Charles both profess themselves content with their apprentice status, however, Eustace's response to his father's enquiry indicates a less cheerful acceptance of citizen standards and customs: 'Father, I say Hawking is a pretty sport, / And Hunting is a Princely exercise; / To ride a great horse, oh tis admirable!' (102–4). This rather undermines Fenella Macfarlane's statement that in Eustace 'we find the drama's most robustly urban voice'; yet Macfarlane is right to observe that in the lines that follow, Eustace seems to express a less specifically gentle attitude towards his apprenticeship:

> Mee thinkes I could endure it for seven yeares,
> Did not my Maister keepe me in too much.
> I cannot goe to breake-fast in a morning
> With my kinde mates and fellow-Prentises,
> But he cries Eustace, one bid Eustace come:
> And my name Eustace is in every roome.
> If I might once a weeke but see a Tilting,
> Six daies I would fall unto my business close,
> And ere the weekes end winne that idle day.
> Hee will not let mee see a mustering,
> Nor on a May-day morning fetch in May. (106–16)[16]

Eustace's complaints about not being allowed time off at weekends and on holidays are surely ones with which apprentices in Heywood's audience could have identified, and, indeed, I would suggest that they locate the play within the debate about the recreational practices of servants and apprentices that I discussed in the last chapter. The decision of the brothers to leave for the Holy Land is treated as an expression of their apprentice identity rather than a rejection of it, as they agree to 'try what London Prentises can doe' (226), and it is paralleled by apprentice theatregoers' temporary neglect of their trades to enjoy vicariously the heroic deeds the brothers are shown achieving. Before battle, Eustace wishes

> that I had with mee
> As many good lads, honest Prentises,
> From *Eastcheape*, *Canwicke-streete*, and *London-stone*,
> To end this battell, as could wish themselves
> Under my conduct if they knew me heere. (776–80)

An important part of the lines' significance comes from the fact that he really does have the apprentices with him, in the theatre audience.

While it is difficult to dispute Stevenson's reading of *The Four Prentices of London* in its general outline, in so far as the play's positive representation of apprentices seems to require them to be depicted in a heroic context, the details of the picture are more problematic. First, the eponymous heroes are not simply weird class hybrids but need to be seen in the context of a city where the sons of gentlemen, if not earls, really were being apprenticed to urban trades. Second, one of those heroes argues not only that his nobility is compatible with apprenticeship but that nobles as well as commoners actually ought to be made to labour – an attitude that hardly bespeaks a commercial class subordinated to an aristocratic system of values. Finally, Heywood takes care to give his heroes desires and frustrations similar to those that apprentices in the audience might have felt; indeed, I have tentatively suggested, the characters' absconding from their trades to fight in the Holy Land is mirrored in apprentice theatregoers' absconding from their trades in order to watch them. This final detail, namely a self-consciousness about how the theatre itself might be implicated in the related concepts of work, idleness and social status, is in evidence in other plays I will examine in this chapter.

One example is *A Woman Killed with Kindness*, written by Heywood and staged by Worcester's Men in 1603. This is a play that seems to be very aware of itself as a piece of non-aristocratic art: as Peter Holbrook has argued, it is remarkable both for its subversion of the expectations set up by the tragic genre and for its 'tendency to situate those expectations (especially the tragic desire for revenge) in the context of a specific social group's code of conduct'.[17] The adulteress Anne Frankford's comment that her husband 'cannot be so base as to forgive me' (13. 140) associates forgiveness with social inferiority, as does her brother Sir Francis Acton's belief that Frankford 'showed too mild a spirit / In the revenge of such a loathed crime'; 'Had it been my case / Their souls at once had from their breasts been freed' (17. 16–17, 20–1).[18] For Holbrook, the status gap between the mere gentleman Frankford and the knight Acton is significant here: 'The play contrasts aristocratic lawlessness, expressed in a code of honour sanctioning violence and revenge in certain situations, with a civic or bourgeois ethic of "kindness."'[19] He points out that the questioning of aristocratic values can also be discerned in the subplot, where (as T. S. Eliot put it) we see 'a man ready to prostitute his sister as payment for a debt of honour': Sir Charles Mountford's request that his sister Susan satisfy with her body the debt he owes his enemy Acton, who redeemed him from prison, seems likely to lead to both their deaths until Acton agrees to marry her.[20] In fact, as I shall argue, the subplot as a whole puts certain aspects of aristocratic identity under sustained scrutiny, including the ethos of conspicuous idleness to which the children's companies had attempted to appeal.

A Woman Killed with Kindness begins by uniting characters from the two plots at the celebration of John Frankford's marriage to Anne. After the couple have been congratulated by Acton, Mountford, Wendoll, Malby and Cranwell, they withdraw to join their other guests; Acton then wonders aloud what he and his fellows should do while the 'mad lads / And country lasses ... / Dance all their country measures, rounds and jigs' (I. 81–2, 84). In his description of the dancers, he uses the fact that they are workers as a means of expressing his disdain for their ability, thereby betraying his sense of work as socially degrading:

> They toil like mill-horses, and turn as round,
> Marry, not on the toe. Ay, and they caper,
> But without cutting. You shall see tomorrow
> The hall floor pecked and dinted like a millstone,
> Made with their high shoes; though their skill be small,
> Yet they tread heavy where their hobnails fall. (I. 86–91)

The comparison of the dancers to mill horses, and of the floor to a millstone, as well as the image of their clodhopping labourers' boots, serve to emphasise the world of work which they cannot leave behind: they are inherently and inescapably workers, even when at their recreations. Mountford responds to Acton's remarks by proposing a more aristocratic pastime:

> SIR CHARLES Well, leave them to their sports. Sir Francis Acton,
> I'll make a match with you: meet me tomorrow
> At Chevy Chase, I'll fly my hawk with yours.
> SIR FRANCIS For what? for what?
> SIR CHARLES Why, for a hundred pound.
> SIR FRANCIS Pawn me some gold of that.
> SIR CHARLES Here are ten angels,
> I'll make them good a hundred pound tomorrow
> Upon my hawk's wing.
> SIR FRANCIS 'Tis a match, 'tis done.
> Another hundred pound upon your dogs,
> Dare you Sir Charles?
> SIR CHARLES I dare. Were I sure to lose,
> I durst do more than that: here's my hand,
> The first course for a hundred pound. (I. 92–102)

The terms in which the knights discuss hawking provide a good example of how, in the early modern period, recreation could provide an opportunity for the performance of social status: as Kathleen E. McLuskie puts it, they 'identify themselves by an effortless expertise in gallant sports'.[21] The hawking match is deferred until tomorrow, when the dancers will, presumably, be back at work. It gives the competitors the opportunity to demonstrate their skill in an accomplishment unavailable to commoners and requiring 'such exotic and valuable properties as hawks'.[22] Finally, it allows them to show off not only their disposable wealth but also the lightness with which they prize it: even if Sir Charles were sure to lose, he would venture a hundred pounds on his dogs. As Sir John Harington says in *A Treatise on Playe* of the high stakes wagered at gaming, 'And whearfore is all this, forsooth? because the beholders may extoll theyr braue myndes, and saye one to another, Did yow ever see Gentlemen that cared so little for theyr money, so braue, so bountifull, etc.'.[23] The idea that one's perceived rank can depend on such apparently trivial contests is made clear in the parting words of Sir Charles: 'If there you miss me, say / I am no gentleman. I'll hold my day' (111–12).

In the scene that follows, Heywood seems to parody the knights' sense of social superiority by showing the house servant, Nick, using pretentious vocabulary and attitudes to distance himself from the farm servants. 'My humour is not compendious: dancing I possess not,' he tells them (2. 6), before going on to lay claim to the fashionable affliction of melancholy (25); when the servants dance at the end of the scene, Nick 'speaks stately and scurvily, the rest after the country fashion' (54 s.d.). The idea that can prove one's high social status through the adoption of a particular mode of speech, demeanour and even attitude towards recreation – the idea exploited by writers for the children's companies at the turn of the century – is made ridiculous by being ascribed to a domestic servant. When we see it again, in the third scene, it produces a less comic outcome. Acton's refusal to grant victory to Mountford's falcon leads to a swaggering exchange of insults:

SIR FRANCIS Come, come, your hawk is but a rifler.
SIR CHARLES How?
SIR FRANCIS Ay, and your dogs are trindle-tails and curs.
SIR CHARLES You stir my blood
You keep not a good hound in all your kennel,
Nor one good hawk upon your perch. (27–31)

The performance of recreation has given way to the performance of honour through calculated insult. Neither party can easily back down with his reputation intact, and the argument escalates into a fight in which Mountford kills Acton's falconer and huntsman. As Sir Charles immediately recognises, excessive punctilio has led him to reject Christian morality: 'My God! what have I done? what have I done? / My rage hath plunged into a sea of blood / In which my soul lies drowned' (42–4).

The irony of Mountford's fall is that a form of behaviour supposedly motivated by rank ends up imperilling that rank. In suing to be pardoned for the murder, Mountford spends 'All the revenues that his father left him' (5. 7), making him the 'poorest knight in England' (17). He now has 'only a house of pleasure, / With some five hundred pounds, reserved / Both to maintain me and my loving sister' (47–9). The maxim, 'what is a gentleman but his pleasure?' is made literal: the pleasure house is, indeed, all that remains of Mountford's hereditary lands.[24] As he explains when the villainous Shafton tries to purchase it, to lose it would be to lose his and his sister's last claim to high social status: 'If this were sold our means should then be quite / Razed from the bead-roll of gentility' (7. 36–7). Accordingly, they have been forced to behave in a way theoretically at odds with their position, to carry out manual labour:

SIR CHARLES You see what hard shift we have made to keep it
Allied still to our own name. This palm you see
Labour hath glowed within; her silver brow,
That never tasted a rough winter's blast
Without mask or fan, doth with a grace
Defy cold winter and his storms outface.
SUSAN Sir, we feed sparing and we labour hard,
We lie uneasy, to reserve to us
And our succession this small plot of ground. (38–46)

As Diana E. Herderson puts it, 'This place, the family's summer home, ties Charles with his ancestors; in his words, Charles gives the family name and place priority over his particular honor as the basis for social identity'.[25] All other manifestations of social status, in behaviour and in the body, are secondary to the imperative of keeping the house, and Charles graphically explains that he has forgotten 'What a new fashion is, how silk or satin / Feels in my hand' (49–50), the names of his servants and of his hounds. These signifiers of gentility have become strange to him; 'To keep this place I have changed myself away' (56).

For my purposes, what is particularly noteworthy about the fact that Charles is 'enforced to follow husbandry' (7. 3), and Susan to milk, is the fact that Heywood seems to sanction Charles's belief that the practice of manual labour does not invalidate his gentility, in contradiction of Harrison's opinion that a gentleman must be able to 'live without manual labor'. Indeed, it is suggested that the change of fortune has brought about a moral growth, turning the murderer into a stoic:

And do we not live well?
Well, I thank God. ...
All things on earth change, some up, some down,
Content's a kingdom, and I wear that crown. (4–7)

Mountford's sense of contentedness proves illusory, however, as Shafton demands the return of the 300 pounds he lent him in Scene 5, plus interest, and Mountford is jailed. His friends and relatives proving recalcitrant, Mountford is eventually freed (against his knowledge and will) through a payment from his enemy Acton, giving rise to a new sense of imprisonment and indebtedness: 'I am not free; I go but under bail' (10. 96). Learning from Susan, however, that Acton 'dotes on me, and oft hath sent me gifts, / Letters, and tokens' (121–2), Mountford ends the scene resolute: 'I have enough. Though poor, my heart is set / In one rich gift to pay back all my debt' (123–4).

'Nothing can make Charles's behavior quite acceptable to a twentieth-century audience', as Henderson writes of his decision to settle his debt by offering Acton his sister, and, indeed, the conclusion of this subplot is uncomfortable in many respects.[26] The readiness with which Susan agrees to be made a chattel, her decision to kill herself before losing her honour, the pleasure with which Charles greets this resolution, the assumption that Acton's offer of marriage to Susan constitutes a happy outcome for all concerned: all of these make the ending problematic. However, I would suggest that as well as relying on assumptions about gender relations and female behaviour that a modern audience will find unpalatable, the ending fails on its own terms, in that Charles gets what he wants by reverting to the very behaviour that has led him to misfortune: Lena Cowen Orlin is quite right when she refers to his offer of Susan to Acton as a 'gamble'.[27] As Acton recognises, Charles offers his sister in the same spirit of aristocratic competitiveness that he displayed over the hawking match:

> Was ever known in any former age
> Such honourable wrested courtesy?
> Lands, honours, lives, and all the world forgo
> Rather than stand engaged to such a foe. (14. 120–3)

Mountford has out-gentled him, displaying in his punctilious payment of the debt an 'honourable wrested courtesy' that Acton is unable to match. The sense that Charles is gambling on this reaction is clear from the subsequent speech in which he reminds Acton of their poverty: '*if* thou hast the heart / To seize her as a rape or lustful prey' (126–7, my italics), to kill Susan and Charles and to stain their house, 'Do them at once on her; all these rely / And perish with her spotted chastity' (131–2). Acton appreciates that he has simply been outbid ('You overcome me in your love, Sir Charles', 133); the only way he can top Mountford's outrageous courtesy is by offering to marry Susan, a strategy that, as she realises, leaves him victorious: 'You still exceed us' (147). A subplot apparently intended to question the notion of gentility as performance and to show true gentility as compatible with dignified labour depends for its resolution on the ethos it originally rejected.

I want to end my discussion of the Henslowe companies by focusing on another two-part play that, like *A Woman Killed with Kindness*, seems intended to articulate a specifically non-aristocratic ethos and that stages the spectacle of work in order to do so. *The Honest Whore* (Prince Henry's Men, 1604 and *c.* 1604–5), written by Thomas Dekker and, in the case of Part 1, Thomas Middleton, has an obvious affinity with Heywood's play in that one of its characters, Candido, is presented as noteworthy for his patience; indeed, Dekker seems to allude to *A Woman Killed with Kindness* in Part 2, when Candido is advised to show less forbearance towards his second wife than towards his first and worries that 'her death, / By my vnkindnesse might be counted murther' (II. 2. 28–9). As with John Frankford, Candido's patience is only one aspect of a more general refusal to aspire to aristocratic behaviour codes that is most obviously illustrated by his speech in praise of citizens' flat caps (Part 2, I. 3. 26–71). Another is his pride in his work as a linen-draper and his belief that it can be reconciled with moral uprightness.

I have made repeated reference in this book to the widely held belief that a gentleman must be able to live without manual labour; many early modern writers, however, believed that this interdiction extended to commercial labour, as is implied by Mulcaster's division of the non-elite commonalty into '*marchauntes* and *manuaries*'.[28] Dudley Digges stated in 1604 his belief that 'To play the Merchants was only for Gentlemen of *Florence*, *Venice*, or the like that are indeede but the better sort of Citizens'; conversely, as William Segar put it two years earlier, the English gentleman lives 'as one that accounteth it no honour to exercise Marchandize'.[29] The explanation usually given for this exclusion is the supposedly dishonest nature of commercial work, which, in John Ferne's words, 'consisteth of most vngentle parts, as doublenes of toong, violation of faith, with the rest of their tromperies and disceites'.[30] Ferne views merchants as professional liars and faith-breakers and, accordingly, goes on to rank them below villeins in the social scale. This view of merchandise is repeated by Henry Peacham in *The Complete Gentleman* (1634), where he says that the practice has been 'accounted base and much derogating from nobility'; 'the ancient Romans never preferred any that exercised merchandise to any eminent place or office in the commonwealth, perhaps agreeing in one with Aristotle, who, speaking of merchants and mechanics, saith: *Vilis est huius modi vita, et virtuti adversa* – This kind of life is base and contrary to virtue'.[31] Peacham goes on, however, to exempt overseas merchants from this criticism, and, in doing so, he follows the example of Cicero, to whom Ferne explicitly alludes and whose *De officiis* was a major influence upon this view of merchandise.[32] Cicero argues that usury, tax-gathering and waged labour are all 'of base reputacion', the first two because they are unpopular, the third because it is servile; 'They moreouer ar to be counted of the baser sorte: who bye of marchants, that oute of hand they retaile again. For, nothing they profit, onlesse they lie apace: and trulie dishonester thing is ther none, than a vaine tonge.'[33] The profits of retail merchandise, Cicero argues, depend on dishonesty: the merchant buys goods wholesale before going on to sell them for more than they are worth.

In recent years, both Theodore B. Leinwand and Ceri Sullivan have shown how early modern merchants responded in print to such criticism, as well as to religious tracts and sermons that denounced them for covetousness and usury. In treatises on merchandise, and in handbooks purporting to instruct merchants in their trade, writers sought to invent a new image of the merchant as morally upright and socially useful; in Leinwand's words, 'to fashion "the merchant" and to find a vocabulary adequate to him'.[34] While Leinwand and Sullivan focus primarily on the ways in which stage plays questioned or satirised the role created for the merchant in such pamphlets (Sullivan examining 'the humor created in the gap between the two images', for instance), a case can be made for Candido's role in *The Honest Whore* as the dramatic equivalent of texts such as *The Marchants Aviso* (1591), in which John Browne advises the novice merchant, 'First seeke the Kingdome of GOD and the righteousnesse thereof: and then all things shall be giuen thee that thou hast neede of'.[35] Like *The Marchants Aviso*, the two plays seem to suggest, first, that a merchant can and should place godliness before other considerations and, second, that such behaviour does not preclude commercial profit. Candido's godliness is demonstrated most obviously in his patience, a virtue that he says is quintessentially Christian:

> It makes men looke like Gods; the best of men
> That ere wore earth about him, was a sufferer,
> A soft meeke, patient, humble, tranquill spirit,
> The first true Gentleman that euer breathd. (Part 1, V. 2. 491–4)

This attitude informs Candido's professional dealings in a way that contradicts the stereotype of the grasping merchant motivated by 'excessive desire of gain', as Richard Barckley put it in 1598.[36] His patience leads him to accept financial loss and the destruction of his assets: in Part 1, a gallant, for a wager, tries to annoy him by demanding a pennyworth of lawn cut from the centre of the piece, while in Part 2, gallants encourage an Irish footman to get angry in Candido's shop and tear some cambric to bits. He invariably treats such behaviour with courteous forbearance: 'Thanke you Gentlemen, / I vse you well, pray know my shop agen' (Part 2, III. 3. 119–20). Candido is equally patient in his domestic life: his wife Viola has a 'strange longing' to make him angry (Part 1, I. 2. 81), which leads her to flirt with her brother, lock up Candido's clothes when he has to attend the Senate, dress his apprentice in Candido's gown and chain and eventually have him confined to Bedlam, but none of these shake his equanimity.

However, while Candido professes to be motivated by Christian morality in refusing to get angry, his attitude seems also to be compatible with commercial success. His wife tells us that he 'haz wealth enough' (I. 2. 54), and Candido provides the following rationale for selling the gallant the pennyworth of lawn:

> We are set heere to please all customers,
> Their humours and their fancies: – offend none:
> We get by many, if we leese by one.
> May be his minde stood to no more then that,
> A penworth serues him, and mongst trades tis found,
> Deny a pennorth, it may crosse a pound. (I. 5. 121–6)

Apparently, patience is good business: a reputation for complaisance will make him more attractive to other potential customers, bringing profits that will cancel out this loss. In Part 2, he similarly reacts to the loss of the cambrics with the words, 'My Customers doe oft for remnants call, / These are two remnants now, no losse at all' (III. 3. 119–20). Not only does Candido demonstrate the practicability of Christian virtues in a commercial context; he also argues that they can be profitable in the long term.

On this reading of *The Honest Whore*, Candido appears to represent the exact phenomenon that Stevenson says is absent from early modern popular literature: a hero from the commercial classes who does not desire or pretend to be a gentleman, who is characterised in terms of his work and who conforms to the demands of Christian morality. The problem is that Candido is more than a little ridiculous. The full title of Part 1 refers to 'The Humours of the Patient Man, and the Longing Wife', and, in large part, his role in the two plays is, indeed, that of the comic eccentric. When, early in Part 1, Viola's brother Fustigo suggests that she make Candido angry by cuckolding him, she replies, 'Puh, he would count such a cut no vnkindenes' (I. 2. 94); in the context of city comedy, where the only thing more undignified than being a cuckold is being a willing cuckold, this sort of patience is not to Candido's credit. Although Fustigo's flirtation with Viola leads only to him getting beaten up by Candido's apprentices, Candido is made to look absurd when Viola locks his gown in a chest and he has to attend the Senate dressed in a carpet with a nightcap on his head. Candido presents this as a victory: he has managed to avoid both the use of violence to break into the chest and the fine he would have incurred from the Senate. '[T]he Fine imposde / For an vn-gowned Senator, is about / Forty Cruzadoes, the Carpet not 'boue foure' (III. 1. 203–5). However, the logic implied by this computation contrasts with Candido's refusal to break open the chest, which seems to be motivated not so much by ethical considerations as by Candido's 'humour', an obsession with non-violence that borders on the pathological:

> O no, breake open chest thats a Theeues office:
> Therein you counsell me against my bloud:
> 'Twould shew impatience that, any meeke meanes
> I would be glad to imbrace. (III. 1. 191–4)

In Part 2, as Alexander Leggatt has suggested, Candido increasingly becomes the comic butt, and this is most obviously the case in the scene where he is made to drink a health to Bots's whore and then arrested for unwittingly buying Matheo's stolen lawn (IV. 3).[37] Arguably, Candido here gets his comeuppance for being concerned only with his own moral standing and not that of the people with whom he does business: as he puts it in Part 1, 'he that meanes to thriue, with patient eye / Must please the diuell, if he come to buy' (I. 5. 127–8).

Lois Potter wrote of Marcello Magni's performance as Candido at Shakespeare's Globe in 1998, 'Is he a passive-aggressive; a genuine saint, a lunatic; or, as the author seems to think, the only sane man in the play? Magni left all possibilities open.'[38] However, this kind of radical ambiguity seems inherent in the play's treatment of Candido, and the Duke's verdict on him at the end of Part 1 is puzzlingly contradictory:

> Twere sinne all women should such husbands haue.
> For euery man must then be his wiues slaue.
> Come therefore you shall teach our court to shine,
> So calme a spirit is worth a golden Mine. (V. 2. 512–14)

Candido is both a paragon of Christian patience and a henpecked husband. Leinwand attributes the unresolved doubleness of his characterisation partly to the mixed audience at the Fortune and partly to the lack of a 'stable social identity' for the merchant citizen in Jacobean England: 'The shopkeepers in the audience at the Fortune were staged as both winning fools and wealthy businessmen. The double bind that distinguished the stage merchant was an accurate articulation of the spectator-merchant's dilemma.'[39] However, I would suggest that it also reflects the problems of reconciling a favourable presentation of a merchant and his work with the generic demands of city comedy. A patient husband can be made a hero in a tragedy like Heywood's; his place in a city comedy, where most of the characters are either exploiters or exploited, is less obvious. A parallel might be drawn with Moll Cutpurse in another Middleton–Dekker collaboration with another oxymoronic title, *The Roaring Girl*. Insisting that she is neither cutpurse nor whore, Moll is not quite part of the city-comedy world and is therefore treated as a freak, 'a monster with two trinckets' (II. 2. 72) like *The Honest Whore*'s 'monstrous patient man' (Part 1, I. 4. 7). And, just as the real Mary Frith sat on the stage of the Fortune theatre in 1610 'in the publique viewe of all the people there p[rese]nte in mans apparrel & playd vppon her lute & sange a songe', Candido is very much a creature of the public stage, despite Leinwand's remarks to the contrary.[40] When Fustigo insults him in Part 1, Candido banishes him to the private theatre of the child companies:

> Are you angry sir, because I namde the foole?
> Trust me, you are not wise, in mine owne house;
> And to my face to play the Anticke thus:
> If youle needs play the madman, choose a stage
> Of lesser compasse, where few eyes may note
> Your actions errour. (III. 1. 57–62)

Conversely, his assumption that the customer is always right works well as a manifesto for a theatre that claims to appeal to the imaginations of a diverse, paying audience: 'We are set heere to please all customers, / Their humours and their fancies: – offend none: / We get by many, if we leese by one' (I. 5. 121–3).

THE CHILDREN'S COMPANIES

My argument that one of Candido's functions in *The Honest Whore* is to show how Christian virtues can be reconciled with commercial success comes into clearer focus when the play is compared with *Eastward Ho!*, performed at the Blackfriars in 1605 and written by Ben Jonson, George Chapman and John Marston. Critics are agreed that as well as being an explicit reply to *Westward Ho!*, performed at Paul's in 1604, *Eastward*

Ho! is a burlesque of dramatic structures and themes familiar from the adult theatre.[41] The figure of the industrious citizen rewarded with high office, as exemplified by Simon Eyre in *The Shoemakers' Holiday*, is parodied in Golding: 'Ta'en into the livery of his company the first day of his freedom! Now (not a week married) chosen commoner and alderman's deputy in a day!' (IV. 2. 50–2). Conversely, the figure of the prodigal, whom we see in *The London Prodigal* (King's Men, 1603–5) as well as in the second part of *The Honest Whore*, is parodied in Quicksilver, whose exaggerated penitence forms the climax of the play. The specific type of drama that the authors have in mind as their satiric target is indicated by the words of Touchstone on hearing of Golding's success:

> I hope to see thee one o' the monuments of our City, and reckoned among her worthies, to be remembered the same day with the Lady Ramsey and grave Gresham, when the famous fable of Whittington and his puss shall be forgotten, and thou and thy acts become the posies for hospitals; when thy name shall be written upon conduits, and thy deeds played i' thy lifetime by the best companies of actors, and be called their get-penny. (IV. 2. 67–75)

In having Touchstone allude to *If You Know Not Me You Know Nobody* and to the lost *Richard Whittington*, Jonson, Chapman and Marston suggest that we should read Golding's rise as a parody of the glorifications of London's commercial luminaries staged by Prince Henry's and Queen Anne's Men. His name, incidentally, may refer to the location where *Richard Whittington* was performed – Golding Lane, the home of the Fortune Theatre.

Although Clifford Leech and Lawrence Manley have both suggested that Touchstone himself may be meant as a parody of Simon Eyre, I would argue that Candido is an equally relevant object of comparison.[42] This is not because of any obvious similarity between the two as characters but, rather, because the authors of *Eastward Ho!* treat satirically in their characterisation of Touchstone the same notion that Dekker and Middleton treat with apparent sincerity in their characterisation of Candido: namely, that commercial profits are compatible with Christian morality. In the first scene, Touchstone angrily rebuts Quicksilver's offer to encourage his gambling friends to become indebted to his master:

> And as for my rising by other men's fall; God shield me! Did I gain my wealth by ordinaries? No! By exchanging of gold? No! By keeping of gallants' company? No! I hired me a little shop, sought low, took small gain, kept no debt-book, garnished my shop for want of plate, with good wholesome thrifty sentences, as 'Touchstone, keep thy shop, and thy shop will keep thee'. (I. 1. 43–9)

Like Candido, Touchstone claims to have been patient in his pursuit of wealth, remaining content with 'small gain'. The difference is that while profits seem to be merely an incidental effect of Candido's Christian patience, for Touchstone they are the prime consideration, and his moral rhetoric is revealed to be little more than cant: 'the play exposes in the conventionally generous ethos of Touchstone and Golding the same pursuit of advantage they expose in others'.[43] Touchstone's use of pious language to cover selfish motives is made clear when, for example, he declines to receive petitioning letters from Quicksilver: 'Son Golding, I will not be tempted; I find mine own easy nature, and I know not what a well-penned subtle letter may work upon it' (V. 2. 3–5). For him, the cardinal virtue of charity is secondary to the bourgeois virtues of diligence, thrift and sobriety, which he venerates because of the rewards they bring rather than for their intrinsic value, and he is more concerned with the material than the spiritual effects of the sins with which he charges Quicksilver: 'You see the issue of your sloth. Of sloth cometh pleasure, of pleasure cometh riot, of riot comes whoring, of whoring comes spending, of spending comes want, of want comes theft, of theft comes hanging; and there is my Quicksilver fixed' (IV. 2. 315–19). Part of Touchstone's satirical function is to make us question the moral stature of a Candido; the fact that this is necessary implies that Candido himself is meant to be morally exemplary.

The reconciliation of profits with patience is not the only public-theatre attitude parodied by *Eastward Ho!*: the playwrights also have Golding insist that, though he was born a gentleman, 'the trade I have learned of my master ... taints not my blood' (III. 2. 104–5), and, elsewhere, that 'From trades, from arts, from valour, honour springs; / These three are founts of gentry, yea of kings' (I. 1. 145–6). However, it would be wrong to conclude from this that *Eastward Ho!* defines itself and its theatre in opposition to the world of work in the same way as the earlier plays of the revived children's companies examined in the last chapter. Rather, it seems to hold that very attitude up to scrutiny in the form of Quicksilver, the prodigal apprentice. From the beginning of the play, Quicksilver uses not only his clothes but also his recreational habits to express his sense of social superiority to Touchstone, entering 'with his hat, pumps, short sword and dagger, and a racket trussed up under his cloak' (I. 1. 0 s.d.). When Touchstone uncloaks Quicksilver to reveal the sporting accessory, Quicksilver's sardonic repetition of his master's catchphrase – 'Work upon that now!' (19) – takes on an additional significance. Later in the scene, he reiterates to Golding the assumption that his gentility is something to be expressed in ostentatious idleness when he counsels his fellow apprentice to

do nothing, be like a gentleman, be idle; the curse of man is labour. Wipe thy bum with testons, and make ducks and drakes with shillings. What, Eastward Ho! Wilt thou cry, 'what is't ye lack?', stand with a bare pate and a dropping nose under a wooden pent-house, and art a gentleman? Wilt thou bear tankards, and may'st bear arms? Be ruled, turn gallant, Eastward Ho! 'Ta ly-rem ly-re ro! Who calls Jeronimo? Speak, here I am!'(114–21)

As Lucy Munro has observed, Quicksilver's repetition of theatrical tags – here, of course, from *The Spanish Tragedy*, II. 5. 4 – is another way in which he tries to express his difference from Touchstone and Golding: 'the language of the theatre – detached from its dramatic context but retaining its talismanic value – can be used as a weapon against the sober virtues of trade'.[44] However, the fact that such strategies are so overt and transparent, not to mention the fact that they conflict with a reality of apprentice status and financial embarrassment, is a measure of the gap between *Eastward Ho!* and earlier children's plays such as *Antonio and Mellida*. Rather than exploiting the practice of conspicuous idleness as a marketing ploy, *Eastward Ho!* dramatises its adoption, in much the same way that (according to Leggatt) it dramatises in Touchstone 'the morality of thrift and industry' that is 'simply assumed' by playwright and audience in plays like *The Shoemakers' Holiday*.[45] In this respect, *Eastward Ho!* has a surprising affinity with *A Woman Killed with Kindness*: both plays highlight, and question, the use of idleness and recreation as means of advertising (or laying claim to) gentle status. However, while Heywood opposes to such behaviour qualities such as patience, industry and integrity, those who profess these virtues are themselves the satirical targets of Jonson, Chapman and Marston. This makes it difficult to be sure where *Eastward Ho!*'s centre of gravity lies, an absence that C. G. Petter seems to recognise when he tentatively posits 'the gentlemanly point of view' as the play's implied norm.[46]

If *Eastward Ho!* signals a move away from the attitude towards work adopted at the Blackfriars theatre at the turn of the century, the play to which it is an ostensible reply, the *Westward Ho!* of Dekker and Webster, seems to indicate a more substantial *rapprochement* between the theatre at St Paul's and London's citizenry. As Clifford Leech points out, while Dekker mildly satirises the citizen values he earlier espoused in *The Shoemakers' Holiday*, he also shows 'city virtue triumphant' when Justiniano's wife withstands the attentions of the old Earl. Even in the main plot, 'Dekker and Webster manage to combine making fun of the citizen class without suggesting any infidelity on the part of their wives'.[47] However, as Leech's remarks indicate, *Westward Ho!* is less interested in the work of citizens than in their sexual escapades and in the chastity of their wives when faced with aristocratic suitors. In fact, perhaps the child-company play of this period that, along with *Eastward Ho!*, concerns itself most with questions of work and idleness is another Blackfriars play, Francis Beaumont's *The Knight of the Burning Pestle* (1607–*c.* 1610), and it may not be a coincidence that this play too is very much a play about the theatre, parodying public-theatre plays such as *The Four Prentices of London* (to which it refers at IV. 49–50) and getting comic mileage out of the gap presumed to exist between public and private theatre cultures.[48] Notoriously, it begins with a citizen climbing onto the stage to complain about the play the actors plan to stage, *The London Merchant*, which he presumes contains more of the 'girds at citizens' (Ind. 8) he has come to expect at the Blackfriars: 'Why could not you be contented, as well as others, with *The Legend of Whittington*, or *The Life and Death of Sir Thomas Gresham, with the Building of the Royal Exchange*, or *The Story of Queen Elenor, with the Rearing of London Bridge upon Wool-sacks*?' (Ind. 18–22). As in *Eastward Ho!*, Gresham and Whittington are used as paradigms of public-theatre citizen hagiography, and they serve to place the Citizen in terms both of his social status and his aesthetic tastes. The play he coerces the company into producing is at once a citizen romance starring his apprentice Rafe, a Cervantean romp of which Rafe is the unwitting dupe, and a city comedy in which the gentleman apprentice Jasper succeeds in marrying his master's daughter.

This is not to say, however, that *The Knight of the Burning Pestle* is simply a class-based satire against the presumed naivety of non-gentle theatregoers. As Alexander Leggatt has noted, recent critics increasingly stress 'the citizens' energy and generosity of spirit, and point out that their play is a lot more fun than *The London Merchant*'.[49] I would suggest that the play's mingled satire and celebration of its fictional citizen audience is paralleled by an equivocal acceptance of non-aristocratic values. For one thing, although Jasper, like the apprentices in *Eastward Ho!*, is of gentle origins, he is not the prodigal that Munro and Michael Hattaway both see him as.[50] His only transgression is to fall in love with his master's daughter; in all other respects he seems perfectly assimilated to the citizen ethos, reminding his master,

> Sir, I do liberally confess I am yours,
> Bound both by love and duty to your service,
> In which my labour hath been all my profit.

I have not lost in bargain, nor delighted
To wear your honest gains upon my back,
Nor have I given a pension to my blood,
Or lavishly in play consumed your stock. (I. 16–22)

Jasper takes care to highlight not only his diligence, competence and frugality but also his sexual continence and avoidance of gambling; in effect, he is a more sympathetic version of Golding, thwarted only by his master's unwillingness to have him marry his daughter. When he returns to his parents, the Merrythoughts, he indignantly rebuts his mother's surmise that 'thou art a waste-thrift, and art run away from thy master that loved thee well' (I. 313–15); 'I ran not from my master, nor return / To have your stock maintain my idleness' (I. 328–9). In fact, it is Jasper's father who is the unthrift; as Mistress Merrythought observes: 'Thou art an old man, and thou canst not work, and thou hast not forty shillings left, and thou eatest good meat, and drinkest good drink, and laughest' (I. 356–9). The reason why Jasper, an eldest son as well as a gentleman, is an apprentice becomes obvious.

However, Beaumont forestalls any condemnation of Old Merrythought on the audience's part by allowing the citizens to judge him first: 'Give me a penny i'th'purse while I live, George' (I. 371). Our reluctance to share the citizens' limited viewpoint encourages a sympathetic response to the object of their criticism; at the same time, however, it may prompt the realisation that part of Old Merrythought's dramatic function is to be a source of irritation to the citizens. As Leggatt points out, while Jonson, Chapman and Marston burlesque the prodigal story by oversimplifying it into Quicksilver's exaggerated fall and repentance, 'Beaumont makes his point by turning the story itself upside down'.[51] The irrepressible Merrythought carouses happily through the rest of the drama, and even the sight of Jasper in his coffin elicits a song rather than a sigh; the prodigal father ultimately triumphs, his elder son betrothed to Luce, his wife and younger son humbled for their resistance to his good cheer. This is not so much a recommendation of carefree drunkenness on Beaumont's part as a calculated reversal of the prodigal story and thwarting of the citizens' desires: 'I do not like this', George complains (V. 267). I would argue, therefore, that Merrythought's rejection of thrift and industry is not simply a continuation of the child companies' earlier distancing of themselves from the world of work. Its significance relates to its reversal of narrative convention more than to any set of social values. Incidentally, another point of difference between *The Knight of the Burning Pestle* and earlier child-company plays is suggested early on, when the speaker of the prologue responds to the request for a play about a grocer with the excuse, 'you should have told us your mind a month since. Our play is ready to begin now' (Ind. 31–2). As Leggatt observes, this 'gives a realistic sense of the lead-time needed to bring a play on stage'; but it also contrasts with the improvisational, amateur aesthetic advanced a few years earlier.[52] In the play that follows, it is the apprentice Rafe who is the improvising amateur and the boys who have put in the weeks of rehearsal.

The Knight of the Burning Pestle is typical of the plays I have discussed so far in this chapter in that, while it uses the idea of work in a similar way to earlier plays staged by the same company, it also marks a significant shift away from their attitude. It relies on the assumption that a citizen and his wife will feel slightly out of place, and potential satirical targets, in the Blackfriars theatre, and that George's status as a worker will give them desires and expectations at odds with the usual run of Blackfriars plays. However, the hero of the play they reject is an exemplary apprentice, and the carefree idleness of his prodigal father is not seriously sanctioned. *Eastward Ho!* makes industrious citizens the object of ridicule and exposes the self-interest that underlies their professions of piety, but it also mocks the practice of conspicuous idleness appealed to by earlier child-company plays. The same practice is, more predictably, questioned by an adult company in *A Woman Killed with Kindness*, a play that argues, like *The Four Prentices of London*, that work is compatible with gentility. It demonstrates this by showing a gentleman ennobled by manual labour; however, whereas *The Shoemakers' Holiday* sustains a celebration of workers right up to its festive climax, the situation in Heywood's play is resolved through a return to aristocratic values. Finally, the two parts of *The Honest Whore* mark perhaps the most thoroughgoing attempt in this decade to present commercial work in positive terms, depicting a merchant who is simultaneously honest, prosperous and happy in his social status; however, Candido is as absurd as he is exemplary and is the object of scorn for his refusal to accept a conventional patriarchal role in his marriage. The festive world of *The Shoemakers' Holiday* has given way to the more predatory environment of city comedy, into which characters like Candido fit only with difficulty.

THE LORD CHAMBERLAIN'S/KING'S MEN

The question of whether the repertory of the Lord Chamberlain's Men (or, as they became in 1603, the King's Men) was designed to attract a different range of theatregoers from Queen Anne's Men and Prince Henry's Men, on the one hand, and the children's companies playing at St Paul's and the Blackfriars, on the other, is a problematic one. Andrew Gurr's argument that *Hamlet* heralded an attempt to compete both with the offerings of the children and with those of the adult companies is attractive, not least because we know that after the King's Men acquired the Blackfriars in 1608 they continued to play at the Globe and, indeed, rebuilt the outdoor theatre when it burned down in 1613.[53] On the other hand, Roslyn Lander Knutson has argued that the company could not have flourished without operating on a similar business model to that which she deduces for the Admiral's Men from Henslowe's diary, one that relied on a rapid turnover of quickly written, conventional plays, the repetition of winning formulae, revivals of old favourites and the imitation of other companies' successes.[54] This view is not incompatible with Gurr's: if a play like *Hamlet* could appeal to a broad spectrum of theatregoers, that is testimony to Shakespeare's expertise as a writer within the repertory system. However, it does suggest that innovative plays like *Hamlet* were probably not typical of the company's output; the posthumous cultural centrality of Shakespeare can lead us to forget that his plays were outnumbered in the repertory by other plays that have since been lost. Knutson suggests that Wentworth Smith's play *The Freeman's Honour* (*c.* 1600–3) sounds like a citizen play along the lines of *The Shoemakers' Holiday*: 'The only clue to the narrative beyond the title provided in the dedicatory epistle to Sir John Swinnerton, a merchant taylor and former lord mayor, is that the play was meant "to dignifie" Swinnerton's company.'[55] Evidently, the genre of citizen hagiography was not limited to Prince Henry's and Queen Anne's Men. In the final section of this chapter, I will begin my discussion of the Lord Chamberlain's/ King's Men by briefly considering two plays that may well owe their survival to their apocryphal association with Shakespeare but which are examples of genres popular with the other adult companies: the Protestant history *Thomas Lord Cromwell* (*c.* 1599–1602) and the prodigal play *The London Prodigal* (1603–5).

As a play dealing with the rise to power of the man who implemented many of Henry VIII's Reformation policies, and his fall at the hands of treacherous plotters led by Stephen Gardiner, Bishop of Winchester, *Thomas Lord Cromwell* ('Written by W. S.') has affinities with plays such as *Sir John Oldcastle* and *Sir Thomas Wyatt*.[56] While Gurr groups the latter two together as 'plays about Protestant heroes', however, Larry S. Champion has argued that *Cromwell*, for one, is more ambivalent than this taxonomy implies.[57] The play depicts its protagonist as a talented scholar and merchant who remembers his roots after being raised to eminence by Wolsey, but it also stresses Cromwell's social and political ambition and tells us that he circumvented the law at Henry's behest; Thomas can be seen as 'heroic overreacher' or 'time-serving scoundrel'.[58] One feature of *Thomas Lord Cromwell* that is of particular importance in creating this dual image of its central character is its treatment of the theme of work.

To an even greater extent than the play to which it is probably closest, *Sir Thomas More, Thomas Lord Cromwell* presents its protagonist's rise as the result not only of talent but also of labour. At the beginning of the play, Hodge, three smiths and two other servants of Cromwell's father complain that they cannot sleep due to the young master's studying out loud:

HODGE	Come masters, I thinke it be past fiue a clock, Is it not time we were at worke: My old Master heele be stirring anon.
FIRST SERVANT	I cannot tell whether my old master will be stirring or no: but I am sure I can hardly take my afternoones nap, for my young Maister *Thomas*, He keepes such a quile in his studie, With the Sunne, and the Moone, and the seauen starres, That I do verily thinke heele read out his wits. (sig. A2^{r})

For a moment, cliché is overturned: instead of the student being disturbed by manual workers, the labourers are irritated by the industriousness of the student. However, the situation reverts after the labourers leave the stage, when Cromwell's soliloquy on the high aspirations that motivate his study is disturbed by their noises off: '*Here within they must beate with their hammers*' (sig. A2^{v}). By allowing the two scenes to mirror one another, the playwright creates an analogy between Cromwell's intellectual work and the manual work of the smiths. The implication that there is a continuity between the two is very striking in the context of a society that commentators tended, as we have seen, to divide into a majority who performed manual labour and a minority who did not. When Cromwell complains that the workers are disturbing his study, the relationship between these two groups is anatomised with unusual frankness:

HODGE	Why how now Maister *Thomas* how now, Will you not let vs worke for you.
CROMWELL	You fret my hart, with making of this noise.
HODGE	How fret your hart, I but *Thomas*, youle Fret your fathers purse if you let vs from working.

SECOND SERVANT I this tis for him to make him a gentleman,
Shal we leaue worke for your musing, thats well I faith.
(sig. A2v)

The argument of the labourers is that far from disturbing Cromwell, they are working for his benefit: they fill his father's purse with the money that goes towards making Cromwell a gentleman. The manual work that enables his studies is made audible, if not visible, on the stage. Their view is echoed by Cromwell's angry father:

OLD CROMWELL Why knaue I say, haue I thus carkde & car'd
And all to keepe thee like a gentleman,
And dost thou let my seruants at their worke:
That sweat for thee knaue, labour thus for thee.
CROMWELL Father their hammers doe offend my studie.
OLD CROMWELL Out of my doores knaue if thou likest it not,
I crie you mercie is your eares so fine:
I tell thee knaue these get when I doe sleepe,
I will not haue my Anuill stand for thee. (sig. A2v)

Again, Cromwell's scholarly privilege is shown to be underwritten both by the care of his father and by the labour of the servants who 'get when I doe sleepe'; the fact that Cromwell Senior, too, lives off the work of others is implied.

An ambivalent attitude towards Cromwell's rise is thus encouraged from the start of the play. On the one hand, we might enjoy seeing him defy the predictions of his father, who mocks Cromwell's promise to build a palace one day where his father's cottage now stands:

You build a house, you knaue youle be a begger,
Now afore God all is but cast away,
That is bestowed vpon this thriftlesse lad,
Well had I bound him to some honest trade:
This had not beene, but it was his mo[t]hers doing,
To send him to the Vniuersitie. (sig. A3r)

On the other hand, Cromwell's success is shown to be the result not only of his own scholarly labours but also of the manual labours of those who have supported his exemption from other forms of work. Furthermore, his speech at the end of the scene, which begins by asking, 'Why should my birth keepe downe my mounting spirit', suggests that he is motivated more by ambition than by any desire to serve his country, or, for that matter, to improve the lot of those whose work has paid for his education.

While *Thomas Lord Cromwell* is remarkable for its demystification of the Tudor economy of labour as a zero-sum game – Old Cromwell's servants work so that Thomas does not have to – it is still a play that would be perfectly at home in the other adult repertories. Cromwell's 'mounting spirit' evidently owes something to the plays by Marlowe already in the repertory of Prince Henry's Men; more sympathetically, Thomas can be seen as a non-aristocratic hero rewarded for his industry. Indeed, prior to his elevation into the world of politics, he works as a merchant in Europe, acquiring a reputation for uprightness: 'We hardly shall finde such a one as he, / To fit our turnes, his dealings were so honest' (sig. B4^{v}). The same is true of *The London Prodigal*, 'By *VVilliam Shakespeare*', according to the title page of its 1605 edition.[59] The play has obvious affinities with the second part of *The Honest Whore*, in which the prodigal Matheo's father-in-law is retained as his servant in disguise; here, the rich merchant Old Flowerdale follows his son as a servingman, testing him by claiming that his father died having written Flowerdale out of his will. The setting is London, and the characters are merchants rather than aristocrats; the play might be said to exemplify a citizen mentality, in that Flowerdale is made to represent sins that can be grouped under the heading of unthriftiness, namely 'Ryot, Swearing, Drunkennes and Pride' (sig. G4^{r}). Old Flowerdale helps his son to marry Luce under false pretences before revealing the trick and getting Flowerdale arrested for debt by his uncle; like Bellafront, and the heroine of *How a Man May Choose a Good Wife from a Bad*, Luce remains devoted to a husband who spurns her and resolves to support him through independent labour. Rejecting his suggestion that she 'turne whore, thats a good trade, / And so perhaps Ile see thee now and then' (sig. E3^{r}), Luce finds employment in disguise as the maid of her sister. By contrast, Flowerdale's degradation is suggested through the various methods he resorts to in the attempt to earn money: highway robbery (sig. F1^{r}), beggary (sig. F3^{v}), a salacious offer of 'secret seruice' to a citizen's wife (sig. F4^{r}). In short, *The London Prodigal* relies on social and moral suppositions that inform plays like *The Honest Whore* and that are satirised in plays like *Eastward Ho!*: that non-aristocratic characters are dramatically interesting; that idleness and unthriftiness are not just foolish but morally disastrous; and that work, even as a servant, is dignified and laudable.

One striking feature of Shakespeare's plays of this period, and perhaps the tendency that leads Gurr to see the King's Men as trying to compete both with the other adult companies and with the children, is the way they can simultaneously rely on assumptions like those that inform

The London Prodigal and appear to reject them. *Antony and Cleopatra* (*c.* 1606–8) is a good case in point, since on a very superficial level it can be read as a prodigal play. Living a life of sensual dissipation with Cleopatra, Antony 'fishes, drinks, and wastes / The lamps of night in revel' (I. 4. 4–5). After being offered the chance of redemption, like Flowerdale, through an advantageous marriage to a dutiful wife, he reverts to his 'Egyptian dish' (II. 7. 126), giving 'his empire / Up to a whore' (III. 6. 66–7). Greater misfortune only begets greater revelling, as Antony seeks to 'drown consideration' (IV. 2. 45); Cleopatra's eventual betrayal of him leads to ultimate catastrophe and suicide. Clearly, this is a gross simplification of the play, but in order for *Antony and Cleopatra* to work, we have to see Antony in the limited terms that his compatriots tend to see him in, as 'The triple pillar of the world transform'd / Into a strumpet's fool' (I. 1. 12–13) – or, to put it another way, to judge him by the moral standards of *The London Prodigal*. However, the reason why this is necessary is that it allows us fully to appreciate the limitations of such a judgement and to understand why ''Tis paltry to be Caesar' (V. 2. 2). If the comparison is not too strained, we would not wish to be Caesar in much the same way that we would not wish to be Golding or Mildred in *Eastward Ho!*: these are characters who are materially successful, calculating and emotionally null. For all his aristocratic status, and his insistence that 'Caesar's no merchant' (V. 2. 183), Octavius's cold acquisitiveness is set up to contrast with Antony's largesse: he 'gets money where / He loses hearts' (II. 1. 13–14), asks Antony how the Egyptians forecast from the flow of the Nile 'if dearth / Or foison follow' (II. 7. 19–20), and feasts his army only after satisfying himself that 'we have store to do't, / And they have earn'd the waste' (IV. 1. 15–16), like Golding asking Touchstone for the 'superfluity and cold meat' (II. 1. 146) from the wedding of Gertrude and Flash to furnish forth his and Mildred's marriage tables. Viewed from this perspective, Antony's readiness to hazard his empire, to engage in acts of conspicuous consumption such as having 'Eight wild-boars roasted whole at a breakfast, and but twelve persons there' (II. 2. 179–80), is not so much prodigality as an aristocratic rejection of the calculating mentality, like the Earl of Southampton 'undermining his estate by losing up to 18,000 crowns on a game of tennis, and staking up to 4,000 crowns during a single evening at cards'.[60]

As I have briefly suggested above, *Antony and Cleopatra* relies on its audience being able to mobilise different sets of attitudes: attitudes that might broadly be said to be representative of different groups in society or, indeed, of different types of theatre in the Jacobean period. *Coriolanus* (*c.* 1608), the last play I want to consider, is similarly informed by contradictory social attitudes or, more specifically, contradictory attitudes towards work; here, however, rather than shaping the audience's response to the hero, they underlie the hero's problematic relationship to the society around him.[61] This relationship has been described by Lars Engle in terms of a refusal to participate in acts of symbolic exchange with the plebeians: for example, whereas Menenius's retailing of the belly fable in the opening scene, regardless of its actual content, indicates a willingness to engage with their grievances, Martius refuses any such engagement, just as he will later on refuse to make the reciprocal gesture of showing his wounds in return for the citizens' acclamation of him as consul. For Engle, this is because of his adherence to 'a hierarchical society in which the value of martial nobility will be fixed, recognised, and nonnegotiable', a society that is threatened by the more fluid exchange values of the marketplace.[62] It is Martius's belief that the worth of military valour transcends valuation that leads him to refuse material recompense for his deeds at Corioles: he 'cannot make my heart consent to take / A bribe to pay my sword' (I. 9. 37–8). And, rather than accepting a reward that might imply that his deeds have an exchange value, he takes the more intangible payment of a name, Coriolanus; as Cominius puts it, he 'rewards / His deeds with doing them' (II. 2. 127–8).

While Engle locates this aspect of the play in relation to James I's 'bringing nobility pervasively and explicitly into the marketplace' through the sale of honours, I would suggest that it should be seen in the context of the assumptions about the impropriety of merchandise for gentlemen that I have already referred to in this chapter.[63] According to Lawrence Stone, it was considered legitimate in the early modern period for nobles to market commodities derived from their own estates, as the first Lord Spencer did with wool and mutton; the line was drawn, however, at buying other goods for resale.

> It was perfectly in order for Sir Percival Willoughby to own ships and transport his coal down the Trent to Lincolnshire, but disreputable to buy corn there to provide a return freight for resale in Nottingham. To persuade him to agree it was urged that 'your worships need nott be seene in the premises, but onely your servantes.'[64]

Similarly, while the role of Martius in restricting the distribution of grain is not made clear in *Coriolanus*, the assertion that if the Citizens kill him 'we'll have corn at our own price' (I. 1. 10–11) implies that he has a financial interest in its sale, as does his resentful insistence later in the play that their war service 'Did not deserve corn gratis' (III. 1. 125). However, like Willoughby avoiding business premises, Martius refuses to present himself as a vendor, suggesting that the price of grain is not negotiable but arrived at by quasi-mystical means: 'Hang 'em! They say? / They'll sit by th' fire, and presume to know / What's done i' th' Capitol ... They say there's grain enough?' (I. 1. 190–2, 196). He also hates the metaphorical position of buyer that he sees the consulship as requiring him to occupy: 'Well then, I pray, your price a' th' consulship?' 'The price is, to ask it kindly' (II. 3. 73–5). Facing banishment, he insists that were he condemned by the plebeians to death, exile, flaying or starvation, 'I would not buy / Their mercy at the price of one fair word' (III. 3. 90–1). This tendency to see any form of interaction with the plebeians in terms of commercial exchange also expresses itself in Coriolanus's punning use of the term 'custom' to describe the tradition of a consul elect dressing in rags to ask for the citizens' acclamation (II. 2. 136, II. 3. 87 ['customary'], 117–18). While Engle sees such attitudes as deriving from Coriolanus's sense that gentility is non-negotiable, I would suggest that they also derive from a sense that negotiation is ungentle. After withdrawing to his house, Coriolanus reminds his mother that she was wont to call the citizens 'woollen vassals, things created / To buy and sell with groats' (III. 2. 9–10); part of the vituperative force of this comes from reducing the citizens to the status of objects no more human than the clothes they wear, but it also depends on the assumption that buying and selling (especially with such small sums as groats) is an inherently ignoble activity.

Coriolanus's rejection of exchange, and of people who make exchange their livelihood, is only one aspect of a more general tendency on his part to define the plebeians as workers and to denigrate them accordingly. Brutus says that he sees the people as 'Of no more soul nor fitness for the world / Than camels in their war, who have their provand / Only for bearing burthens' (II. 1. 250–2); this refusal to look beyond their status as manual labourers is expressed again late in the play when Coriolanus declines to 'capitulate / Again with Rome's mechanics' (V. 3. 82–3). Indeed, I would suggest that the drama itself encourages us to perceive Rome as essentially a two-class society divided into those who carry out manual and mercantile work and those who do not: its opening, after all, depicts producers rising up against consumers and hoarders, and Menenius's didactic fable pits against the body's other members an 'idle and unactive' belly (I. 1. 99), 'never bearing / Like labor with the rest' (100–1). The same character's first words in the play, 'What work's, my countrymen, in hand?' (54), allude to the rioters' status as labourers, and he and Cominius return to this theme in their invective against the tribunes after news of Coriolanus's return arrives in Rome: 'you have made good work!' (IV. 6. 79, 146; V. 1. 15), 'You have made fair work' (IV. 6. 88, 100), 'You have made fair hands, / You and your crafts! You have crafted fair!' (IV. 6. 117–18) and, most lavishly,

> You have made good work,
> You and your apron-men; you that stood so much
> Upon the voice of occupation and
> The breath of garlic-eaters! (IV. 6. 95–8)

All of these lines invoke the people whom the tribunes supposedly represent: workers, handicraftsmen, men of occupation. The claim of Brutus and Sicinius to speak for such people is the first thing the patricians reach for when seeking to abuse them.

The fact that the language of work – indeed, the word 'work' itself, obsessively – is so ostentatiously used and with such negative overtones in the latter half of the play is strikingly at odds with its more positive use in a very different context in the first half. At the gates of Corioles, Martius prays to Mars to 'make us quick in work' (I. 4. 10); later in the act, when Titus Lartius tries to dissuade him from going to fight alongside Cominius, he insists that, 'My work hath yet not warm'd me' (I. 5. 17). When he meets Aufidius in combat, he boasts that in Corioles he 'made what work I pleas'd' (I. 8. 9), and in the subsequent scene, Cominius praises 'this thy day's work' (I. 9. 1), similarly referring in his eulogy before the Senate to 'that worthy work perform'd / By Martius Caius Coriolanus' (II. 2. 45–6). Of course, 'work' here is not always understood in the sense of 'labour', often meaning something closer to 'deeds'. However, the frequent use of the same word elsewhere in the play to refer to manual and commercial labour (and labourers) creates an unlikely affinity between Coriolanus's martial exploits and the activities of the class he despises. The same is true of the moment when Volumnia imagines the wounded Martius going forth into battle 'Like to a harvest-man that's task'd to mow / Or all or lose his hire' (I. 3. 36–7): the image alludes to the figure of Death as Grim Reaper, but, more unexpectedly, it also seems to portray Martius as a hired manual labourer.

The use of the language of work, by other characters and by Martius himself, to describe his deeds on the battlefield is consistent with his scornful use of the language of idleness, or rather beggary, to describe his obligation to solicit popular acclaim in order to become Consul. Brutus recalls that Martius swore, if he stood for the office, never to observe the custom, 'Nor, showing (as the manner is) his wounds / To th' people, beg their stinking breaths' (II. 1. 235–6); as Martius explains, in surly manner, to the Third Citizen, ''twas never my desire yet to trouble the poor with begging' (II. 3. 69–70). Bidding the citizens adieu, he observes, 'There's in all two worthy voices begg'd. I have your alms' (II. 3. 80–1). Dressed in 'woolvish toge' (115) and claiming to have 'wounds to show you' (76–7), Coriolanus sardonically plays up to the role of counterfeit beggar of the kind described by Thomas Harman:

> And with stoute audacyte, [he] demaundeth where he thinketh hee maye be bolde, and circomspecte ynough as he sethe cause to aske charitie, rufully and lamentably, that it would make a flyntey hart to relent, and pytie his miserable estate, howe he hath bene maymed and broused in the warres, & perauenture some wyll shew youe som outward wounde, whiche he gotte at some dronken fraye.[65]

Indeed, Coriolanus tells the Fourth Citizen that, in order to obtain the good opinion of the people, he will 'practice the insinuating nod and be off to them most counterfeitly' (II. 3. 99–100).

Coriolanus's view of his martial exploits as labour, and his perception of seeking the citizens' acclamation as idleness and beggary, is not exactly incompatible with his rejection of manual and commercial work; however, I would suggest that the two should, at least, be seen as distinct attitudes informed by different sets of assumptions and prejudices. The first is the notion, encouraged by the Reformation, by humanism and by 'the increased social importance of the industrious sort of people', that to categorise an activity as work is to valorise it; in Chapter 3, I examined how Shakespeare draws upon this in his histories of the 1590s. The second is the view of work as degrading and incompatible with gentility, an attitude derived from the medieval tripartite model of society but also shaped by early modern anxieties regarding social mobility and exploited, I argued in Chapter 4, by the renascent children's companies. One effect of the coexistence of these attitudes is to give Coriolanus two ostensibly contrasting reasons for being unwilling to 'capitulate ... with Rome's mechanics': first, because to do so would be a form of beggary; second, because to do so would be a form of exchange analogous to the work of merchants, the more demeaning for being carried out with people who buy and sell, or work with their hands, in order to earn a living. I would argue that the reason why these attitudes can be reconciled is because both suspicion of exchange and hatred of idleness are eminently compatible with the theatrical metaphors that inform Coriolanus's arguments. Coriolanus and Volumnia alike repeatedly refer to the adoption of a conciliatory attitude towards the plebeians in terms of role play – he calling it 'a part / That I shall blush in acting' (II. 2. 144–5) and 'a part which never / I shall discharge to th' life' (III. 2. 105–6); she, rather more optimistically, asking him to 'perform a part / Thou hast not done before' (III. 2. 109–10). As Geoffrey Miles observes, Volumnia's words imply a perception of her son's military prowess, too, as role play rather than a straightforward expression of his true nature.[66] Coriolanus, however, seems to share the absolutist conception of self that Jonas Barish ascribes to Puritan opponents of the stage:

> If it was possible truly to know the 'uniform, distinct and proper being' one had received from God, then it was possible either to affirm that being in all of one's acts – to be 'such in truth' as one was 'in show' – or to deny it by disguise or pretense.[67]

To smile like a knave, weep like a schoolboy, wheedle and bow like a beggar is objectionable to Coriolanus because it is to be untrue to himself:

> I will not do't,
> Lest I surcease to honor mine own truth,
> And by my body's action teach my mind
> A most inherent baseness. (III. 2. 120–3)

Coriolanus's words also bespeak the assumption of writers against the stage that to play a part is to risk becoming the part one plays:

> For who will call hym a wise man that plaieth the parte of a foole and a vice? Who can call him a Christian, who plaieth the part of a Deuill, *th*e sworne enemie of Christ? Who can call hym a iust man, that plaieth the parte of a dissemblyng Hipocrite? And to bee breefe, who can call him a straight dealing man, who plaieth a Cosener's trick?[68]

Like Stubbes, Coriolanus sees what he is doing as cozenage: 'I'll mountebank their loves' (III. 2. 132). His perception of it as beggary, too, recalls Stubbes's criticism of actors for living 'vppon beggyng of euery one that comes', as well as the fact that unlicensed actors were classified as rogues, vagabonds and sturdy beggars.[69]

However, as I remarked earlier, Coriolanus describes his unwilling interaction with Rome's commoners not just in terms of beggary but also in terms of commercial exchange, and we are repeatedly reminded that the venue for this interaction is the 'market-place' (II. 1. 233; II. 2. 159; III. 1. 31; III. 1. 330; III. 2. 93; III. 2. 104; III. 2. 131). What he receives there is not just charity but payment: he laments having to 'crave the hire which first we do deserve' (II. 3. 114) and to show the citizens his scars, 'As if

I had receiv'd them for the hire / Of their breath only' (II. 2. 149–50). The idea of meeting the common people, the 'beast / With many heads' (IV. 1. 1–2), in the marketplace, and of being paid in breath, or 'voices' (II. 2. 140; II. 3. 1; II. 3. 36; II. 3. 45; and *passim*), irresistibly calls to mind Thomas Dekker's well-known formulation of 1609:

> The theatre is your poets' Royal Exchange upon which their Muses – that are now turned to merchants – meeting, barter away that light commodity of words for a lighter ware than words – plaudits and the breath of the great beast which, like the threatenings of two cowards, vanish all into air.[70]

As David Hawkes has argued, the fact that the theatre was a place of exchange, where poetry (and, according to some accusations, sex) could be bought and sold, seems to have been one of the things that exercised critics of the theatre such as Anglo-Phile Eutheo, who complained that the playwright 'writeth for reward' and so 'flattereth for commoditie', and Stephen Gosson, who called theatres 'markets of bawdry, where choise w*ith*out shame hath bene as free, as it is for your money in the royall exchaung'.[71] In *Coriolanus*, the trope is reversed, and the marketplace is treated as a theatrical arena. As the citizens wait for Coriolanus to appear in his humble gown, the Third Citizen invokes a contractual relation mirroring that between players and audience:

> FIRST CITIZEN Once if he do require our voices, we ought not to deny him.
> SECOND CITIZEN We may, sir, if we will.
> THIRD CITIZEN We have power in ourselves to do it, but it is a power that we have no power to do; for if he show us his wounds and tell us his deeds, we are to put our tongues into those words and speak for them; so, if he tell us his noble deeds, we must also tell him our noble acceptance of them. Ingratitude is monstrous. (II. 3. 1–9)

The wounds and words of Coriolanus demand a grateful response from the citizens: vocal acclamation, 'plaudits and the breath of the great beast', in return for showing and telling.[72] As such, while his self-display is presented as a form of beggary, it is also presented as a form of work, acting; and this is possible because acting is a form of work that is also a form of beggary.

Conclusion

In the last chapter, I identified both continuities and changes in the dramatic treatment of work by the adult and the children's companies after 1601. The adult companies continued to associate themselves (though not exclusively) with London's citizens through depicting manual and commercial work as morally upstanding (*The Honest Whore*) and compatible with gentle status (*The Four Prentices of London*), as well as highlighting the perils of idleness and dissolution (*The London Prodigal*). For their part, the Children of the Chapel satirised the former two claims in *Eastward Ho!* and rewarded an ostentatiously idle and dissolute character at the end of *The Knight of the Burning Pestle*. However, the fact that Jasper in the latter play is a paragon of dutiful industriousness and that the eponymous heroes of *The Four Prentices of London* are sons of the Earl of Bouillon precludes any easy identification of adults or children with particular sectional interests; furthermore, in these years, dramatists began to demonstrate a willingness to question the assumptions on which the companies' divergent treatments of work had been founded. The aristocratic culture of conspicuous leisure comes in for sustained interrogation in *A Woman Killed with Kindness*, but it is also satirised in *Eastward Ho!*; conversely, even in *The Honest Whore*, Candido is as ridiculous as he is impressive. I concluded the chapter with a discussion of *Antony and Cleopatra* and *Coriolanus*, two plays whose calculated juxtaposition of aristocratic and non-aristocratic discourses about work and idleness seems to stem less from an uncertainty about audience composition (as, perhaps, in *Hamlet*) than from a desire to exploit their dramatic possibilities. Antony is such an ambivalent figure because we are invited to judge him by two sets of standards; one way in which Coriolanus's confusion about his own role in relation to the citizens of Rome is expressed is through his holding two radically opposed valuations of work simultaneously.

One aspect of *Coriolanus* that makes it a particularly appropriate play with which to end the main part of this book is the manner in which its treatment of work is shaped by the theatrical environment in which it was produced. Not only does Coriolanus compare himself to an actor: in doing so, he draws on anti-theatrical discourses that variously condemned playing for its commercialism and for its idleness, and this permits his ostensibly paradoxical perception of engagement with Rome's citizens both as a demeaning form of exchange and as a form of beggary. Elsewhere in this book, I have argued that Hamlet's 'otiation', his studied performance of idleness, aligns him with the professional actor, who works while appearing not to. And Prince Hal's suggestion that his youthful dissipation is work rather than idleness is facilitated not only by theatrical metaphors of spectacle and disrobing but also by the fact that Shakespeare and other Elizabethan dramatists had already used their plays to suggest that such deceptions might be a form of work. In all of these cases, the controversial professional status of playing influences stage depiction of work and idleness.

A second controversy that affected the way work and play were treated on the stage was that surrounding audience composition. The right of prentices and servants to be in theatre audiences was repeatedly called into question by London's civic governors; it was questioned in a different way after 1599 by the dramatists writing for the children's companies, who sought to present their playhouses as socially exclusive spaces. In the years that followed, playing companies seem to have taken opposing positions in relation to work, in a way that was influenced by work's implication in questions of social status: the Admiral's/Prince Henry's Men, the Earl of Worcester's/Queen Anne's Men and, to some extent, the Lord Chamberlain's/King's Men staged at least some plays that stressed the dignity and respectability of work, as well as its compatibility with high social status, while these attitudes were satirised and parodied in some of the plays performed at the Blackfriars.

A pertinent question is whether the King's Men began to treat work in a different way after their own move to the Blackfriars, where they probably first performed in 1610 when theatres reopened after a lengthy plague outbreak.[1] The fashionable neighbourhood, the small size of the theatre, the consequent high prices and their own status as schoolboys had enabled the Children of the Chapel to advertise their performances there as socially exclusive in 1600; one might expect that the King's Men would have taken advantage of the first three of these circumstances to present their own partial relocation as a move upmarket. However, the company appears to have been slow to capitalise in this way on its new playing space. 'Title pages of company plays began to advertise performance at the

Blackfriars ahead of the Globe only in the 1620s', while the King's Men carried on performing at the Globe and rebuilt it when it burned down in 1613; evidently, they continued to place importance on that theatre and the socially mixed clientele it represented.[2] One play of 1610 that does identify strongly with the new theatre is Jonson's *The Alchemist*, whose location in a house 'here, in the *friers*' (I. I. 17) enables numerous metatheatrical analogies between Lovewit's residence and the playhouse – and, as several critics have noted, between the way Doll, Face and Subtle delude their clients with misleading spectacles and the way the King's Men entice money from the Blackfriars audience with theatrical entertainment.[3] The implied comparison with a whore, a rogue servant and a fake magician is hardly one that elevates the King's Men socially; nor do the Blackfriars audience gain much credit for being represented by the likes of Abel Drugger and Epicure Mammon. Though the play displays a marked ambivalence about the transaction taking place between actors and audience, however, one thing it does emphasise is the effort that the three cozeners put into defrauding their customers, keeping up a constant stream of talk, regularly changing disguise and reacting to unforeseen difficulties with brilliant improvisation. R. L. Smallwood makes an interesting comparison with the kind of drama that Jonson had mocked in *Eastward Ho!*: 'Like the business men of the earlier citizen plays, Face and Subtle and Doll work hard in their trade and display great energy and resourcefulness in their pursuit of profit.'[4] The analogy Jonson draws between the three central characters and professional actors, influenced though it may be by anti-theatrical discourses that associated playing with cozenage, has the inevitable side effect of making the Blackfriars theatre a place of work. Moreover, the epistle Jonson added to the 1612 printed text of the play serves to distance his own authorial labours, his 'diligence' in the art of poetry (11), from the more questionable work of the play's main characters, warning the reader 'thou wert neuer more fair in the way to be cos'ned (then in this Age) in *Poetry*, especially in Playes' (4–5). Jonson's text anticipates the energetic but morally dubious work of Face, Subtle and Doll with a contrasting image of the poet labouring conscientiously in his own 'house in the Black-Friars', the location given at the end of his 1607 epistle to *Volpone* (145n); his final sentence, 'For it is onely the disease of the vnskilfull, to thinke rude things greater then polish'd: or scatter'd more numerous then compos'd' (33–5), magisterially invokes the artifice of which *The Alchemist* is a product.

A number of critics have regarded another early Blackfriars play, Shakespeare's *The Tempest* (1611), as engaged in a kind of dialogue with

The Alchemist, positing Shakespeare as the implied target of Jonson's Epistle to the Reader and citing the plays' mutual observance of the unities of time and place, their central mage figures and their shared thematic concern with the nature of theatrical illusion as evidence of their intertextuality.[5] Like *The Alchemist*, *The Tempest* invites its audience to recognise parallels between the magical illusions created by its characters and the dramatic spectacles produced by the King's Men: as early as the second scene, the revelation that the first scene's storm was a work of Prospero's 'art' (I. 2. 1) and that 'There's no harm done' (15) reminds us that what we perceived as a tempest was a piece of theatrical art that left the actors wet but unhurt. Recently, Douglas Bruster and Daniel Vitkus have extended the analogy so far as to see the play as echoing the division of labour within the Jacobean playhouse, Bruster comparing Prospero to a playwright or director, Ariel to a boy actor, and the disobedient Caliban to Will Kemp, still active in Shakespeare's memory if long absent from his playing company.[6] Without proposing so specific a reading, it is possible to identify a number of instances where *The Tempest* emphasises the labour that goes into the making of illusion, including Ariel's references to the 'toil' and 'pains' (I. 2. 242) that Prospero makes him undergo in carrying out 'our work' (V. 1. 5), Prospero's own talk of needing to 'perform / Much business' (III. 1. 95–6) and his anticipation of an end to his 'labors' (IV. 1. 264). Indeed, beyond this interest in theatrical labour, *The Tempest* is remarkable for its willingness to show characters engaged in physical work: the mariners trying to keep the ship afloat in the first scene and Caliban and Ferdinand carrying logs in II. 2 and III. 1. If the island, like *The Alchemist*'s house in the Friars, is analogous to the Blackfriars theatre, then it implies a placing space much more amenable to the idea of work than it had been a decade before.

And yet, if the island is a place of work, it is also a place of fantasies about idleness. For Gonzalo, it is a blank canvas onto which to project his ideal of a commonwealth in which there would be 'No occupation, all men idle, all' (II. 1. 155) and where 'All things in common nature should produce / Without sweat or endeavor' (160–1) – a vision readily parodied by Antonio as a state whose subjects would be 'all idle – whores and knaves' (167). Caliban, perhaps short-sightedly, welcomes servitude to Stephano as offering freedom from the work he carried out for Prospero:

> No more dams I'll make for fish,
> Nor fetch in firing
> At requiring,
> Nor scrape trenchering, nor wash dish. (II. 2. 180–3)

Prospero's own presence on the isle is a product of his reluctance to shoulder the cares of rule: 'the liberal arts ... being all my study, / The government I cast upon my brother, / And to my state grew stranger' (I. 2. 73–6). He speaks disdainfully about Antonio's knowledge of 'how to grant suits, / How to deny them, who t' advance, and who / To trash for overtopping' (79–81), but his words are not far from those of the Gardener in *Richard II* who lamented the King's failure to check the growth of proud nobles as 'Superfluous branches / We lop away' (III. 4. 63–4). The skills Antonio is expert in are, for the Gardener, precisely those in which the work of a ruler resides. Unwilling to do this work, Prospero has ended up on an island where the native Caliban does the menial jobs and he himself has been able to devote his full attention to study, to fantasies of revenge and to Miranda's education.

Miranda has been described as 'a figure of an idealized spectatorship', and a significant part of her role in *The Tempest* is, indeed, to act as an audience: to Prospero's narrative of how they came to be on the island, to his harsh treatment of Ferdinand and to Ferdinand's log-carrying.[7] As Ferdinand describes it, 'My sweet mistress / Weeps when she sees me work, and says such baseness / Had never like executor' (III. 1. 11–13); while she is unable to share his labour (25–8), the experience of watching it excites her sympathy. But her presence also changes the nature of what Ferdinand is doing, transforming it from work into something other than work: 'The mistress which I serve quickens what's dead, / And makes my labors pleasures' (6–7). Ferdinand could mean that being Miranda's servant makes the work pleasurable for him, or he could mean that Miranda herself derives a tearful pleasure from watching someone suffer in her service; in the metatheatrical context of *The Tempest*, which reflects continually on its own status as drama, both meanings are relevant. The island, like an early modern playhouse, is both a place of work and a place for escape from work; Ferdinand, like an early modern actor, is both working and playing, his physical exertions turned into recreation by the presence of an idle audience.

Notes

INTRODUCTION

1. Keith Thomas (ed.), *The Oxford Book of Work* (Oxford: Oxford University Press, 1999), pp. v–vi.
2. Philip Sidney, *The Complete Works of Sir Philip Sidney*, ed. Albert Feuillerat, 4 vols. (Cambridge: Cambridge University Press, 1922–6), Vol. III, p. 39.
3. Stephen Gosson, *Playes Confuted in Fiue Actions* (London, 1582), sigs. D1^{r}, D4^{v}.
4. Thomas, *Oxford Book of Work*, p. xiii.
5. The text of all quotations is as in J. A. Simpson and E. S. C. Weiner (eds.), *The Oxford English Dictionary*, 2nd edn, 20 vols. (Oxford: Clarendon Press, 1989).
6. Mary Ellen Rickey and Thomas B. Stroup (eds.), *Certaine Sermons or Homilies Appointed to Be Read in Churches in the Time of Queen Elizabeth I (1547–1571): A Facsimile Reproduction of the Edition of 1623* (Gainesville, Fla.: Scholars' Facsimiles & Reprints, 1968), pp. 253, 249–51.
7. Richard H. Hall, with contributions by Robert T. Buttram, *Sociology of Work: Perspectives, Analyses, and Issues* (Thousand Oaks, Calif.: Pine Forge Press, 1994), pp. 3, 5; Keith Grint, *The Sociology of Work: An Introduction*, 2nd edn (Cambridge: Polity Press, 1998), pp. 1, 3, 11.
8. Maurice Hunt, *Shakespeare's Labored Art: Stir, Work, and the Late Plays* (New York: Peter Lang, 1995), pp. 7, 259, 275, 260.
9. According to the *Annual Survey of Hours and Earnings*, in 2003 the average hourly earnings for women in the United Kingdom, excluding overtime, were £10.70, which amounted to 80.5 per cent of the average for men (£13.29). Chris Daffin, *Annual Survey of Hours and Earnings: An Analysis of Historical Data 1998–2003* (Newport: Office of National Statistics, 2004), p. 6.
10. Amy Louise Erickson, *Women and Property in Early Modern England* (London: Routledge, 1993), p. 24. See also T(homas). E(dgar). (ed.), *The Lawes Resolvtions of Womens Rights; or, The Lawes Provision for Woemen* (London, 1632), pp. 129–30: while 'That which the Husband hath is his owne', 'That which the Wife hath is the Husbands'.
11. Lloyd E. Berry (ed.), *The Geneva Bible: A Facsimile of the 1560 Edition* (Madison, Wisc.: University of Wisconsin Press, 1969).
12. John Dod and Robert Cleaver, *A Godlie Forme of Hovseholde Government: For the Ordering of Private Families, According to the Direction of Gods Word*

(London, 1612), sig. F3[v]; Henry Smith, *A Preparatiue to Mariage* (London, 1591), p. 76.

13. Ste. B., *Covnsel to the Husband: To the Wife Instruction* (London, 1608), pp. 46–7.
14. Lorna Hutson, *The Usurer's Daughter: Male Friendship and Fictions of Women in Sixteenth-Century England* (London: Routledge, 1994), p. 21; Baldassare Castiglione, *The Book of the Courtier from the Italian of Count Baldassare Castiglione: Done into English by Sir Thomas Hoby Anno 1561*, ed. W. E. Henley (London: David Nutt, 1900), p. 224; Thomas Smith, *De republica anglorum*, ed. Mary Dewar (Cambridge: Cambridge University Press, 1982), p. 58; Thomas Heywood, *Gynaikeion; or, Nine Bookes of Various History Concerninge Women; Inscribed by the Names of the Nine Muses* (1624), p. 180. See also *Xenophons Treatise of Hovseholde*, trans. Gentian Hervet (London, 1534), fols. 23[r]–23[v]; Aristotle, *Metaphysics, X–XIV, Oeconomica, Magna Moralia*, trans. Hugh Tredennick and G. Cyril Armstrong, *Aristotle in Twenty-Three Volumes*, (Cambridge, Mass.: Harvard University Press, 1935, repr. 1990), Vol. XVIII, p. 333.
15. Hutson, *Usurer's Daughter*, p. 29.
16. Ronda A. Arab, 'Work, Bodies and Gender in *The Shoemaker's Holiday*', *Medieval and Renaissance Drama in England* 13 (2000), pp. 182–212 (pp. 197–8).
17. Linda Woodbridge, *Women and the English Renaissance: Literature and the Nature of Womankind, 1540–1620* (Brighton: Harvester Press; Urbana, Ill.: University of Illinois Press, 1984), pp. 174–5. For a recent survey of such scenes in the drama, see Leslie Thomson, '"As Proper a Woman as Any in Cheap": Women in Shops on the Early Modern Stage', *Medieval and Renaissance Drama in England* 16 (2003), pp. 145–61.
18. Garrett A. Sullivan Jr., '"All Thinges Come into Commerce": Women, Household Labor, and the Spaces of Marston's *The Dutch Courtesan*', *Renaissance Drama*, n.s., 27 (1996), pp. 19–46.
19. Mary Wack, 'Women, Work, and Plays in an English Medieval Town', in Susan Frye and Karen Robertson (eds.), *Maids and Mistresses, Cousins and Queens: Women's Alliances in Early Modern England* (New York: Oxford University Press, 1999), pp. 33–51.
20. Patricia Fumerton, *Unsettled: The Culture of Mobility and the Working Poor in Early Modern England* (Chicago, Ill.: University of Chicago Press, 2006), pp. 26, 16, 55.
21. Fiona McNeill, *Poor Women in Shakespeare* (Cambridge: Cambridge University Press, 2007), p. 18–19.
22. See Tom Rutter, 'Playing Work: The Uses of Labour on the Shakespearean Stage', unpublished Ph.D. thesis, University of London (2003), pp. 244–85.

WORK IN SIXTEENTH-CENTURY ENGLAND

1. Although my contention that the meaning of work changed between the Middle Ages and the early modern period is not meant to be understood with reference to the word 'work' itself, the *OED* does point to some

suggestive developments. 'Out of work', meaning 'having no work to do, unemployed, workless' first appears in 1599, in *Henry V* (I. 2. 114) (*OED* 'work', *sb.*, III. 27). 'A literary or musical composition' had been a work since the fourteenth century ('work', *sb.*, II. 13), but the word did not connote 'high artistic quality' ('work', *sb.*, II. 14) until well into the sixteenth. The fact that Ben Jonson was mocked for publishing his 'Workes' in 1616 indicates the novelty of using the word to refer to plays; see Ben Jonson, *Ben Jonson*, ed. C. H. Herford and Percy and E. M. Simpson, 11 vols. (Oxford: Clarendon Press, 1925–52), Vol. IX, p. 13. By 1581, a works could be a place of manufacture, as in 'iron workes' ('work', *sb.*, II. 18), reflecting the beginnings of a factory system in England.

2. David Aers, *Chaucer, Langland and the Creative Imagination* (London: Routledge & Kegan Paul, 1980), pp. 1–37 (p. 2).
3. Quoted in G. R. Owst, *Literature and Pulpit in Medieval England: A Neglected Chapter in the History of English Letters and of the English People* (Cambridge: Cambridge University Press, 1933), p. 554.
4. Georges Duby, *The Three Orders: Feudal Society Imagined*, trans. Arthur Goldhammer (Chicago, Ill.: University of Chicago Press, 1980), pp. 1–4, 99–104, 30, 54, 276.
5. Quoted in Duby, *The Three Orders*, pp. 284, 274.
6. Lloyd E. Berry (ed.), *The Geneva Bible: A Facsimile of the 1560 Edition* (Madison,Wisc.: University of Wisconsin Press, 1969).
7. Thomas Aquinas, *Summa theologica*, trans. the Fathers of the English Dominican Provinces, 22 vols. (London: Burns Oates & Washbourne, (1921?–1934), Vol. XIV, p. 243.
8. James M. Dean (ed.), *Medieval English Political Writings* (Kalamazoo, Mich.: Medieval Institute Publications, 1996), p. 140.
9. Jacques Le Goff, *Medieval Civilization, 400–1500*, trans. Julia Barrow (Oxford: Basil Blackwell, 1988), p. 261.
10. Aers, *Chaucer, Langland*, pp. 1, 4; William Langland, *The Vision of Piers Plowman: A Critical Edition of the B-Text Based on Trinity College Cambridge MS B.15.17*, ed. A. V. C. Schmidt, 2nd edn (London: Everyman, 1995), pp. 7, 96.
11. Cary J. Nederman and Kate Langdon Forhan (eds.), *Medieval Political Theory – A Reader: The Quest for the Body Politic, 1100–1400* (London: Routledge, 1993), p. 224.
12. Quoted in Owst, *Literature and Pulpit*, p. 550.
13. Mary Ellen Rickey and Thomas B. Stroup (eds.), *Certaine Sermons or Homilies Appointed to be Read in Churches in the Time of Queen Elizabeth I (1547–1571): A Facsimile Reproduction of the Edition of 1623* (Gainesville, Fla.: Scholars' Facsimiles & Reprints, 1968), pp. 249–50.
14. Thomas Elyot, *The Boke Named the Gouernour*, ed. Henry Herbert Stephen Croft, 2 vols. (London: C. Kegan Paul, 1880), Vol. I, pp. 6–7.
15. W. S., *A Compendious or Brief Examination of Certayne Ordinary Complaints, of Diuers of our Country Men in these our Dayes* (London, 1581), fol. 6[r]. According to Halkett and Laing, W. S. put his name in 1581 to a work written

in 1549; see Samuel Halkett and John Laing, *A Dictionary of Anonymous and Pseudonymous Publications in the English Language*, 3rd edn, rev. John Horden (Harlow: Longman, 1980), p. 39.

16. John Cotta, *A Short Discoverie of the Vnobserved Dangers of Seuerall Sorts of Ignorant and Vnconsiderate Practisers of Physicke in England* (London, 1612), p. 75; William Fulbecke, *A Direction or Preparatiue to the Study of the Lawe* (London, 1600), fol. 13ᵛ.
17. Hugh Latimer, *The Works of Hugh Latimer*, ed. George Elwes Corrie, 2 vols. (Cambridge: Cambridge University Press, 1844–5), Vol. I, p. 215.
18. Thomas Smith, *De republica anglorum*, ed. Mary Dewar (Cambridge: Cambridge University Press, 1982), p. 72. See also William Harrison, *The Description of England*, ed. Georges Edelen (Ithaca, NY: Cornell University Press, 1968), p. 114; William Segar, *Honor Military, and Ciuill, Contained in Foure Bookes* (London, 1602), p. 228. On the relationship between similar passages in Smith and Harrison, see Appendix 3 in Smith, *De republica anglorum*, pp. 157–62.
19. Francis Bacon, *The Essayes or Counsels, Civill and Morall*, ed. Michael Kiernan (Cambridge, Mass.: Harvard University Press, 1985), pp. 124–9, 110.
20. Gerrard Winstanley, *The Works of Gerrard Winstanley*, ed. George H. Sabine (Ithaca, NY: Cornell University Press, 1941), p. 579.
21. Christopher Hill, *Milton and the English Revolution* (London: Faber & Faber, 1977), p. 5.
22. Rickey and Stroup (eds.), *Certaine Sermons or Homilies*, sig. a2ᵛ.
23. Jacques Le Goff, *Time, Work, and Culture in the Middle Ages*, trans. Arthur Goldhammer (Chicago, Ill.: University of Chicago Press, 1980), pp. 58–70 (pp. 62, 68, 64).
24. Sybil M. Jack, *Trade and Industry in Tudor and Stuart England* (London: George Allen & Unwin, 1977), pp. 15–65.
25. C. G. A. Clay, *Economic Expansion and Social Change: England 1500–1700*, 2 vols. (Cambridge: Cambridge University Press, 1984), Vol. I, pp. 1–3.
26. Thomas More, *Utopia*, ed. Edward Surtz and J. H. Hexter, The Complete Works of St Thomas More, 4 (New Haven, Conn.: Yale University Press, 1965), pp. 64–71; Thomas Starkey, *A Dialogue between Pole and Lupset*, ed. T. F. Mayer, Camden Fourth Series, 37 (London: Royal Historical Society, 1989), pp. 52–3, 59.
27. Christopher Hill, *Society and Puritanism in Pre-Revolutionary England* (London: Secker & Warburg, 1964), pp. 124–5.
28. D. C. Coleman, *The Economy of England, 1450–1750* (Oxford: Oxford University Press, 1977), pp. 23, 29.
29. Coleman, *Economy of England*, p. 50; Christopher Hill, *Reformation to Industrial Revolution*, 2nd edn (Harmondsworth: Penguin, 1969), p. 53.
30. A. L. Beier, *Masterless Men: The Vagrancy Problem in England, 1560–1640* (London: Methuen, 1985), p. 21 and *passim*; Paul Slack, *Poverty and Policy in Tudor and Stuart England* (London: Longman, 1988), pp. 22–7, 63–9.
31. R. H. Tawney and Eileen Power (eds.), *Tudor Economic Documents: Being Select Documents Illustrating the Economic and Social History of Tudor*

England, 3 vols. (London: Longmans, Green, 1924; repr. 1951), Vol. I, p. 339, Vol. II, p. 332.

32. Hill, *Society and Puritanism*, p. 139.
33. Max Weber, *The Protestant Ethic and the Spirit of Capitalism*, trans. Talcott Parsons (New York: Charles Scribner's Sons; London: George Allen & Unwin, 1930; repr. 1956). For criticism of Weber, see R. H. Tawney, *Religion and the Rise of Capitalism: A Historical Study* (London: John Murray, 1926; repr. Harmondsworth: Penguin, 1972), pp. 311–13; Christopher Hill, *Change and Continuity in Seventeenth-Century England* (London: Weidenfeld & Nicolson, 1974), pp. 81–102.
34. Martin Luther, *Reformation Writings of Martin Luther*, trans. Bertram Lee Woolf, 2 vols. (London: Lutterworth Press, 1952–56), Vol. I, pp. 116, 371, 375.
35. Tawney, *Religion*, pp. 101, 119, 199, 230–1. Or, more generally, according to Hill's reading, Protestantism's 'appeal to inner conviction, and the rejection of the routine of ceremonies through which the priesthood imposed its authority' made it easier for the commercial classes to overcome traditional objections to their behaviour (Hill, *Change and Continuity*, p. 99).
36. Thomas Becon, *The Worckes of Thomas Becon*, 3 vols. (London, 1564), Vol. I, sig. $A4^{v}$.
37. William Perkins, *The Works of that Famovs and Worthie Minister of Christ, in the Vniversitie of Cambridge, M. W. Perkins* (Cambridge, 1603), sig. $Kkkk1^{v}$, pp. 909, 903, 906.
38. Lorna Hutson, *The Usurer's Daughter: Male Friendship and Fictions of Women in Sixteenth-Century England* (London: Routledge, 1994), p. 21.
39. *Xenophons Treatise of Hovseholde*, trans. Gentian Hervet (London, 1534), fols. 14^{r}–15^{v}.
40. Cicero, *Marcus Tullius Ciceroes Thre Bokes of Duties, to Marcus his Sonne, Turned oute of Latine into English, by Nicolas Grimalde*, ed. Gerald O'Gorman (Washington, DC: Folger Shakespeare Library; London: Associated University Presses, 1990), Introduction, pp. 15, 13.
41. Cicero, *De officiis*, trans. Walter Miller (London: William Heinemann; Cambridge, Mass.: Harvard University Press, 1913; repr. 1938), pp. 73–5, 125.
42. Brendan Bradshaw, 'Transalpine Humanism', in J. H. Burns and Mark Goldie (eds.), *The Cambridge History of Political Thought, 1450–1700* (Cambridge: Cambridge University Press, 1991), pp. 95–131 (pp. 105, 115, 106).
43. More, *Utopia*, pp. 102–3, 126–7.
44. Louis A. Montrose, 'Professing the Renaissance: The Poetics and Politics of Culture', in H. Aram Veeser (ed.), *The New Historicism* (New York: Routledge, 1989), pp. 15–36 (p. 20).
45. H. Aram Veeser, 'Introduction', in *The New Historicism*, pp. ix–xvi (p. xii).
46. Stephen Greenblatt, *Shakespearean Negotiations: The Circulation of Social Energy in Renaissance England* (Berkeley, Calif.: University of California Press, 1988), p. 19.
47. David Perkins, *Is Literary History Possible?* (Baltimore, Md.: Johns Hopkins University Press, 1992), pp. 148, 150.

48. Walter Cohen, 'Political Criticism of Shakespeare', in Jean E. Howard and Marion F. O'Connor (eds.), *Shakespeare Reproduced: The Text in History and Ideology* (New York: Routledge, 1987), pp. 18–46, pp. 33–4.
49. Perkins, *Is Literary History Possible?*, p. 132.
50. Scott McMillin and Sally-Beth MacLean, *The Queen's Men and Their Plays* (Cambridge: Cambridge University Press, 1998), pp. 18–36.
51. Richard Dutton, *Mastering the Revels: The Regulation and Censorship of English Renaissance Drama* (Basingstoke: Macmillan, 1991), pp. 194–204, 46.
52. Roslyn Lander Knutson, *The Repertory of Shakespeare's Company, 1594–1613* (Fayetteville, Ark.: University of Arkansas Press, 1991), p. 40.
53. Andrew Gurr, *Playgoing in Shakespeare's London*, 2nd edn (Cambridge: Cambridge University Press, 1996), p. 158.

'VPON THE WEKE DAIES AND WORKE DAIES AT CONUENIENT TIMES': ACTING AS WORK IN ELIZABETHAN ENGLAND

1. John Stephens, *Essayes and Characters: Ironicall, and Instrvctive* (London, 1615), p. 295; Thomas Overbury, *New and Choise Characters, of Seuerall Authors: Together with that Exquisite and Vnmatcht Poeme, The Wife* (London, 1615), sigs. $M5^v$–$M6^r$. See also Glynne Wickham, Herbert Berry and William Ingram (eds.), *English Professional Theatre, 1530–1660* (Cambridge: Cambridge University Press, 2000), pp. 179–81.
2. Philip Sidney, *The Complete Works of Sir Philip Sidney*, ed. Albert Feuillerat, 4 vols. (Cambridge: Cambridge University Press, 1922–6), Vol. III, p. 7.
3. In order to avoid repetitiousness, however, I use the two words interchangeably in this book.
4. E. K. Chambers, *The Elizabethan Stage*, 4 vols. (Oxford: Clarendon Press, 1923), Vol. I, p. 309.
5. M. C. Bradbrook, *The Rise of the Common Player: A Study of Actor and Society in Shakespeare's England* (London: Chatto & Windus, 1962), p. 37.
6. Wilfrid R. Prest, *The Rise of the Barristers: A Social History of the English Bar, 1590–1640* (Oxford: Clarendon Press, 1986), p. 2.
7. Gerald Eades Bentley, *The Profession of Player in Shakespeare's Time, 1590–1642* (Princeton, NJ: Princeton University Press, 1984), p. 6.
8. David Kathman, 'Grocers, Goldsmiths, and Drapers: Freemen and Apprentices in the Elizabethan Theater', *Shakespeare Quarterly* 55 (2004), pp. 1–49 (p. 3).
9. Bradbrook, *Rise of the Common Player*, p. 39.
10. David Galloway (ed.), *Records of Early English Drama: Norwich 1540–1642* (Toronto: University of Toronto Press, 1984), pp. 1–56. The exception is 'certen spanyardes and ytalyans who dawnsyd antyck [...] & played dyu*er*se p*ro*per bayne ffeetes', to whom a payment was recorded in 1546–7 (p. 21). In two instances from 1541–2 and 1542–3, payments to unnamed players are recorded, though in the latter case the recipients may have been the Earl of Arundel's players, who are named shortly afterwards (pp. 5–8).

11. See David M. Bevington, *From 'Mankind' to Marlowe: Growth of Structure in the Popular Drama of Tudor England* (Cambridge, Mass.: Harvard University Press, 1962) and *Tudor Drama and Politics: A Critical Approach to Topical Meaning* (Cambridge, Mass.: Harvard University Press, 1968); Glynne Wickham, *Early English Stages 1300 to 1600*, 2nd edn, 4 vols. (London: Routledge & Kegan Paul, 1980–2002); Suzanne R. Westfall, *Patrons and Performance: Early Tudor Household Revels* (Oxford: Clarendon Press, 1990); Paul Whitfield White, *Theatre and Reformation: Protestantism, Patronage, and Playing in Tudor England* (Cambridge: Cambridge University Press, 1993); and the ongoing *Records of Early English Drama.*
12. Bevington, *From 'Mankind' to Marlowe*, pp. 11, 15–17. Bevington points out that *Mankind*'s actors solicit the audience for money; the variety of placenames in the script, simple stage, small number of properties and cast of six suggest itinerancy.
13. Anne Barton (Anne Righter), *Shakespeare and the Idea of the Play* (London: Chatto & Windus, 1962), p. 20.
14. Michael D. Bristol, *Carnival and Theater: Plebeian Culture and the Structure of Authority in Renaissance England* (New York: Methuen, 1985), p. 3.
15. R. W. Ingram (ed.), *Records of Early English Drama: Coventry* (Toronto: University of Toronto Press; London: Manchester University Press, 1981), p. 149.
16. Wickham, *Early English Stages*, Vol. I, p. 113. See also Harold C. Gardiner, *Mysteries' End: An Investigation of the Last Days of the Medieval Religious Stage* (New Haven, Conn.: Yale University Press; London: Oxford University Press, 1946), pp. 46–93.
17. Alexandra F. Johnston, 'The City as Patron: York', in Paul Whitfield White and Suzanne R. Westfall (eds.), *Shakespeare and Theatrical Patronage in Early Modern England* (Cambridge: Cambridge University Press, 2002), pp. 150–75 (p. 173).
18. Wickham, *Early English Stages*, Vol. I, p. 115.
19. Lawrence M. Clopper (ed.), *Records of Early English Drama: Chester* (Toronto: University of Toronto Press; London: Manchester University Press, 1979), p. 97.
20. Westfall, *Patrons and Performance*, pp. 125, 122, 156, 118–19. Bale's career as a writer, and possibly actor, of Reformation plays is dealt with in detail in White, *Theatre and Reformation*, pp. 12–41.
21. John Foxe, *Acts and Monuments*, ed. S. R. Cattley, rev. Josiah Pratt, 8 vols. (London: Religious Tract Society, 1877), Vol. VI, pp. 31, 57, quoted in White, *Theatre and Reformation*, p. 44.
22. Westfall, *Patrons and Performance*, pp. 123–4.
23. Galloway, *Records of Early English Drama: Norwich 1540–1642*, pp. 1–48.
24. Ingram, *Records of Early English Drama: Coventry*, pp. xxxiii, 265–302.
25. A. L. Beier, *Masterless Men: The Vagrancy Problem in England 1560–1640* (London: Methuen, 1985), pp. 9–10, 21; see also Paul Slack, *Poverty and Policy in Tudor and Stuart England* (London: Longman, 1988), p. 13.
26. Earlier Tudor vagrancy statutes that make no reference to actors include 11 Hen. VII (1494), c. 2; 22 Hen. VIII (1530), c. 12; and 27 Hen. VIII (1535), c. 25, although both the first and third of these prohibit the playing of unlawful

games. See Owen Ruffhead (ed.), *The Statutes at Large, from Magna Charta, to the Twenty-Fifth Year of the Reign of King George the Third, Inclusive*, rev. Charles Runnington, 10 vols. (London: Charles Eyre & Andrew Strahan; William Woodfall & Andrew Strahan, 1786), Vol. II, pp. 73, 147, 229.

27. Wickham et al., *English Professional Theatre*, pp. 62–3.
28. Galloway, *Records of Early English Drama: Norwich 1540–1642*, p. 98.
29. Galloway, *Records of Early English Drama: Norwich 1540–1642*, p. 91.
30. Peter H. Greenfield, 'Touring', in John D. Cox and David Scott Kastan (eds.), *A New History of Early English Drama* (New York: Columbia University Press, 1997), pp. 251–68 (pp. 258–9).
31. Andrew Gurr, *The Shakespearian Playing Companies* (Oxford: Clarendon Press, 1996), p. 19.
32. The Red Lion theatre had been built at Whitechapel in 1567: see Janet S. Loengard, 'An Elizabethan Lawsuit: John Brayne, His Carpenter, and the Building of the Red Lion Theatre', *Shakespeare Quarterly* 34 (1983), pp. 298–310. However, Herbert Berry points out that this was not 'an imposing structure built to house plays for many years' and doubts whether it should be called the first permanent London playhouse: see Herbert Berry, 'The First Public Playhouses, Especially the Red Lion', *Shakespeare Quarterly* 40 (1989), pp. 133–48 (p. 145).
33. Chambers, *Elizabethan Stage*, Vol. I, p. 277.
34. Richard Dutton, *Mastering the Revels: The Regulation and Censorship of English Renaissance Drama* (Basingstoke: Macmillan, 1991), pp. 30–1.
35. Charles Whitney, 'The Devil His Due: Mayor John Spencer, Elizabethan Civic Antitheatricalism, and *The Shoemaker's Holiday*', *Medieval and Renaissance Drama in England* 14 (2001), pp. 168–85 (p. 171–2).
36. William Ingram, *The Business of Playing: The Beginnings of the Adult Professional Theater in Elizabethan London* (Ithaca, NY: Cornell University Press, 1992), pp. 135–6.
37. Scott McMillin and Sally-Beth MacLean, *The Queen's Men and their Plays* (Cambridge: Cambridge University Press, 1998), p. 9.
38. Act of Common Council, 6 December 1574, Lansdowne MS 20.10, fols. 23–5, British Library. A modernised version is given in Wickham, Berry and Ingram (eds.), *English Professional Theatre*, pp. 73–7.
39. Ingram, *Business of Playing*, p. 129.
40. E. K. Chambers and W. W. Greg (eds.), 'Dramatic Records of the City of London: The Remembrancia', Malone Society *Collections*, Vol. I, Pt. 1 (Oxford: Malone Society, 1907), p. 48.
41. Chambers, *Elizabethan Stage*, Vol. IV, p. 291.
42. Chambers and Greg, 'The Remembrancia', pp. 68–9, 76, 80. Interestingly, the Privy Council accepts this charge in its order of June 1600 limiting the number of playhouses in London to two:

> it is manifestly knowen and graunted that the multitude of the saide houses, and the mysgouerment of them hath bin and is dayly occasion, of the ydle ryoutous, and dissolute living of great Nombers of people, that leavinge all such honest and painefull course of life as they should followe doe meete and assemble there.

Restricting licensed companies to two performances a week, the order notes that 'these stage plaies, by the multitude of houses and company of players haue bin to frequent not servinge for recreation but invitinge and callinge the people dayly from their trade and worke to myspend their tyme' (Order of the Privy Council, 22 June 1600, Privy Council, PC 2/25, p. 223, National Archives). Modernised extracts from this document are given in Wickham, et al., *English Professional Theatre*, pp. 106–9.

43. Grindal to Lord Burghley, 22 February 1563–4, Lansdowne MS 7.62 fol. 141^r, British Library. A modernised extract is given in Wickham, et al., *English Professional Theatre*, p. 55.
44. Margreta de Grazia, 'World Pictures, Modern Periods, and the Early Stage', in John D. Cox and David Scott Kastan (eds.), *A New History of Early English Drama*, pp. 7–21 (p. 13).
45. Ingram, *Business of Playing*, pp. 146, 135; Wickham, *Early English Stages*, Vol. II, Pt. 1, p. 196.
46. Thomas Blanke to Lord Burghley, 14 January 1582–3, Lansdowne MS 37.4, fol. 8, British Library; Chambers and Greg, 'The Remembrancia', pp. 58–62.
47. Chambers and Greg, 'The Remembrancia', p. 67.
48. Gurr, *Shakespearian Playing Companies*, pp. 196–7.
49. Wickham et al., *English Professional Theatre*, pp. 538–9.
50. Kathleen E. McLuskie and Felicity Dunworth [*sic*]: 'Patronage and the Economics of Theater', in John D. Cox and David Scott Kastan (eds.), *A New History of Early English Drama*, pp. 423–40 (p. 431).
51. R. A. Foakes (ed.), *Henslowe's Diary*, 2nd edn (Cambridge: Cambridge University Press, 2002), p. 284.
52. Herbert Berry, 'Brayne, John (*c.* 1541–1586)', *Oxford Dictionary of National Biography* (Oxford University Press, 2004), available online at www.oxforddnb.com/view/article/68128, accessed 21 June 2007; S. P. Cerasano, 'Henslowe, Philip (*c.* 1555–1616)', *Oxford Dictionary of National Biography* (Oxford University Press, 2004), available online at www.oxforddnb.com/view/article/12991, accessed 21 June 2007.
53. Chambers and Greg, 'The Remembrancia', p. 46.
54. Corporation of London, *c.* 1584, Lansdowne MS 20.13, fol. 38, British Library. On the dating of this document, see the transcription in E. K. Chambers and W. W. Greg (eds.), 'Dramatic Records from the Lansdowne Manuscripts', Malone Society *Collections*, Vol. I, Pt. 2 (Oxford: Malone Society, 1908), pp. 168–74.
55. Bradbrook, *Rise of the Common Player*, p. 67; Gurr, *Shakespearian Playing Companies*, pp. 30–1.
56. Anglo-phile Eutheo and Salvianus, *A Second and Third Blast of Retrait from Plaies and Theaters* (London, 1580).
57. See Laura Levine, *Men in Women's Clothing: Anti-Theatricality and Effeminization, 1579–1642* (Cambridge: Cambridge University Press, 1994);

Jean E. Howard, *The Stage and Social Struggle in Early Modern England* (London: Routledge, 1994), pp. 22–46; David Scott Kastan, 'Is There a Class in This (Shakespearean) Text?', *Renaissance Drama*, n.s., 24 (1993), pp. 101–21; Jonas A. Barish, *The Antitheatrical Prejudice* (Berkeley, Calif.: University of California Press, 1981), p. 2.

58. John Northbrooke, *A Treatise Wherein Dicing, Dauncing, Vaine Playes or Enterluds with Other Idle Pastimes &c. Commonly Vsed on the Sabboth Day, Are Reproued by the Authoritie of the Word of God and Auntient Writers* (London, [1577?]), pp. 22, 29, 50, 32, 58, 59–65.
59. Stephen Gosson, *The Schoole of Abuse: Conteining a Plesaunt Inuectiue Against Poets, Pipers, Plaiers, Iesters, and Such Like Caterpillers of a Commonwelth* (London, 1579), sigs. A1^{v}, A3^{r}, A7^{v}, A4^{v}, B6^{v}, B8^{v}–C3^{v}, C6^{r}.
60. Thomas Lodge, *The Complete Works of Thomas Lodge (1580–1623)*, 4 vols. (Glasgow: Hunterian Club, 1883; repr. New York, Russell & Russell, 1963), Vol. I, pp. 33–45. *The Defence of Poesie*, too, may have been intended as a reply to Gosson, who was unwise in dedicating *The Schoole of Abuse* to Sidney. See Edmund Spenser, *The Works of Edmund Spenser: A Variorum Edition*, ed. Edwin Greenlaw and others, 10 vols. (Baltimore, Md.: Johns Hopkins Press, 1932–49), Vol. X, p. 6.
61. Russell Fraser, *The War Against Poetry* (Princeton, NJ: Princeton University Press, 1970), p 4.
62. Philip Stubbes, *The Anatomie of Abuses* (London, 1583), sig. B5^{v}.
63. Eutheo, *Second and Third Blast*, sig. A2^{r}, pp. 43–4, 66, 75–7, 110–11, 121–2.
64. Stephen Gosson, *Markets of Bawdrie: The Dramatic Criticism of Stephen Gosson*, ed. Arthur F. Kinney (Salzburg: Institut für Englische Sprache und Literatur, 1974), p. 18.
65. Stephen Gosson, *Playes Confuted in Fiue Actions* (London, 1582), sigs. B3^{r}, C3^{r}, C7^{v}, G6^{v}, G7^{v}.
66. William Rankins, *A Mirrovr of Monsters* (London, 1587), fols. 2^{r}–2^{v}, 8^{r}–9^{v}.
67. Gosson, *Playes Confuted*, sig. F1^{v}.
68. Stephen Roy Miller (ed.), *The Taming of a Shrew* (Oxford: Malone Society, 1998), pp. 5–6.
69. Peter Thomson, *Shakespeare's Professional Career* (Cambridge: Cambridge University Press, 1992), p. 93.
70. Tiffany Stern, *Rehearsal from Shakespeare to Sheridan* (Oxford: Clarendon Press, 2000), p. 53.
71. Wickham et al., *English Professional Theatre*, p. 283.
72. On the dating of *John a Kent*, and its relationship to *The Wise Man*, see Anthony Munday, *An Edition of Anthony Munday's 'John a Kent and John a Cumber'*, ed. Arthur E. Pennell (New York: Garland, 1980), pp. 43–54. Roslyn Lander Knutson challenges the identification of the two plays in 'Play Identifications: *The Wise Man of West Chester and John a Kent and John a Cumber; Longshanks and Edward I*', *Huntington Library Quarterly* 47 (1984), pp. 1–11.

73. Quoted in Celeste Turner, *Anthony Mundy: An Elizabethan Man of Letters* (Berkeley, Calif.: University of California Press; Cambridge: Cambridge University Press, 1928), p. 59; Tracey Hill, *Anthony Munday and Civic Culture: Theatre, History and Power in Early Modern London, 1580–1633* (Manchester: Manchester University Press, 2004), p. 2. The case for identifying Munday with Anglo-Phile Eutheo is made by John Dover Wilson in 'Anthony Munday, Pamphleteer and Pursuivant', *Modern Language Review* 4 (1909), pp. 484–90.
74. Line references in the text are to Anthony Munday, *John a Kent and John a Cumber*, ed. Muriel St. Clare Byrne (Oxford: Malone Society, 1923).
75. W. W. Greg (ed.), *The Book of Sir Thomas More*, 2nd edn (Oxford: Malone Society, 1961), pp. xxxiv–xxxv, xxxviii–xxxix. Line references in the text are to this edition. More recently, Vittorio Gabrieli and Giorgio Melchiori have concluded that 'the authorship of the original Book should be attributed to Anthony Munday in the same measure as that of the three parts of *Henry VI* is acknowledged Shakespeare's', Anthony Munday et al., *Sir Thomas More*, ed. Vittorio Gabrieli and Giorgio Melchiori (Manchester: Manchester University Press, 1990), p. 14. John Jowett assigns 'at a minimum, over one-third of the original text' to Henry Chettle; the scene discussed here, however (Scene 9), is attributed to Munday. John Jowett, 'Henry Chettle and the Original Text of *Sir Thomas More*', in T. H. Howard-Hill (ed.), *Shakespeare and 'Sir Thomas More': Essays on the Play and its Shakespearian Interest* (Cambridge: Cambridge University Press, 1989), pp. 131–49 (pp. 147–8).
76. Thomas More, *The History of King Richard III*, ed. Richard S. Sylvester, The Complete Works of St Thomas More, 2 (New Haven, Conn.: Yale University Press, 1963), p. 81.
77. Charles R. Forker and Joseph Candido, 'Wit, Wisdom, and Theatricality in *The Book of Sir Thomas More*', *Shakespeare Studies* 13 (1980), pp. 85–104 (p. 88).
78. William Roper, *The Life of Sir Thomas More*, in Richard S. Sylvester and Davis P. Harding (eds.), *Two Early Tudor Lives* (New Haven, Conn.: Yale University Press, 1962), p. 198.
79. Greg (ed.), *Book of Sir Thomas More*, p. xix.
80. Nora Johnson has noted the significance of More's dinner guests, who include the Lord Mayor and his wife. She suggests that in having the players stage a moral interlude before this audience, Munday is making reference to the ongoing negotiations between Corporation and Privy Council, challenging the argument of the former that dramatic entertainments were useless and unedifying. Nora Johnson, *The Actor as Playwright in Early Modern Drama* (Cambridge: Cambridge University Press, 2003), p. 93.
81. For a recent survey, see William Shakespeare, *The Taming of the Shrew*, ed. Ann Thompson, rev. edn (Cambridge: Cambridge University Press, 2003), pp. 172–81.
82. Stern, however, argues that the mechanicals are 'not ... criticized for being amateurs. They are criticized because they are "hempen home-spuns", "rude mechanicals" – this is social criticism, not theatrical criticism' (*Rehearsal from Shakespeare to Sheridan*, p. 29).

83. I. A. Shapiro notes the similarity between Bottom's and Turnop's acting troupes in 'Shakespeare and Mundy', *Shakespeare Survey* 14 (1961), pp. 25–33 (p. 28).
84. Chambers, *Elizabethan Stage*, Vol. I, p. 267.
85. McMillin and MacLean, *The Queen's Men*, p. 31.
86. Patent for Leicester's Men, 10 May 1574, Patent Rolls, C 66/1116, memb. 36, National Archives. A modernised version is given in Wickham *et al.*, *English Professional Theatre*, p. 206.
87. Chambers, *Elizabethan Stage*, Vol. IV, p. 278.
88. Chambers and Greg, 'The Remembrancia', pp. 50, 52–3, 66.
89. Even if the play was written for an aristocratic wedding, as some critics have suggested, the title page of the 1600 Quarto advertises it as having been 'sundry times publickely acted' by the Lord Chamberlain's Men. For a survey (and eventual rejection) of the arguments for *A Midsummer Night's Dream* as an occasional play, see Gary Jay Williams, *Our Moonlight Revels: 'A Midsummer Night's Dream' in the Theatre* (Iowa City, Iowa: University of Iowa Press, 1997), pp. 1–18.
90. Line references in the text are to Anthony Munday, *The Downfall of Robert Earl of Huntingdon*, ed. John C. Meagher (Oxford: Malone Society, 1965).
91. Stern, *Rehearsal from Shakespeare to Sheridan*, p. 51.
92. Turner, *Anthony Mundy*, p. 119; Foakes, *Henslowe's Diary*, p. 102.
93. Munday, *The Downfall*, p. vii.
94. See also lines 1587–1607, 2491–3.
95. Hill, *Anthony Munday*, p. 62.

'THOUGH HE BE A KING, YET HE MUST LABOUR': WORK AND NOBILITY IN SHAKESPEARE'S HISTORIES

1. David Riggs, *Shakespeare's Heroical Histories: 'Henry VI' and Its Literary Tradition* (Cambridge, Mass.: Harvard University Press, 1971), p. 84.
2. Lawrence Stone, *The Crisis of the Aristocracy, 1558–1641* (Oxford: Clarendon Press, 1965), p. 56.
3. Keith Wrightson, *English Society, 1580–1680* (London: Hutchinson, 1982), p. 23.
4. Richard Mulcaster, *Positions Wherin those Primitive Circvmstances Be Examined, Which Are Necessarie for the Training Vp of Children, Either for Skill in their Booke, or Health in their Bodie* (London, 1581), p. 198.
5. William Harrison, *The Description of England*, ed. Georges Edelen (Ithaca, NY: Cornell University Press, 1968), p. 114.
6. Peter Laslett, *The World We Have Lost* (London: Methuen, 1965), p. 26.
7. John Davies of Hereford, *Microcosmos: The Discovery of the Little World, with the Government Thereof* (Oxford, 1603), p. 215; see also Katherine Duncan-Jones, *Ungentle Shakespeare: Scenes from his Life* (London: Arden Shakespeare, 2001), pp. 91–103.
8. Christopher Hill, *Society and Puritanism in Pre-Revolutionary England* (London: Secker & Warburg, 1964), p. 139.

9. Lloyd E. Berry (ed.), *The Geneva Bible: A Facsimile of the 1560 Edition* (Madison, Wisc.: University of Wisconsin Press, 1969).
10. Hugh Latimer, *The Works of Hugh Latimer*, ed. George Elwes Corrie, 2 vols. (Cambridge: Cambridge University Press, 1844–5), Vol. I, pp. 214–15.
11. William Perkins, *The Works of that Famovs and Worthie Minister of Christ, in the Vniversitie of Cambridge, M. W. Perkins* (Cambridge, 1603), p. 910.
12. Laurence Humphrey, *The Nobles; or, Of Nobilitye: The Original Nature, Dutyes, Right, and Christian Institucion Thereof* (London, 1563), sig. B6^{v}.
13. Humphrey, *The Nobles*, sig. K1^{r}.
14. Quoted in G. R. Owst, *Literature and Pulpit in Medieval England: A Neglected Chapter in the History of English Letters and of the English People* (Cambridge: Cambridge University Press, 1933), pp. 550, 554.
15. Edmund Dudley, *The Tree of Commonwealth*, ed. D. M. Brodie (Cambridge: Cambridge University Press, 1948), pp. 66–7.
16. *The Book of the Courtier from the Italian of Count Baldassare Castiglione: Done into English by Sir Thomas Hoby Anno 1561*, ed. W. E. Henley (London: David Nutt, 1900), p. 48.
17. Thomas Elyot, *The Boke Named the Gouernour*, ed. Henry Herbert Stephen Croft, 2 vols. (London: C. Kegan Paul, 1880), Vol. I, p. 169.
18. Mervyn James, *Society, Politics and Culture: Studies in Early Modern England* (Cambridge: Cambridge University Press, 1986), pp. 308–415 (pp. 309, 357–70).
19. Stone, *Crisis*, pp. 251–7, 239, 265.
20. Elyot, *Gouernour*, Vol. II, p. 27.
21. Humphrey, *The Nobles*, sigs. A5^{r}, H1^{r}, I2^{r}, I6^{v}–I7^{r}, D3^{r}.
22. Mary Ellen Rickey and Thomas B. Stroup (eds.), *Certaine Sermons or Homilies Appointed to Be Read in Churches in the Time of Queen Elizabeth I (1547–1571): A Facsimile Reproduction of the Edition of 1623* (Gainesville, Fla.: Scholars' Facsimiles & Reprints, 1968), p. 250.
23. See Rickey and Stroup, *Certaine Sermons or Homilies*, p. vii.
24. John Jewell, *An Exposition upon the Two Epistles of the Apostle St. Paul to the Thessalonians*, ed. Peter Hall (London: B. Wertheim, 1841), p. 274. See also Latimer, *Works*, Vol. I, p. 214, 'I know no man hath a greater labour than a King'.
25. Thomas Tymme, *The Figure of Antichriste, with the Tokens of the End of the World, Most Plainly Disciphered by a Catholike and Diuine Exposition of the Second Epistle of Paul to the Thessalonians* (London, 1586), sigs. K6^{v}, K7^{r}.
26. Elizabeth I, *Collected Works*, ed. Leah S. Marcus, Janel Mueller and Mary Beth Rose (Chicago, Ill.: University of Chicago Press, 2000), p. 331.
27. Alfred Hart, *Shakespeare and the Homilies and Other Pieces of Research into the Elizabethan Drama* (Melbourne: Melbourne University Press, 1934), pp. 27, 75, 23.
28. E. M. W. Tillyard, *Shakespeare's History Plays* (London: Chatto & Windus, 1944), pp. 320–1.
29. Jonathan Dollimore, *Radical Tragedy: Religion, Ideology and Power in the Drama of Shakespeare and his Contemporaries* (Brighton: Harvester Press, 1984), pp. 90, 8.

30. Stephen Greenblatt, *Shakespearean Negotiations: The Circulation of Social Energy in Renaissance England* (Berkeley, Calif.: University of California Press, 1988), p. 65.
31. Phyllis Rackin, *Stages of History: Shakespeare's English Chronicles* (London: Routledge, 1990), pp. 46, 27.
32. John Stephens, *Essayes and Characters: Ironicall, and Instrvctive* (London, 1615), pp. 296–7.
33. Lucy De Bruyn, *Mob-rule and Riots: The Present Mirrored in the Past* (London: Regency Press, 1981), p. 13.
34. Rackin, *Stages of History*, p. 219; Richard Wilson, *Will Power: Essays on Shakespearean Authority* (Hemel Hempstead: Harvester Wheatsheaf, 1993), p. 42; Richard Helgerson, *Forms of Nationhood: The Elizabethan Writing of England* (Chicago, Ill.: University of Chicago Press, 1992), p. 212.
35. Stephen Longstaffe, '"A short report and not otherwise": Jack Cade in *2 Henry VI*', in Ronald Knowles (ed.), *Shakespeare and Carnival: After Bakhtin* (Basingstoke: Macmillan, 1998), pp. 13–35.
36. William Shakespeare, *King Henry VI Part 2*, ed. Ronald Knowles, Arden Shakespeare, 3rd series (London: Thomas Nelson & Sons, 1999), pp. 98, 100, 103.
37. Riggs, *Shakespeare's Heroical Histories*, pp. 115–16.
38. Dudley, *The Tree of Commonwealth*, p. 66.
39. Rickey and Stroup, *Certaine Sermons or Homilies*, p. 251.
40. Helgerson, *Forms of Nationhood*, p. 207.
41. Shakespeare, *King Henry VI Part 2*, ed. Knowles, p. 102.
42. Shakespeare, *King Henry VI Part 2*, ed. Knowles, pp. 98–9; Riggs, *Shakespeare's Heroical Histories*, p. 124.
43. See Quentin Skinner, *The Foundations of Modern Political Thought*, 2 vols. (Cambridge: Cambridge University Press, 1978), Vol. I, p. 195.
44. William Shakespeare, *King Richard II*, ed. Charles R. Forker, Arden Shakespeare, 3rd series (London: Thomson Learning, 2002), pp. 1, 3; see also Rackin, *Stages of History*, p. 119.
45. Graham Holderness, '*Richard II*', in Graham Holderness, Nick Potter and John Turner, *Shakespeare: The Play of History* (Basingstoke: Macmillan, 1987), pp. 20–40, p. 40.
46. Rackin, *Stages of History*, p. 67.
47. William Shakespeare, *King Richard II*, ed. Andrew Gurr, 2nd edn (Cambridge: Cambridge University Press, 2003), p. 121, II. 3. 165n.
48. Harrison, *Description*, p. 183.
49. Rickey and Stroup, *Certaine Sermons or Homilies*, pp. 250–1.
50. Humphrey, *The Nobles*, sig. D2^{v}.
51. Shakespeare, *King Richard II*, ed. Forker, p. 23.
52. Elizabeth I, *Collected Works*, p. 342.
53. Shakespeare, *King Richard II*, ed. Forker, p. 395, IV. 1. 179n; Edward Hall, *The Vnion of the Two Noble and Illustrate Famelies of Lancastre & Yorke* (London, 1548), fol. viii^{v}.

54. William Shakespeare, *The Second Part of King Henry IV*, ed. Giorgio Melchiori (Cambridge: Cambridge University Press, 1989), p. 3.
55. Humphrey, *The Nobles*, sig. K2r.
56. Shakespeare, *King Richard II*, ed. Forker, p. 159.
57. References in the text are to Christopher Marlowe, *Edward II*, ed. Charles Forker (Manchester: Manchester University Press, 1994).
58. Tillyard, *Shakespeare's History Plays*, p. 265; see also J. Dover Wilson, *The Fortunes of Falstaff* (Cambridge: Cambridge University Press, 1943), pp. 15–35.
59. Robert Ornstein, *A Kingdom for a Stage: The Achievement of Shakespeare's History Plays* (Cambridge, Mass.: Harvard University Press, 1972), p. 139.
60. Graham Holderness, *Shakespeare's History* (Dublin: Gill & Macmillan; New York: St. Martin's Press, 1985), p. 97.
61. David Ruiter, *Shakespeare's Festive History: Feasting, Festivity, Fasting and Lent in the Second Henriad* (Aldershot: Ashgate, 2003), p. 70.
62. William Shakespeare, *King Henry IV Part 1*, ed. David Scott Kastan, Arden Shakespeare, 3rd series (London: Arden Shakespeare, 2002), p. 151, I. 2. 24n.
63. C. L. Barber, *Shakespeare's Festive Comedy: A Study of Dramatic Form and its Relation to Social Custom* (Princeton, NJ: Princeton University Press, 1959), pp. 195–6.
64. Holderness, *Shakespeare's History*, pp. 100–1; Ruiter, *Shakespeare's Festive History*, p. 104.
65. Riggs, *Shakespeare's Heroical Histories*, p. 157.
66. Greenblatt, *Shakespearean Negotiations*, p. 49.
67. Raphael Holinshed, *The Chronicles of England, Scotland and Ireland*, 2nd edn, 3 vols. (London, 1587), Vol. III, p. 553, quoted in William Shakespeare, *King Henry V*, ed. T. W. Craik, Arden Shakespeare, 3rd series (London: Routledge, 1995), p. 287, IV. 3. 16–18n.
68. James Shapiro, *1599: A Year in the Life of William Shakespeare* (London: Faber & Faber 2005), pp. 185–6.

'WE MAY SHUT VP OUR SHOPS, AND MAKE HOLIDAY': WORKERS AND PLAYHOUSES, 1599–1601

1. Lukas Erne, *Shakespeare as Literary Dramatist* (Cambridge: Cambridge University Press, 2003), p. 224.
2. William Shakespeare, *The First Quarto of King Henry V*, ed. Andrew Gurr (Cambridge: Cambridge University Press, 2000), p. 2.
3. James P. Bednarz, 'When did Shakespeare Write the Choruses of *Henry V*?', *Notes and Queries* 53 (2006), pp. 486–9.
4. The first performance of *The Shoemakers' Holiday* was evidently some time between 15 July 1599, when Henslowe lent Samuel Rowley and Thomas Downton three pounds to buy the book from Dekker, and New Year's Day 1600, when the play was performed at Court. See R. A. Foakes (ed.), *Henslowe's Diary*, 2nd edn (Cambridge: Cambridge University Press, 2002), p. 122; Thomas Dekker, *The Dramatic Works of Thomas Dekker*, ed. Fredson

Bowers, 4 vols. (Cambridge: Cambridge University Press, 1953–61), Vol. I, p. 7. I follow Bowers in placing the apostrophe after the terminal 's' of 'Shoemakers'.

5. L. D. Timms, 'Dekker's *The Shoemaker's Holiday* and Elizabeth's Accession Day', *Notes and Queries* 32 (1985), p. 58.
6. Marta Straznicky, 'The End(s) of Discord in *The Shoemaker's Holiday*', *Studies in English Literature* 36 (1996), pp. 357–72 (p. 361).
7. David Farmer, *The Oxford Dictionary of Saints*, 4th edn (Oxford: Oxford University Press, 1997), pp. 244–5; Jacobus de Voragine, (*The Golden Legend*), trans. (William Caxton?) (London, 1527).
8. Thomas Deloney, *The Novels of Thomas Deloney*, ed. Merritt E. Lawlis (Bloomington, Ind.: Indiana University Press, 1961), p. 92.
9. Farmer, *Oxford Dictionary of Saints*, p. 117.
10. Thomas Dekker, *The Shoemaker's Holiday*, ed. R. L. Smallwood and Stanley Wells (Manchester: Manchester University Press; Baltimore, Md.: Johns Hopkins University Press, 1979), p. 16.
11. There may also be a sectarian dimension to Dekker's decision in that the apocryphal patron saint he gives his shoemakers is one without a feast day in the Roman Catholic calendar.
12. Alison A. Chapman, 'Whose Saint Crispin's Day Is It? Shoemaking, Holiday Making, and the Politics of Memory in Early Modern England', *Renaissance Quarterly* 54 (2001), pp. 1467–94 (p. 1467).
13. David Cressy, *Bonfires and Bells: National Memory and the Protestant Calendar in Elizabethan and Stuart England* (Berkeley, Calif.: University of California Press; London: Weidenfeld & Nicolson, 1989), pp. 6–7.
14. Christopher Hill, *Society and Puritanism in Pre-Revolutionary England* (London: Secker & Warburg, 1964), pp. 121, 128.
15. Firke's words resonate interestingly with the case of Calvinist Geneva, where the traditional Wednesday holiday for prentices was abolished in 1561. See Hill, *Society and Puritanism*, p. 121.
16. Charles Whitney, '"Usually in the werking Daies": Playgoing Journeymen, Apprentices, and Servants in Guild Records, 1582–92', *Shakespeare Quarterly* 50 (1999), pp. 433–58 (pp. 455, 435).
17. Louis B. Wright, *Middle-Class Culture in Elizabethan England* (Chapel Hill, NC: University of North Carolina Press, 1935), p. 626.
18. David Scott Kastan, 'Workshop and/as Playhouse: Comedy and Commerce in *The Shoemaker's Holiday*', *Studies in Philology* 84 (1987), pp. 324–37 (p. 325).
19. Straznicky, 'The End(s) of Discord', p. 358.
20. Charles Whitney, 'The Devil His Due: Mayor John Spencer, Elizabethan Civic Antitheatricalism, and *The Shoemaker's Holiday*', *Medieval and Renaissance Drama in England* 14 (2001), pp. 168–85 (pp. 180, 170–5, 169).
21. Richard Wilson, *Will Power: Essays on Shakespearean Authority* (Hemel Hempstead: Harvester Wheatsheaf, 1993), p. 42; Richard Helgerson, *Forms of Nationhood: The Elizabethan Writing of England* (Chicago, Ill.: University of Chicago Press, 1992), p. 212; Thomas Nashe, *The Works of Thomas Nashe*,

ed. Ronald B. McKerrow, 2nd edn, rev. F. P. Wilson, 5 vols. (Oxford: Basil Blackwell, 1958), Vol. I, p. 214.

22. Chapman, 'Whose Saint Crispin's Day Is It?', pp. 1470–1.
23. Alexander Leggatt, *Jacobean Public Theatre* (London: Routledge, 1992), p. 30.
24. Wilson, *Will Power*, pp. 46–7.
25. See Foakes (ed.), *Henslowe's Diary*, pp. xxx–xxxi; Neil Carson, *A Companion to Henslowe's Diary* (Cambridge: Cambridge University Press, 1988), p. 69. Steve Sohmer has also raised the intriguing possibility that *Julius Caesar*'s first performance may have been on the summer solstice, 12 June by the Julian calendar. The fact that this did not coincide with the official Midsummer Day on 22 June may inform the play's interest in licensed and illicit holidays. See Steve Sohmer, *Shakespeare's Mystery Play: The Opening of the Globe Theatre 1599* (Manchester: Manchester University Press, 1999), pp. 45–6.
26. Andrew Gurr, *Playgoing in Shakespeare's London*, 2nd edn (Cambridge: Cambridge University Press, 1996), p. 23.
27. More recently, Gurr has suggested that as early as 1594, the company may have intended to play outdoors in the summer and at inns inside the City during the winter but that John Spencer managed to obstruct their designs. See Andrew Gurr, *The Shakespeare Company, 1594–1642* (Cambridge: Cambridge University Press, 2004), pp. 2–4.
28. David Farley-Hills, *Shakespeare and the Rival Playwrights, 1600–1606* (London: Routledge, 1990), pp. 7–8.
29. Richard Brome, *The Antipodes*, ed. Ann Haaker (London: Edward Arnold, 1967), p. 40 (II. 2. 46).
30. David Wiles, *Shakespeare's Clown: Actor and Text in the Elizabethan Playhouse* (Cambridge: Cambridge University Press, 1987), pp. x, 43–7, 136, 158–61.
31. Will Kemp, *Kemps Nine Daies VVonder* (London, 1601), sig. $D3^r$.
32. Andrew Gurr, *The Shakespearian Playing Companies* (Oxford: Clarendon Press, 1996), p. 347.
33. Reavley Gair, *The Children of Paul's: The Story of a Theatre Company, 1553–1608* (Cambridge: Cambridge University Press, 1982), pp. 116, 121, 119.
34. Michael Shapiro, *Children of the Revels: The Boy Companies of Shakespeare's Time and Their Plays* (New York: Columbia University Press, 1977), p. 111.
35. See Gurr, *Playgoing*, p. 69; Ann Jennalie Cook, *The Privileged Playgoers of Shakespeare's London, 1576–1642* (Princeton, NJ: Princeton University Press, 1981), pp. 140–1; Gair, *Children of Paul's*, pp. 119, 127.
36. Alfred Harbage, *Shakespeare and the Rival Traditions* (New York: Macmillan, 1952), pp. 29, 43–6.
37. Cook, *Privileged Playgoers*, pp. 8, 128–9.
38. Gurr, *Playgoing*, p. 65.
39. See Leggatt, *Jacobean Public Theatre*, p. 28; Roslyn Lander Knutson, *Playing Companies and Commerce in Shakespeare's Time* (Cambridge: Cambridge University Press, 2001), p. 18; Lucy Munro, *Children of the Queen's Revels: A Jacobean Theatre Repertory* (Cambridge: Cambridge University Press, 2005), pp. 61–6.

40. Gurr, *Playgoing*, p. 27.
41. Munro, *Children of the Queen's Revels*, p. 61.
42. Tiffany Stern, *Rehearsal from Shakespeare to Sheridan* (Oxford: Clarendon Press, 2000), p. 43.
43. Gair, *Children of Paul's*, pp. 44, 80; Shapiro, *Children of the Revels*, p. 15; Munro, *Children of the Queen's Revels*, p. 37.
44. See Richard Dutton, '*Hamlet, An Apology for Actors*, and the Sign of the Globe' *Shakespeare Survey* 41 (1988), pp. 35–43.
45. Keith Wrightson, *English Society, 1580–1680* (London: Hutchinson, 1982), p. 26.
46. William Harrison, *The Description of England*, ed. Georges Edelen (Ithaca, NY: Cornell University Press, 1968), pp. 113–14.
47. Laurence Humphrey, *The Nobles; or, Of Nobilitye: The Original Nature, Dutyes, Right, and Christian Institucion Thereof* (London, 1563), sigs. G6v-G7r; Richard Mulcaster, *Positions Wherin those Primitive Circvmstances Be Examined, Which Are Necessarie for the Training Vp of Children, Either for Skill in their Booke, or Health in their Bodie* (London, 1581), p. 194.
48. Lawrence Stone, *The Crisis of the Aristocracy, 1558–1641* (Oxford: Clarendon Press, 1965), pp. 39, 67, 754.
49. Stone, *Crisis*, pp. 184–7.
50. Barnaby Rich, *Roome for a Gentleman, or the Second Part of Favltes* (London, 1609), fols 2^{v}–3^{r}.
51. Sir Thomas Smith, *De republica anglorum*, ed. Mary Dewar (Cambridge: Cambridge University Press, 1982), p. 72; on Smith's use of Harrison (and vice versa), see Apprendix 3, pp. 157–62. See also William Segar, *Honor Military, and Ciuill, Contained in Four Bookes* (London, 1602), p. 228.
52. Robert Burton, *The Anatomy of Melancholy*, ed. Thomas C. Faulkner, Nicolas K. Kiessling and Rhonda L. Blair, 6 vols. (Oxford: Clarendon Press, 1989–2000), Vol. I, p. 240.
53. Maurice Ashley, *England in the Seventeenth Century*, 3rd edn (Harmondsworth: Penguin, 1961), p. 18.
54. Marcia Vale, *The Gentleman's Recreations: Accomplishments and Pastimes of the English Gentleman, 1580–1630* (Cambridge: D. S. Brewer; Totowa, Rowman & Littlefield, 1977), p. 2.
55. Thomas Dekker, *Thomas Dekker*, ed. E. D. Pendry (London: Edward Arnold, 1967), p. 100.
56. Knutson, *Playing Companies and Commerce*, pp. 21–47, 38.
57. Gurr, *Shakespearian Playing Companies*, pp. 244, 299; *Playgoing*, p. 157.
58. Judith Bronfman, 'Griselda, Renaissance Woman', in Anne M. Haselkorn and Betty S. Travitsky (eds.), *The Renaissance Englishwoman in Print: Counterbalancing the Canon* (Amherst, Masse: University of Massachusetts Press, 1990), pp. 211–23; see also Lee Bliss, 'The Renaissance Griselda: A Woman for All Seasons', *Viator: Medieval and Renaissance Studies* 23 (1992), pp. 301–43.
59. Bliss, 'The Renaissance Griselda', p. 327.

60. Cyrus Hoy, *Introductions, Notes, and Commentaries to Texts in 'The Dramatic Works of Thomas Dekker' Edited by Fredson Bowers*, 4 vols. (Cambridge: Cambridge University Press, 1980), Vol. I, p. 174. On the Bishops' Ban and dramatic satire, see Oscar James Campbell, *Comicall Satyre and Shakespeare's 'Troilus and Cressida'* (San Marino, Calif.: Huntington Library Publications, 1938), p. vii; on the relationship between *Patient Grissil* and satirical comedy, see Tom Rutter, '*Patient Grissil* and Jonsonian Satire', *Studies in English Literature* 48 (2008) (in press).
61. Dekker, *Shoemaker's Holiday*, p. 52.
62. Gurr, *Playgoing*, pp. 156–7.
63. Annabel Patterson, *Shakespeare and the Popular Voice* (Cambridge, Mass.: Basil Blackwell, 1989), pp. 100, 13–15, 95.
64. Robert Weimann, *Author's Pen and Actor's Voice: Playing and Writing in Shakespeare's Theatre*, ed. Helen Higbee and William West (Cambridge: Cambridge University Press, 2000), pp. 161, 152; Peter Burke, *Popular Culture in Early Modern Europe*, rev. edn (Aldershot: Scolar Press; Brookfield, Vt.: Ashgate, 1994), p. 272.
65. Brian Vickers, 'Leisure and Idleness in the Renaissance: The Ambivalence of Otium', *Renaissance Studies* 4 (1990), pp. 1–37, 107–54 (p. 136); *The Works of Edmund Spenser: A Variorum Edition*, ed. Edwin Greenlaw and others, 10 vols. (Baltimore, Md.: Johns Hopkins Press, 1932–49), Vol. I, p. 120.
66. See Malcolm Bull, *The Mirror of the Gods: Classical Mythology in Renaissance Art* (London: Allen Lane, 2005), pp. 97–9.
67. Burton, *Anatomy of Melancholy*, Vol. I, p. 238. As Hodge the smith puts it in *Thomas Lord Cromwell*, when made to disguise himself as the Earl of Bedford, 'My Nobilitie is wonderfull melancholie: / Is it not most Gentleman like to be melancholie', W. S., *The True Chronicle Historie of the Whole Life and Death of Thomas Lord Cromwell* (London, 1602), sig. $C4^v$.
68. Jonathan Goldberg, 'Hamlet's Hand', *Shakespeare Quarterly* 39 (1988), pp. 307–27 (p. 322) (Goldberg's ellipsis).
69. Frank Whigham, *Ambition and Privilege: The Social Tropes of Elizabethan Courtesy Theory* (Berkeley, Calif.: University of California Press, 1984), p. 95.
70. George Puttenham, *The Arte of English Poesie* (London, 1589), pp. 251–2.

'WORK UPON THAT NOW!': LABOUR AND STATUS ON THE STAGE, 1599–1610

1. Glynne Wickham, Herbert Berry and William Ingram (eds.), *English Professional Theatre, 1530–1660* (Cambridge: Cambridge University Press, 2000), p. 423; Andrew Gurr, *The Shakespearian Playing Companies* (Oxford: Clarendon Press, 1996), p. 239.
2. Wickham et al., *English Professional Theatre*, p. 423; Gurr, *Shakespearian Playing Companies*, p. 320.
3. Andrew Gurr, *Playgoing in Shakespeare's London*, 2nd edn (Cambridge: Cambridge University Press, 1996), pp. 156, 67–73.

4. Thomas Heywood, *If You Know Not Me You Know Nobody Part II*, ed. Madeleine Doran (Oxford: Malone Society, 1935), p. 1532.
5. Barbara J. Baines, *Thomas Heywood* (Boston, Mass.: Twayne, 1984), p. 33; Laura Caroline Stevenson, *Praise and Paradox: Merchants and Craftsmen in Elizabethan Popular Literature* (Cambridge: Cambridge University Press, 1984), p. 145. On the representation of citizens in aristocratic terms, see also Walter Cohen, *Drama of a Nation: Public Theater in Renaissance England and Spain* (Ithaca, NY: Cornell University Press, 1985), p. 192; Charles W. Crupi, 'Ideological Contradictions in Part I of Heywood's *Edward IV*: "Our Musicke Runs ... Much upon Discords" ', *Medieval and Renaissance Drama in England* 7 (1995), pp. 224–56; Lawrence Manley, *Literature and Culture in Early Modern London* (Cambridge: Cambridge University Press, 1995), pp. 128–31.
6. In the dedication of the first edition (1615), Heywood excuses the play's deficiency in 'that accuratenesse both in Plot and Stile, that these more Censorious dayes with greater curiousity acquire', pleading that 'as *Playes* were then some fifteene or sixteene yeares agoe it was in the fashion'; Thomas Heywood, *The Four Prentices of London: A Critical, Old-Spelling Edition*, ed. Mary Ann Weber Gasior (New York: Garland, 1980) p. 2 (further references in the text are to this edition, by line number). I do not see any reason to follow Gasior in positing a date earlier than that of the late 1590s implied by Heywood; as Roslyn Lander Knutson has argued, Henslowe's references to a *Jerusalem* in 1592 and a *Godfrey of Bouillon* in 1594 may signal only 'the theatrical popularity of the subject of the conquest of Jerusalem'. See Heywood, *Four Prentices*, pp. xi–xv; Roslyn Lander Knutson, *Playing Companies and Commerce in Shakespeare's Time* (Cambridge: Cambridge University Press, 2001), p. 58; R. A. Foakes (ed.), *Henslowe's Diary*, 2nd edn (Cambridge: Cambridge University Press, 2002), pp. 17, 22–5, 28, 31.
7. Stevenson, *Praise and Paradox*, p. 115.
8. Stevenson, *Praise and Paradox*, p. 187.
9. Lisa H. Cooper, 'Chivalry, Commerce, and Conquest: Heywood's *The Four Prentices of London*', in Curtis Perry (ed.), *Material Culture and Cultural Materialisms in the Middle Ages and Renaissance* (Turnhout, Belgium: Brepolis, 2001), pp. 159–75 (p. 163).
10. Christopher Brooks, 'Apprenticeship, Social Mobility and the Middling Sort, 1550–1800', in Jonathan Barry and Christopher Brooks (eds.), *The Middling Sort of People: Culture, Society and Politics in England, 1550–1800* (Basingstoke: Macmillan, 1994), pp. 52–83 (p. 61).
11. Richard Grassby, 'Social Mobility and Business Enterprise in Seventeenth-Century England', in Donald Pennington and Keith Thomas (eds.), *Puritans and Revolutionaries: Essays in Seventeenth-Century History Presented to Christopher Hill* (Oxford: Clarendon Press, 1978), pp. 355–81 (p. 359).
12. Brooks, 'Apprenticeship', p. 80.
13. John Ferne, *The Blazon of Gentrie* (London, 1586), pp. 7–8.

14. Thomas Smith, *De republica anglorum*, ed. Mary Dewar (Cambridge: Cambridge University Press, 1982), p. 140.
15. Theodora A. Jankowski, 'The Development of Middle-Class Identity and the "Problem" of the "Gentle" Apprentice', in Michelle M. Sauer (ed.), *Proceedings of the 11th Annual Northern Plains Conference on Early British Literature* (Minot, ND: Minot State University Printing Services, 2003), pp. 1–17, p. 2.
16. Fenella Macfarlane, 'To "Try What London Prentices Can Do": Merchant Chivalry as Representational Strategy in Thomas Heywood's *The Four Prentices of London*', *Medieval and Renaissance Drama in England* 13 (2001), pp. 136–64 (p. 149).
17. Peter Holbrook, *Literature and Degree in Renaissance England: Nashe, Bourgeois Tragedy, Shakespeare* (Newark, NJ: University of Delaware Press; London: Associated University Presses, 1994), p. 102.
18. References in the text are to Thomas Heywood, *A Woman Killed with Kindness*, ed. Brian Scobie (London: A & C Black; New York: W. W. Norton, 1985, repr. 1991), by scene and line number.
19. Holbrook, *Literature and Degree*, p. 102.
20. T. S. Eliot, *Elizabethan Essays* (London: Faber & Faber, 1934), p. 109.
21. Kathleen E. McLuskie, 'Introduction', in Kathleen E. McLuskie and David Bevington (eds.), *Plays on Women* (Manchester: Manchester University Press, 1999), pp. 42.
22. Edward Berry, *Shakespeare and the Hunt: A Cultural and Social Study* (Cambridge: Cambridge University Press, 2001), p. 107.
23. John Harington, *Nugae Antiquae: Being a Miscellaneous Collection of Original Papers in Prose and Verse*, ed. Henry Harington, 2 vols. (London: W. Frederick, 1769–75), Vol. II, p. 17.
24. Maurice Ashley, *England in the Seventeenth Century*, 3rd edn (Harmondsworth: Penguin, 1961), p. 18.
25. Diana E. Henderson, 'Many Mansions: Reconstructing *A Woman Killed with Kindness*', *Studies in English Literature* 26 (1996), pp. 277–94 (p. 284).
26. Henderson, 'Many Mansions', p. 287.
27. Lena Cowen Orlin, *Private Matters and Public Culture in Post-Reformation England* (Ithaca, NY: Cornell University Press, 1994), p. 175.
28. Richard Mulcaster, *Positions Wherin those Primitive Circvmstances Be Examined, Which Are Necessarie for the Training Vp of Children, Either for Skill in their Booke, or Health in their Bodie* (London, 1581), p. 198.
29. Thomas Digges and Dudley Digges, *Four Paradoxes; or, Politique Discourses* (London, 1604), p. 77; William Segar, *Honor Military, and Ciuill, Contained in Four Bookes* (London, 1602), p. 230.
30. Ferne, *Blazon of Gentrie*, p. 7.
31. Henry Peacham, *'The Complete Gentleman', 'The Truth of Our Times', and 'The Art of Living in London'*, ed. Virgil B. Heltzel (Ithaca, NY: Cornell University Press, 1962), pp. 21–2.
32. Ferne, *Blazon of Gentrie*, p. 72.

33. *Marcus Tullius Ciceroes Thre Bokes of Duties, to Marcus his Sonne, Turned Oute of Latine into English, by Nicolas Grimalde*, ed. Gerald O' Gorman (Washington, DC: Folger Shakespeare Library; London: Associated University Presses, 1990), p. 106.
34. Theodore B. Leinwand, *The City Staged: Jacobean City Comedy, 1603–1613* (Madison, Wisc.: University of Wisconsin Press, 1986), p. 25.
35. Ceri Sullivan, *The Rhetoric of Credit: Merchants in Early Modern Writing* (Madison, Wisc.: Fairleigh Dickinson University Press; London: Associated University Presses, 2002), p. 22; J(ohn). B(rowne)., *The Marchants Avizo* (London, 1591), p. 61.
36. Richard Barckley, *A Discourse of the Felicitie of Man; or, His Summum bonum* (London, 1598), p. 368.
37. Alexander Leggatt, *Jacobean Public Theatre* (London: Routledge, 1992), p. 152.
38. Lois Potter, 'A Stage Where Every Man Must Play a Part?', *Shakespeare Quarterly* 50 (1999), pp. 74–86 (p. 79).
39. Leinwand, *City Staged*, pp. 73, 91.
40. Cyrus Hoy, *Introductions, Notes, and Commentaries to Texts in 'The Dramatic Works of Thomas Dekker' Edited by Fredson Bowers*, 4 vols. (Cambridge: Cambridge University Press, 1980), Vol. III, p. 1; Leinwand, *City Staged*, p. 70.
41. See Ben Jonson, George Chapman and John Marston, *Eastward Ho!*, ed. C. G. Petter (London: Ernest Benn, 1973; repr. London, A & C Black; New York: Norton, 1994), p. xxviii; Clifford Leech, 'Three Times Ho and a Brace of Widows: Some Plays for the Private Theatre', in David Galloway (ed.), *The Elizabethan Theatre III* (London: Macmillan, 1973), pp. 14–32, pp. 21–2; Alexander Leggatt, *Citizen Comedy in the Age of Shakespeare* (Toronto: University of Toronto Press, 1973), p. 51; Manley, *Literature and Culture*, p. 445–6. References to *Eastward Ho!* in the text are to Petter's edition, by act, scene and line number.
42. Leech, 'Three Times Ho', p. 24; Manley, *Literature and Culture*, p. 445.
43. Manley, *Literature and Culture*, p. 445.
44. Thomas Kyd, *The Works of Thomas Kyd*, ed. Frederick S. Boas (Oxford: Clarendon Press, 1901, repr. 1955); Lucy Munro, *Children of the Queen's Revels: A Jacobean Theatre Repertory* (Cambridge: Cambridge University Press, 2005), p. 75. In *Eastward Ho!*, see especially II. 1. 100–33.
45. Leggatt, *Citizen Comedy*, p. 49.
46. Jonson et al., *Eastward Ho!*, p. xxxv.
47. Leech, 'Three Times Ho', pp. 17–18.
48. Francis Beaumont, *The Knight of the Burning Pestle*, ed. Michael Hattaway (London: Ernest Benn; New York: W. W. Norton, 1969). References in the text are to this edition, by act and line number.
49. Alexander Leggatt, 'The Audience as Patron: *The Knight of the Burning Pestle*', in Paul Whitfield White and Suzanne R. Westfall (eds.), *Shakespeare and Theatrical Patronage in Early Modern England* (Cambridge: Cambridge University Press, 2002), pp. 295–315, p. 310. Leggatt cites Ronald F. Miller, 'Dramatic Form and Dramatic Imagination in Beaumont's *Knight of the Burning Pestle*', *English Literary Renaissance* 8 (1978), 67–84; Lee Bliss, *Francis*

Beaumont (Boston, Mass.: Twayne, 1987), pp. 46–7; and Francis Beaumont, *The Knight of the Burning Pestle*, ed. Sheldon P. Zitner (Manchester: Manchester University Press, 1984), pp. 20–37.

50. Munro, *Children of the Queen's Revels*, p. 59; Beaumont, *Knight of the Burning Pestle*, ed. Hattaway, p. xv.
51. Leggatt, *Citizen Comedy*, p. 53n.
52. Leggatt, 'Audience as Patron', p. 311.
53. Andrew Gurr, *The Shakespeare Company, 1594–1642* (Cambridge: Cambridge University Press, 2004), pp. 10, 36.
54. Roslyn Lander Knutson, *The Repertory of Shakespeare's Company 1594–1613* (Fayetteville, Ark.: University of Arkansas Press, 1991), pp. 13–14, 40, 61, 65–6.
55. Knutson, *Repertory*, p. 88.
56. W. S., *The True Chronicle Historie of the Whole Life and Death of Thomas Lord Cromwell* (London, 1602). Further references in the text are to this edition, by signature.
57. Gurr, *Playgoing*, p. 154.
58. Larry S. Champion, 'Dramatic Strategy and Political Ideology in *The Life and Death of Thomas, Lord Cromwell*', *Studies in English Literature* 29 (1989), pp. 218–36 (p. 226).
59. William Shakespeare (attr.), *The London Prodigall* (London, 1605). References in the text are to this edition, by signature.
60. Lawrence Stone, *The Crisis of the Aristocracy, 1558–1641* (Oxford: Clarendon Press, 1965), p. 569.
61. On the date of *Coriolanus*, see William Shakespeare, *Coriolanus*, ed. R. B. Parker (Oxford: Clarendon Press, 1994), pp. 2–7. Harbage dates the play more broadly as 1605–*c.* 1610.
62. Lars Engle, *Shakespearean Pragmatism: Market of His Time* (Chicago, Ill.: University of Chicago Press, 1993), p. 164.
63. Engle, *Shakespearean Pragmatism*, p. 174.
64. Stone, *Crisis*, p. 336.
65. Thomas Harman, *A Caveat or Warening, for Commen Cvrsetors Vvlgarely Called Vagabones* (London, 1567), sig. B2^{r}.
66. Geoffrey Miles, *Shakespeare and the Constant Romans* (Oxford: Clarendon Press, 1996), p. 158.
67. Jonas A. Barish, *The Antitheatrical Prejudice* (Berkeley, Calif.: University of California Press, 1981), p. 94.
68. Philip Stubbes, *The Anatomie of Abuses* (London, 1583), sigs. N5^{v}–N6^{r}. See also Anglo-Phile Eutheo and Salvianus, *A Second and Third Blast of Retrait from Plaies and Theaters* (London, 1580), pp. 111–12: 'And as for those stagers themselues, are they not commonlie such kind of men in their conuersation, as they are in profession? Are they not as variable in hart, as they are in their partes? are they not as good practisers of Bawderie, as inactors?'.
69. Stubbes, *Anatomie of Abuses*, sig. N6^{r}.
70. Thomas Dekker, *Thomas Dekker*, ed. E. D. Pendry (London: Edward Arnold, 1967), p. 98.

71. David Hawkes, 'Idolatry and Commodity Fetishism in the Anti-Theatrical Controversy', *Studies in English Literature* 39 (1998–9), pp. 255–273; Eutheo, *Second and Third Blast*, p. 109; Stephen Gosson, *Playes Confuted in Fiue Actions* (London, 1582), sig. G5[v].
72. On the early modern theatre as 'discretionary compact struck between performers and audience', see Jean-Christophe Agnew, *Worlds Apart: The Market and the Theater in Anglo-American Thought, 1550–1750* (Cambridge: Cambridge University Press, 1986), pp. 110–11.

CONCLUSION

1. See J. Leeds Barroll, 'Shakespeare and the Second Blackfriars Theatre', *Shakespeare Studies* 33 (2005), pp. 156–70.
2. Andrew Gurr, *The Shakespeare Company, 1594–1642* (Cambridge: Cambridge University Press, 2004), p. 160.
3. R. L. Smallwood, ' "Here, in the Friars": Immediacy and Theatricality in *The Alchemist*', *Review of English Studies* 32 (1981), pp. 142–60; see also Andrew Gurr, 'Who Is Lovewit? What Is He?', in Richard Cave, Elizabeth Schafer and Brian Woolland (eds.), *Ben Jonson and Theatre: Performance, Practice and Theory* (London: Routledge, 1999), pp. 5–19.
4. Smallwood, ' "Here, in the Friars" ', p. 146.
5. See, for example, Harry Levin, 'Two Magian Comedies: *The Tempest* and *The Alchemist*', *Shakespeare Survey* 22 (1971), pp. 47–58; Gurr, 'Who Is Lovewit?'; David Lucking, 'Carrying Tempest in His Hand and Voice: The Figure of the Magician in Jonson and Shakespeare', *English Studies* 85 (2004), pp. 297–310.
6. Douglas Bruster, 'Local *Tempest*: Shakespeare and the Work of the Early Modern Playhouse', *Journal of Medieval and Renaissance Studies* 25 (1995), pp. 33–53 (p.33); Daniel Vitkus, ' "Meaner Ministers": Mastery, Bondage, and Theatrical Labor in *The Tempest*', in Richard Dutton and Jean E. Howard (eds.), *A Companion to Shakespeare's Works* (Malden, Mass.: Blackwell, 2003), Vol. IV: *The Poems, Problem Comedies, Late Plays* (2003), pp. 408–26.
7. Bruster, 'Local *Tempest*', p. 33.

Bibliography

MANUSCRIPTS

Lansdowne MS 7.62, British Library (Edmund Grindal to Lord Burghley, 22 February 1563–4).
Lansdowne MS 20.10, British Library (Act of Common Council, 6 December 1574).
Lansdowne MS 20.13, British Library (Corporation of London, *c.* 1584).
Lansdowne MS 37.4, British Library (Thomas Blanke to Lord Burghley, 14 January 1582–3).
Patent Rolls, C 66/1116, memb. 36, National Archives (Patent for Leicester's Men, 10 May 1574).
Privy Council, PC 2/25, p. 223, National Archives (Order of the Privy Council, 22 June 1600).

BOOKS

Where applicable, entries are followed by their Short-Title Catalogue number as given in A. W. Pollard and G. R. Redgrave, *A Short-Title Catalogue of Books Printed in England, Scotland, & Ireland, and of English Books Printed Abroad 1475–1640*, 2nd edn, rev. W. A. Jackson, F. S. Ferguson and Katharine F. Pantzer, 2 vols. (London: Bibliographical Society, 1986). For works published before 1700, the place of publication is London unless otherwise stated.

Aers, David, *Chaucer, Langland and the Creative Imagination* (London: Routledge & Kegan Paul, 1980).
Agnew, Jean-Christophe, *Worlds Apart: The Market and the Theater in Anglo-American Thought, 1550–1750* (Cambridge: Cambridge University Press, 1986).
Aquinas, Thomas, *Summa theologica*, trans. the Fathers of the English Dominican Provinces, 22 vols. (London: Burns Oates & Washbourne, [1921?]–1934).
Arab, Ronda A., 'Work, Bodies and Gender in *The Shoemaker's Holiday*', *Medieval and Renaissance Drama in England* 13 (2000), pp. 182–212.
Aristotle, *Metaphysics, X–XIV, Oeconomica, Magna Moralia*, trans. Hugh Tredennick and G. Cyril Armstrong, Aristotle in Twenty-Three Volumes, 18 (Cambridge, Mass.: Harvard University Press, 1935, repr. 1990).

Ashley, Maurice, *England in the Seventeenth Century*, 3rd edn (Harmondsworth: Penguin, 1961).

B., Ste., *Covnsel to the Husband: To the Wife Instruction* (1608) STC 1069.

Bacon, Francis, *The Essayes or Counsels, Civill and Morall*, ed. Michael Kiernan (Cambridge, Mass.: Harvard University Press, 1985).

Baines, Barbara J., *Thomas Heywood* (Boston, Mass.: Twayne, 1984).

Barber, C. L., *Shakespeare's Festive Comedy: A Study of Dramatic Form and its Relation to Social Custom* (Princeton, NJ: Princeton University Press, 1959).

Barckley, Richard, *A Discourse of the Felicitie of Man; or, His Summum bonum* (1598) STC 1381.

Barish, Jonas A., *The Anti-Theatrical Prejudice* (Berkeley, Calif.: University of California Press, 1981).

Barroll, J. Leeds, 'Shakespeare and the Second Blackfriars Theatre', *Shakespeare Studies* 33 (2005), pp. 156–70.

Barry, Jonathan, and Christopher Brooks (eds.), *The Middling Sort of People: Culture, Society and Politics in England, 1550–1800* (Basingstoke: Macmillan, 1994).

Barton, Anne (as Anne Righter), *Shakespeare and the Idea of the Play* (London: Chatto & Windus, 1962).

Beaumont, Francis, *The Knight of the Burning Pestle*, ed. Michael Hattaway (London: Ernest Benn; New York: W. W. Norton, 1969).

Beckerman, Bernard, *Shakespeare at the Globe: 1599–1609* (New York: Macmillan, 1962).

Becon, Thomas, *The Worckes of Thomas Becon*, 3 vols. (1564) STC 1710.

Bednarz, James P., 'When did Shakespeare Write the Choruses of *Henry V*?', *Notes and Queries* 53 (2006), pp. 486–9.

Beier, A. L., *Masterless Men: The Vagrancy Problem in England 1560–1640* (London: Methuen, 1985).

Bentley, Gerald Eades, *The Profession of Player in Shakespeare's Time 1590–1642* (Princeton, NJ: Princeton University Press, 1984).

Berry, Edward, *Shakespeare and the Hunt: A Cultural and Social Study* (Cambridge: Cambridge University Press, 2001).

Berry, Herbert, 'The First Public Playhouses, Especially the Red Lion', *Shakespeare Quarterly* 40 (1989), pp. 133–48.

'Brayne, John (*c.* 1541–1586)', *Oxford Dictionary of National Biography* (Oxford University Press, 2004), available online at www.oxforddnb.com/view/article/68128, accessed 21 June 2007.

Berry, Lloyd E. (ed.), *The Geneva Bible: A Facsimile of the 1560 Edition* (Madison, Wisc.: University of Wisconsin Press, 1969).

Bevington, David M., *From 'Mankind' to Marlowe: Growth of Structure in the Popular Drama of Tudor England* (Cambridge, Mass.: Harvard University Press, 1962).

Tudor Drama and Politics: A Critical Approach to Topical Meaning (Cambridge, Mass.: Harvard University Press, 1968).

Bliss, Lee, *Francis Beaumont* (Boston, Mass.: Twayne, 1987).

'The Renaissance Griselda: A Woman for All Seasons', *Viator: Medieval and Renaissance Studies* 23 (1992), pp. 301–43.

Bolton, Edmund, *The Cities Advocate, in this Case or Question of Honor and Armes; Whether Apprentiship Extinguisheth Gentry?* (1629) STC 3219.

Bradbrook, M. C., *The Rise of the Common Player: A Study of Actor and Society in Shakespeare's England* (London: Chatto & Windus, 1962).

Bradshaw, Brendan, 'Transalpine Humanism', in J. H. Burns and Mark Goldie (eds.), *The Cambridge History of Political Thought 1450–1700* (Cambridge: Cambridge University Press, 1991), pp. 95–131.

Bristol, Michael D., *Carnival and Theater: Plebeian Culture and the Structure of Authority in Renaissance England* (New York: Methuen, 1985).

Brome, Richard, *The Antipodes*, ed. Ann Haaker (London: Edward Arnold, 1967).

Bronfman, Judith, 'Griselda, Renaissance Woman', in Anne M. Haselkorn and Betty S. Travitsky (eds.), *The Renaissance Englishwoman in Print: Counterbalancing the Canon* (Amherst, Mass.: University of Massachusetts Press, 1990), pp. 211–23.

Brooks, Christopher, 'Apprenticeship, Social Mobility and the Middling Sort, 1550–1800', in Jonathan Barry and Christopher Brooks (eds.), *The Middling Sort of People: Culture, Society and Politics in England, 1550–1800* (Basingstoke: Macmillan, 1994), pp. 52–83.

B(rowne), J(ohn), *The Marchants Avizo* (1591) STC 3908.5.

Bruster, Douglas, *Drama and the Market in the Age of Shakespeare* (Cambridge: Cambridge University Press, 1992).

'Local *Tempest*: Shakespeare and the Work of the Early Modern Playhouse', *Journal of Medieval and Renaissance Studies* 25 (1995), pp. 33–53.

Bull, Malcolm, *The Mirror of the Gods: Classical Mythology in Renaissance Art* (London: Allen Lane, 2005).

(Bullinger, Heinrich), *The Christen State of Matrimonye*, trans. Miles Coverdale (Antwerp, 1541) STC 4045.

Burke, Peter, *Popular Culture in Early Modern Europe*, rev. edn (Aldershot: Scolar Press; Brookfield, Vt.: Ashgate, 1994).

Burnett, Mark Thornton, *Masters and Servants in English Renaissance Drama and Culture: Authority and Obedience* (Basingstoke: Macmillan, 1997).

Burns, J. H., and Mark Goldie (eds.), *The Cambridge History of Political Thought, 1450–1700* (Cambridge: Cambridge University Press, 1991).

Burton, Robert, *The Anatomy of Melancholy*, ed. Thomas C. Faulkner, Nicolas K. Kiessling and Rhonda L. Blair, 6 vols. (Oxford: Clarendon Press, 1989–2000).

Cahn, Susan, *Industry of Devotion: The Transformation of Women's Work in England, 1500–1660* (New York: Columbia University Press, 1987).

Campbell, Oscar James, *Comicall Satyre and Shakespeare's 'Troilus and Cressida'* (San Marino, Calif.: Huntington Library Publications, 1938).

Carson, Neil, *A Companion to Henslowe's Diary* (Cambridge: Cambridge University Press, 1988).

Castiglione, Baldassare, *The Book of the Courtier from the Italian of Count Baldassare Castiglione: Done into English by Sir Thomas Hoby Anno 1561*, ed. W. E. Henley (London: David Nutt, 1900).

Cave, Richard, Elizabeth Schafer and Brian Woolland (eds.), *Ben Jonson and Theatre: Performance, Practice and Theory* (London: Routledge, 1999).

Cerasano, S. P., 'Henslowe, Philip (*c.* 1555–1616)', *Oxford Dictionary of National Biography* (Oxford University Press, 2004), available online at www.oxforddnb.com/view/article/12991, accessed 21 June 2007.

Chambers, E. K., *The Elizabethan Stage*, 4 vols. (Oxford: Clarendon Press, 1923).

Chambers, E. K. and W. W. Greg (eds.), 'Dramatic Records from the Lansdowne Manuscripts', Malone Society *Collections*, 1.2 (Oxford: Malone Society, 1908).

(eds.), 'Dramatic Records of the City of London: The Remembrancia', in Malone Society *Collections*, 1.1 (Oxford: Malone Society, 1907).

Champion, Larry S., 'Dramatic Strategy and Political Ideology in *The Life and Death of Thomas, Lord Cromwell*', *Studies in English Literature* 29 (1989), pp. 218–36

Chapman, Alison A., 'Whose Saint Crispin's Day Is It? Shoemaking, Holiday Making, and the Politics of Memory in Early Modern England', *Renaissance Quarterly* 54 (2001), pp. 1467–94.

Charles, Lindsey, and Lorna Duffin (eds.), *Women and Work in Pre-Industrial England* (Beckenham: Croom Helm, 1985).

Cicero, Marcus Tullius, *De officiis*, trans. Walter Miller (London: William Heinemann; Cambridge, Mass.: Harvard University Press, 1913; repr. 1938).

Marcus Tullius Ciceroes Thre Bokes of Duties, to Marcus his Sonne, Turned oute of Latine into English, by Nicolas Grimalde, ed. Gerald O'Gorman (Washington, DC: Folger Shakespeare Library; London: Associated University Presses, 1990).

Clark, Alice, *Working Life of Women in the Seventeenth Century*, 3rd edn (London: Routledge, 1992).

Clay, C. G. A., *Economic Expansion and Social Change: England 1500–1700*, 2 vols. (Cambridge: Cambridge University Press, 1984).

Clopper, Lawrence M. (ed.), *Records of Early English Drama: Chester* (Toronto: University of Toronto Press; London: Manchester University Press, 1979).

Cohen, Walter, *Drama of a Nation: Public Theater in Renaissance England and Spain* (Ithaca, NY: Cornell University Press, 1985).

'Political Criticism of Shakespeare', in Jean E. Howard and Marion F. O'Connor (eds.), *Shakespeare Reproduced: The Text in History and Ideology* (New York: Routledge, 1987), pp. 18–46.

Coleman, D. C., *The Economy of England, 1450–1750* (Oxford: Oxford University Press, 1977).

Cook, Ann Jennalie, *The Privileged Playgoers of Shakespeare's London, 1576–1642* (Princeton, NJ: Princeton University Press, 1981).

Cooper, Lisa H., 'Chivalry, Commerce, and Conquest: Heywood's *The Four Prentices of London*', in Curtis Perry (ed.), *Material Culture and Cultural*

Materialisms in the Middle Ages and Renaissance (Turnhout, Belgium: Brepolis, 2001), pp. 159–75.

Cotta, John, *A Short Discoverie of the Vnobserved Dangers of Seuerall Sorts of Ignorant and Vnconsiderate Practisers of Physicke in England* (1612) STC 5833.

Cox, John D. and David Scott Kastan (eds.), *A New History of Early English Drama* (New York: Columbia University Press, 1997).

Cressy, David, *Bonfires and Bells: National Memory and the Protestant Calendar in Elizabethan and Stuart England* (Berkeley, Calif.: University of California Press; London: Weidenfeld & Nicolson, 1989).

Crupi, Charles W., 'Ideological Contradictions in Part I of Heywood's *Edward IV*: "Our Musicke Runs ... Much upon Discords" ', *Medieval and Renaissance Drama in England* 7 (1995), pp. 224–56.

Daffin, Chris, *Annual Survey of Hours and Earnings: An Analysis of Historical Data, 1998–2003* (Office of National Statistics, 2004).

Davies, John, of Hereford, *Microcosmos: The Discovery of the Little World, With the Government Thereof* (Oxford, 1603) STC 6333.

Dean, James M. (ed.), *Medieval English Political Writings*, (Kalamazoo, Mich.: Medieval Institute Publications, 1996).

De Bruyn, Lucy, *Mob-Rule and Riots: The Present Mirrored in the Past* (London: Regency Press, 1981).

De Grazia, Margreta, 'World Pictures, Modern Periods, and the Early Stage', in John D. Cox and David Scott Kastan (eds.), *A New History of Early English Drama* (New York: Columbia University Press, 1997), pp. 7–21.

Dekker, Thomas, *The Dramatic Works of Thomas Dekker*, ed. Fredson Bowers, 4 vols. (Cambridge: Cambridge University Press, 1953–61).

Thomas Dekker, ed. E. D. Pendry (London: Edward Arnold, 1967).

The Shoemaker's Holiday, ed. R. L. Smallwood and Stanley Wells (Manchester: Manchester University Press; Baltimore, Md.: Johns Hopkins University Press, 1979).

Deloney, Thomas, *The Novels of Thomas Deloney*, ed. Merritt E. Lawlis (Bloomington, Ind.: Indiana University Press, 1961).

Digges, Thomas and Dudley Digges, *Four Paradoxes; or, Politique Discourses* (1604) STC 6872.

Dod, John and Robert Cleaver, *A Godlie Forme of Hovseholde Government: For the Ordering of Private Families, According to the Direction of Gods Word* (1612) STC 5386.

Dollimore, Jonathan, *Radical Tragedy: Religion, Ideology and Power in the Drama of Shakespeare and his Contemporaries* (Brighton: Harvester Press, 1984).

Duby, Georges, *The Three Orders: Feudal Society Imagined*, trans. Arthur Goldhammer (Chicago, Ill.: University of Chicago Press, 1980).

Dudley, Edmund, *The Tree of Commonwealth*, ed. D. M. Brodie (Cambridge: Cambridge University Press, 1948).

Duncan-Jones, Katherine, *Ungentle Shakespeare: Scenes from his Life* (London: Arden Shakespeare, 2001).

Dutton, Richard, '*Hamlet, An Apology for Actors*, and the Sign of the Globe' *Shakespeare Survey* 41 (1988), pp. 35–43.

Mastering the Revels: The Regulation and Censorship of English Renaissance Drama (Basingstoke: Macmillan, 1991).

Dutton, Richard and Jean E. Howard (eds.), *A Companion to Shakespeare's Works*, Vol. IV: *The Poems, Problem Comedies, Late Plays* (Malden, Mass.: Blackwell, 2003).

E(dgar), T(homas) (ed.), *The Lawes Resolvtions of Womens Rights; or, The Lawes Provision for Woemen* (1632) STC 7437.

Eliot, T. S., *Elizabethan Essays* (London: Faber & Faber, 1934).

Elizabeth I, *Collected Works*, ed. Leah S. Marcus, Janel Mueller and Mary Beth Rose (Chicago, Ill.: University of Chicago Press, 2000).

Elyot, Thomas, *The Boke Named the Gouernour*, ed. Henry Herbert Stephen Croft, 2 vols. (London: C. Kegan Paul, 1880).

Engle, Lars, *Shakespearean Pragmatism: Market of his Time* (Chicago, Ill.: University of Chicago Press, 1993).

Erickson, Amy Louise, *Women and Property in Early Modern England* (London: Routledge, 1993).

Erne, Lukas, *Shakespeare as Literary Dramatist* (Cambridge: Cambridge University Press, 2003).

Eutheo, Anglo-Phile and Salvianus, *A Second and Third Blast of Retrait from Plaies and Theaters* (1580) STC 21677.

Farley-Hills, David, *Shakespeare and the Rival Playwrights, 1600–1606* (London: Routledge, 1990).

Farmer, David, *The Oxford Dictionary of Saints*, 4th edn (Oxford: Oxford University Press, 1997).

Ferne, John, *The Blazon of Gentrie* (1586) STC 10824.

Foakes, R. A. (ed.), *Henslowe's Diary*, 2nd edn (Cambridge: Cambridge University Press, 2002).

Forker, Charles R., and Joseph Candido, 'Wit, Wisdom, and Theatricality in *The Book of Sir Thomas More*', *Shakespeare Studies* 13 (1980), pp. 85–104.

Fraser, Russell, *The War Against Poetry* (Princeton, NJ: Princeton University Press, 1970).

Frye, Susan and Karen Robertson (eds.), *Maids and Mistresses, Cousins and Queens: Women's Alliances in Early Modern England* (New York: Oxford University Press, 1999).

Fulbecke, William, *A Direction or Preparatiue to the Study of the Lawe* (1600) STC 11410.

Fumerton, Patricia, *Unsettled: The Culture of Mobility and the Working Poor in Early Modern England* (Chicago, Ill.: University of Chicago Press, 2006).

Gair, Reavley, *The Children of Paul's: The Story of a Theatre Company, 1553–1608* (Cambridge: Cambridge University Press, 1982).

Galloway, David (ed.), *The Elizabethan Theatre III* (London: Macmillan, 1973).

(ed.), *Records of Early English Drama: Norwich, 1540–1642* (Toronto: University of Toronto Press, 1984).

Gardiner, Harold C., *Mysteries' End: An Investigation of the Last Days of the Medieval Religious Stage* (New Haven, Conn.: Yale University Press; London: Oxford University Press, 1946).

Gibbons, Brian, *Jacobean City Comedy*, 2nd edn (London: Methuen, 1980).

Goldberg, Jonathan, 'Hamlet's Hand', *Shakespeare Quarterly* 39 (1988), pp. 307–27.

Gosson, Stephen, *The Schoole of Abuse: Conteining a Plesaunt Inuectiue Against Poets, Pipers, Plaiers, Iesters, and Such Like Caterpillers of a Commonwelth* (1579) STC 12097.5.

Playes Confuted in Fiue Actions (1582) STC 12095.

Markets of Bawdrie: The Dramatic Criticism of Stephen Gosson, ed. Arthur F. Kinney (Salzburg: Institut für Englische Sprache und Literatur, 1974).

Grassby, Richard, 'Social Mobility and Business Enterprise in Seventeenth-Century England', in Donald Pennington and Keith Thomas (eds.), *Puritans and Revolutionaries: Essays in Seventeenth-Century History Presented to Christopher Hill* (Oxford: Clarendon Press, 1978), pp. 355–81.

Greenblatt, Stephen, *Shakespearean Negotiations: The Circulation of Social Energy in Renaissance England* (Berkeley, Calif.: University of California Press, 1988).

Greenfield, Peter H., 'Touring', in John D. Cox and David Scott Kastan (eds.), *A New History of Early English Drama* (New York: Columbia University Press, 1997), pp. 251–68.

Greg, W. W. (ed.), *The Book of Sir Thomas More*, 2nd edn (Oxford: Malone Society, 1961).

Griffiths, Paul, *Youth and Authority: Formative Experiences in England 1560–1640* (Oxford: Clarendon Press, 1996).

Grint, Keith, *The Sociology of Work: An Introduction*, 2nd edn (Cambridge: Polity Press, 1998).

Gurr, Andrew, 'Money or Audiences: The Impact of Shakespeare's Globe', *Theatre Notebook* 42 (1988), pp. 3–14.

Playgoing in Shakespeare's London, 2nd edn (Cambridge: Cambridge University Press, 1996).

The Shakespearian Playing Companies (Oxford: Clarendon Press, 1996).

'Who Is Lovewit? What Is He?', in Richard Cave, Elizabeth Schafer and Brian Woolland (eds.), *Ben Jonson and Theatre: Performance, Practice and Theory* (London: Routledge, 1999), pp. 5–19.

The Shakespeare Company, 1594–1642 (Cambridge: Cambridge University Press, 2004).

Halkett, Samuel and John Laing, *A Dictionary of Anonymous and Pseudonymous Publications in the English Language*, 3rd edn, rev. John Horden (Harlow: Longman, 1980).

Hall, Edward, *The Vnion of the Two Noble and Illustrate Famelies of Lancastre & Yorke* (1548) STC 12721.

Hall, Richard H., with contributions by Robert T. Buttram, *Sociology of Work: Perspectives, Analyses, and Issues* (Thousand Oaks, Calif.: Pine Forge Press, 1994).

Harbage, Alfred, *Annals of English Drama, 975–1700: An Analytical Record of All Plays, Extant or Lost, Chronologically Arranged and Indexed by Authors, Titles, Dramatic Companies, &c.*, rev. S. Schoenbaum (London: Methuen, 1964).

Shakespeare and the Rival Traditions (New York: Macmillan, 1952).

Harington, John, *Nugae Antiquae: Being a Miscellaneous Collection of Original Papers in Prose and Verse*, ed. Henry Harington, 2 vols. (London: W. Frederick, 1769–75).

Harman, Thomas, *A Caveat or Warening, for Commen Cvrsetors Vvlgarely Called Vagabones* (1567) STC 12787.

Harrison, William, *The Description of England*, ed. Georges Edelen (Ithaca, NY: Cornell University Press, 1968).

Hart, Alfred, *Shakespeare and the Homilies and Other Pieces of Research into the Elizabethan Drama* (Melbourne: Melbourne University Press, 1934).

Haselkorn, Anne M., and Betty S. Travitsky (eds.), *The Renaissance Englishwoman in Print: Counterbalancing the Canon* (Amherst, Mass.: University of Massachusetts Press, 1990).

Hawkes, David, 'Idolatry and Commodity Fetishism in the Antitheatrical Controversy', *Studies in English Literature* 39 (1998–9), pp. 255–73.

Helgerson, Richard, *Forms of Nationhood: The Elizabethan Writing of England* (Chicago, Ill.: University of Chicago Press, 1992).

Henderson, Diana E., 'Many Mansions: Reconstructing *A Woman Killed with Kindness*', *Studies in English Literature* 26 (1996), pp. 277–94.

Heywood, Thomas, *Gynaikeion; or, Nine Bookes of Various History Concerninge Women; Inscribed by the Names of the Nine Muses* (1624) STC 13326.

If You Know Not Me You Know Nobody Part II, ed. Madeleine Doran (Oxford: Malone Society, 1935).

The Four Prentices of London: A Critical, Old-Spelling Edition, ed. Mary Ann Weber Gasior (New York: Garland, 1980).

A Woman Killed with Kindness, ed. Brian Scobie (London: A & C Black; New York: W. W. Norton, 1985, repr. 1991).

Hill, Christopher, *Society and Puritanism in Pre-Revolutionary England* (London: Secker & Warburg, 1964).

Reformation to Industrial Revolution, 2nd edn (Harmondsworth: Penguin, 1969).

Change and Continuity in Seventeenth-Century England (London: Weidenfeld & Nicolson, 1974).

Milton and the English Revolution (London: Faber & Faber, 1977).

Hill, Tracey, *Anthony Munday and Civic Culture: Theatre, History and Power in Early Modern London, 1580–1633* (Manchester: Manchester University Press, 2004).

Holbrook, Peter, *Literature and Degree in Renaissance England: Nashe, Bourgeois Tragedy, Shakespeare* (Newark, NJ: University of Delaware Press; London: Associated University Presses, 1994).

Holderness, Graham, *Shakespeare's History* (Dublin: Gill & Macmillan; New York: St. Martin's Press, 1985).

'*Richard II*', in Graham Holderness, Nick Potter and John Turner, *Shakespeare: The Play of History* (Basingstoke: Macmillan, 1987), pp. 20–40.

Howard, Jean E., *The Stage and Social Struggle in Early Modern England* (London: Routledge, 1994).

Howard, Jean E. and Marion F. O'Connor (eds.), *Shakespeare Reproduced: The Text in History and Ideology* (New York: Routledge, 1987).

Howard-Hill, T. H. (ed.), *Shakespeare and* Sir Thomas More*: Essays on the Play and its Shakespearian Interest* (Cambridge: Cambridge University Press, 1989).

Hoy, Cyrus, *Introductions, Notes, and Commentaries to Texts in 'The Dramatic Works of Thomas Dekker' Edited by Fredson Bowers*, 4 vols. (Cambridge: Cambridge University Press, 1980).

Humphrey, Laurence, *The Nobles; or, Of Nobilitye: The Original Nature, Dutyes, Right, and Christian Institucion Thereof* (1563) STC 13964.

Hunt, Maurice, *Shakespeare's Labored Art: Stir, Work, and the Late Plays* (New York: Peter Lang, 1995).

Hutson, Lorna, *The Usurer's Daughter: Male Friendship and Fictions of Women in Sixteenth-Century England* (London: Routledge, 1994).

Ingram, R. W. (ed.), *Records of Early English Drama: Coventry*, (Toronto: University of Toronto Press; Manchester: Manchester University Press, 1981).

Ingram, William, *The Business of Playing: The Beginnings of the Adult Professional Theater in Elizabethan London* (Ithaca, NY: Cornell University Press, 1992).

Jack, Sybil M., *Trade and Industry in Tudor and Stuart England* (London: George Allen & Unwin, 1977).

James, Mervyn, *Society, Politics and Culture: Studies in Early Modern England* (Cambridge: Cambridge University Press, 1986).

Jankowski, Theodora A., 'Historicizing and Legitimating Capitalism: Thomas Heywood's *Edward IV* and *If You Know Not Me, You Know Nobody*', *Medieval and Renaissance Drama in England* 7 (1995), pp. 305–37.

'The Development of Middle-Class Identity and the "Problem" of the "Gentle" Apprentice', in Michelle M. Sauer (ed.), *Proceedings of the 11th Annual Northern Plains Conference on Early British Literature* (Minot, ND: Minot State University Printing Services, 2003), pp. 1–17.

Jewell, John, *An Exposition upon the Two Epistles of the Apostle St. Paul to the Thessalonians*, ed. Peter Hall (London: B. Wertheim, 1841).

Johnson, Nora, *The Actor as Playwright in Early Modern Drama* (Cambridge: Cambridge University Press, 2003).

Johnston, Alexandra F., 'The City as Patron: York', in Paul Whitfield White and Suzanne R. Westfall (eds.), *Shakespeare and Theatrical Patronage in Early Modern England* (Cambridge: Cambridge University Press, 2002), pp. 150–75.

Jonson, Ben, *Ben Jonson*, ed. C. H. Herford and Percy and E. M. Simpson, 11 vols. (Oxford: Clarendon Press, 1925–52).

Jonson, Ben, George Chapman and John Marston, *Eastward Ho!*, ed. C. G. Petter (London: Ernest Benn, 1973; repr. London, A & C Black; New York: Norton, 1994).

Jowett, John, 'Henry Chettle and the Original Text of *Sir Thomas More*', in T. H. Howard-Hill (ed.), *Shakespeare and 'Sir Thomas More': Essays on the*

Play and its Shakespearian Interest (Cambridge: Cambridge University Press, 1989), pp. 131–49.
Kaplan, Joel H., 'Virtue's Holiday: Thomas Dekker and Simon Eyre', *Renaissance Drama*, n.s., 2 (1969), 103–22.
Kastan, David Scott, 'Workshop and/as Playhouse: Comedy and Commerce in *The Shoemaker's Holiday*', *Studies in Philology* 84 (1987), pp. 324–37.
'Is There a Class in This (Shakespearean) Text?', *Renaissance Drama*, n.s., 24 (1993), pp. 101–21.
Kathman, David, 'Grocers, Goldsmiths, and Drapers: Freemen and Apprentices in the Elizabethan Theater', *Shakespeare Quarterly* 55 (2004), pp. 1–49.
Kemp, Will, *Kemps Nine Daies VVonder* (1601) STC 14923.
Knights, L. C., *Drama and Society in the Age of Jonson* (London: Methuen, 1937; repr. 1977).
Knowles, Ronald (ed.), *Shakespeare and Carnival: After Bakhtin* (Basingstoke: Macmillan, 1998).
Knutson, Roslyn Lander, 'Play Identifications: *The Wise Man of West Chester* and *John a Kent and John a Cumber*; *Longshanks* and *Edward I*', *Huntington Library Quarterly* 47 (1984), pp. 1–11.
The Repertory of Shakespeare's Company, 1594–1613 (Fayetteville, AK.: University of Arkansas Press, 1991).
Playing Companies and Commerce in Shakespeare's Time (Cambridge: Cambridge University Press, 2001).
Kyd, Thomas, *The Works of Thomas Kyd*, ed. Frederick S. Boas (Oxford: Clarendon Press, 1901, repr. 1955).
Langland, William, *The Vision of Piers Plowman: A Critical Edition of the B-Text Based on Trinity College Cambridge MS B.15.17*, ed. A. V. C. Schmidt, 2nd edn (London: Everyman, 1995).
Laslett, Peter, *The World We Have Lost* (London: Methuen, 1965).
Latimer, Hugh, *The Works of Hugh Latimer*, ed. George Elwes Corrie, 2 vols. (Cambridge: Cambridge University Press, 1844–5).
Leech, Clifford, 'Three Times Ho and a Brace of Widows: Some Plays for the Private Theatre', in David Galloway (ed.), *The Elizabethan Theatre III* (London: Macmillan, 1973), pp. 14–32.
Leggatt, Alexander, *Citizen Comedy in the Age of Shakespeare* (Toronto: University of Toronto Press, 1973).
Jacobean Public Theatre (London: Routledge, 1992).
'The Audience as Patron: *The Knight of the Burning Pestle*', in Paul Whitfield White and Suzanne R. Westfall (eds.), *Shakespeare and Theatrical Patronage in Early Modern England* (Cambridge: Cambridge University Press, 2002), pp. 295–315.
Le Goff, Jacques, *Time, Work, and Culture in the Middle Ages*, trans. Arthur Goldhammer (Chicago, Ill.: University of Chicago Press, 1980)
Medieval Civilization, 400–1500, trans. Julia Barrow (Oxford: Basil Blackwell, 1988).

Leinwand, Theodore B., *The City Staged: Jacobean City Comedy, 1603–1613* (Madison, Wisc.: University of Wisconsin Press, 1986).

Theatre, Finance and Society in Early Modern England (Cambridge: Cambridge University Press, 1999).

Levin, Harry, 'Two Magian Comedies: *The Tempest* and *The Alchemist*', *Shakespeare Survey* 22 (1971), pp. 47–58.

Levine, Laura, *Men in Women's Clothing: Anti-Theatricality and Effeminization, 1579–1642* (Cambridge: Cambridge University Press, 1994).

Lodge, Thomas, *The Complete Works of Thomas Lodge [1580–1623]*, 4 vols. (Glasgow: Hunterian Club, 1883; repr. New York, Russell & Russell, 1963).

Loengard, Janet S., 'An Elizabethan Lawsuit: John Brayne, His Carpenter, and the Building of the Red Lion Theatre', *Shakespeare Quarterly* 34 (1983), pp. 298–310.

Longstaffe, Stephen, '"A Short Report and Not Otherwise": Jack Cade in *2 Henry VI*', in Ronald Knowles (ed.), *Shakespeare and Carnival: After Bakhtin* (Basingstoke: Macmillan, 1998), pp. 13–35.

Lucking, David, 'Carrying Tempest in His Hand and Voice: The Figure of the Magician in Jonson and Shakespeare', *English Studies* 85 (2004), pp. 297–310.

Luther, Martin, *Reformation Writings of Martin Luther*, trans. Bertram Lee Woolf, 2 vols. (London: Lutterworth Press, 1952–6).

Macfarlane, Fenella, 'To "Try What London Prentices Can Do": Merchant Chivalry as Representational Strategy in Thomas Heywood's *The Four Prentices of London*', *Medieval and Renaissance Drama in England* 13 (2001), pp. 136–64.

McLuskie, Kathleen E., *Renaissance Dramatists* (Hemel Hempstead: Harvester Wheatsheaf, 1989).

Dekker and Heywood: Professional Dramatists (Basingstoke: Macmillan, 1994).

McLuskie, Kathleen E. and David Bevington (eds.), *Plays on Women* (Manchester: Manchester University Press, 1999).

McLuskie, Kathleen and Felicity Dunworth (misspelled 'Dunsworth'), 'Patronage and the Economics of Theater', in John D. Cox and David Scott Kastan (eds.), *A New History of Early English Drama* (New York: Columbia University Press, 1997), pp. 423–40.

McMillin, Scott and Sally-Beth MacLean, *The Queen's Men and their Plays* (Cambridge: Cambridge University Press, 1998).

McNeill, Fiona, *Poor Women in Shakespeare* (Cambridge: Cambridge University Press, 2007).

Maney, A. S., and R. L. Smallwood (eds.), *MHRA Style Book: Notes for Authors, Editors, and Writers of Theses*, 5th edn, rev. Derek Brown and others (Leeds: Modern Humanities Research Association, 1999).

Manley, Lawrence, *Literature and Culture in Early Modern London* (Cambridge: Cambridge University Press, 1995).

Mann, David, *The Elizabethan Player: Contemporary Stage Representation* (London: Routledge, 1991).

Marcus, Leah S., *The Politics of Mirth: Jonson, Herrick, Milton, Marvell, and the Defence of Old Holiday Pastimes* (Chicago, Ill.: University of Chicago Press, 1986).

Marlowe, Christopher, *Edward II*, ed. Charles Forker (Manchester: Manchester University Press, 1994).

Marston, John, *The Plays of John Marston*, ed. H. Harvey Wood, 3 vols. (Edinburgh: Oliver & Boyd, 1934–9).

Miles, Geoffrey, *Shakespeare and the Constant Romans* (Oxford: Clarendon Press, 1996).

Miller, Stephen Roy (ed.), *The Taming of a Shrew* (Oxford: Malone Society, 1998).

Minchinton, W. E. (ed.), *Wage Regulation in Pre-Industrial England* (Newton Abbot: David & Charles, 1972).

Montrose, Louis A., 'Professing the Renaissance: The Poetics and Politics of Culture', in H. Aram Veeser (ed.), *The New Historicism* (New York: Routledge, 1989), pp. 15–36.

The Purpose of Playing: Shakespeare and the Cultural Politics of Elizabethan Theatre (Chicago, Ill.: University of Chicago Press, 1996).

More, Thomas, *The History of King Richard III*, ed. Richard S. Sylvester, The Complete Works of St Thomas More, 2 Vols. (New Haven, Conn.: Yale University Press, 1963).

Utopia, ed. Edward Surtz and J. H. Hexter, The Complete Works of St Thomas More, 4 (New Haven, Conn.: Yale University Press, 1965).

Mulcaster, Richard, *Positions Wherin Those Primitive Circvmstances Be Examined, Which Are Necessarie for the Training Vp of Children, Either for Skill in Their Booke, or Health in Their Bodie* (1581) STC 18253a.

Mullaney, Stephen, *The Place of the Stage: License, Play, and Power in Renaissance England* (Chicago, Ill.: University of Chicago Press, 1988).

Munday, Anthony, *John a Kent and John a Cumber*, ed. Muriel St. Clare Byrne (Oxford: Malone Society, 1923).

The Downfall of Robert Earl of Huntingdon, ed. John C. Meagher (Oxford: Malone Society, 1965).

An Edition of Anthony Munday's 'John a Kent and John a Cumber', ed. Arthur E. Pennell (New York: Garland, 1980).

Munday, Anthony *et al.*, *Sir Thomas More*, ed. Vittorio Gabrieli and Giorgio Melchiori (Manchester: Manchester University Press, 1990).

Munro, Lucy, *Children of the Queen's Revels: A Jacobean Theatre Repertory* (Cambridge: Cambridge University Press, 2005).

Nashe, Thomas, *The Works of Thomas Nashe*, ed. Ronald B. McKerrow, 2nd edn, rev. F. P. Wilson, 5 vols. (Oxford: Basil Blackwell, 1958).

Nederman, Cary J., and Kate Langdon Forhan (eds.), *Medieval Political Theory – A Reader: The Quest for the Body Politic, 1100–1400* (London: Routledge, 1993).

Northbrooke, John, *A Treatise Wherein Dicing, Dauncing, Vaine Playes or Enterluds with Other Idle Pastimes &c. Commonly Vsed on the Sabboth Day,*

Are Reproued by the Authoritie of the Word of God and Auntient Writers (1577?) STC 18670.
Orgel, Stephen, *Impersonations: The Performance of Gender in Shakespeare's England* (Cambridge: Cambridge University Press, 1996).
Orlin, Lena Cowen, *Private Matters and Public Culture in Post-Reformation England* (Ithaca, NY: Cornell University Press, 1994).
Ornstein, Robert, *A Kingdom for a Stage: The Achievement of Shakespeare's History Plays* (Cambridge, Mass.: Harvard University Press, 1972).
Overbury, Thomas, *New and Choise Characters, of Seuerall Authors: Together with that Exquisite and Vnmatcht Poeme, The Wife* (1615) STC 18908.
Owst, G. R., *Literature and Pulpit in Medieval England: A Neglected Chapter in the History of English Letters and of the English People* (Cambridge: Cambridge University Press, 1933).
Patterson, Annabel, *Shakespeare and the Popular Voice* (Cambridge, Mass.: Basil Blackwell, 1989).
Peacham, Henry, *'The Complete Gentleman', 'The Truth of Our Times', and 'The Art of Living in London'*, ed. Virgil B. Heltzel (Ithaca, NY: Cornell University Press, 1962).
Pennington, Donald, and Keith Thomas (eds.), *Puritans and Revolutionaries: Essays in Seventeenth-Century History Presented to Christopher Hill* (Oxford: Clarendon Press, 1978).
Perkins, David, *Is Literary History Possible?* (Baltimore, Md.: Johns Hopkins University Press, 1992).
Perkins, William, *The Works of that Famovs and Worthie Minister of Christ, in the Vniversitie of Cambridge, M. W. Perkins* (Cambridge, 1603) STC 19647.
Perry, Curtis (ed.), *Material Culture and Cultural Materialisms in the Middle Ages and Renaissance* (Turnhout, Belgium: Brepolis, 2001).
Pollard, A. W., and G. R. Redgrave, *A Short-Title Catalogue of Books Printed in England, Scotland, & Ireland, and of English Books Printed Abroad 1475–1640*, 2nd edn, rev. W. A. Jackson, F. S. Ferguson and Katharine F. Pantzer, 2 vols. (London: Bibliographical Society, 1986).
Potter, Lois, 'A Stage Where Every Man Must Play a Part?', *Shakespeare Quarterly* 50 (1999), pp. 74–86.
Prest, Wilfrid R., *The Rise of the Barristers: A Social History of the English Bar, 1590–1640* (Oxford: Clarendon Press, 1986).
(ed.), *The Professions in Early Modern England* (London: Croom Helm, 1987).
Puttenham, George, *The Arte of English Poesie* (1589) STC 20519.
Rackin, Phyllis, *Stages of History: Shakespeare's English Chronicles* (London: Routledge, 1991).
Rankins, William, *A Mirrovr of Monsters* (1587) STC 20699.
Rich, Barnaby, *Roome for a Gentleman; or, The Second Part of Favltes* (1609) STC 20985.
Rickey, Mary Ellen and Thomas B. Stroup (eds.), *Certaine Sermons or Homilies Appointed to be Read in Churches in the Time of Queen Elizabeth I*

(1547–1571): A Facsimile Reproduction of the Edition of 1623 (Gainesville, Fla.: Scholars' Facsimiles & Reprints, 1968).

Riggs, David, *Shakespeare's Heroical Histories: 'Henry VI' and Its Literary Tradition* (Cambridge, Mass.: Harvard University Press, 1971).

Ruffhead, Owen (ed.), *The Statutes at Large, from Magna Charta, to the Twenty-fifth Year of the Reign of King George the Third, Inclusive*, rev. Charles Runnington, 10 vols. (London: Charles Eyre & Andrew Strahan; William Woodfall & Andrew Strahan, 1786).

Ruiter, David, *Shakespeare's Festive History: Feasting, Festivity, Fasting and Lent in the Second Henriad* (Aldershot: Ashgate, 2003).

Rutter, Tom, 'Playing Work: The Uses of Labour on the Shakespearean Stage', unpublished Ph.D. thesis, University of London (2003).

'Fit Hamlet, Fat Hamlet, and the Problems of Aristocratic Labour', *Cahiers Elisabéthains* 68 (2005), pp. 27–32.

'The Actors in *Sir Thomas More*', *Shakespeare Yearbook 2005*, n.s., 16 (2007), pp. 227–44.

'*Patient Grissil* and Jonsonian Satire', *Studies in English Literature* 48 (2008) (in press).

S., W., *A Compendious or Brief Examination of Certayne Ordinary Complaints, of Diuers of our Country Men in these our Dayes* (1581) STC 23134.

The True Chronicle Historie of the Whole Life and Death of Thomas Lord Cromwell (1602) STC 21532.

Sauer, Michelle M. (ed.), *Proceedings of the 11th Annual Northern Plains Conference on Early British Literature* (Minot, ND: Minot State University Printing Services, 2003).

Segar, William, *Honor Military, and Ciuill, Contained in Foure Bookes* (1602) STC 22164.

Shakespeare, William (attr.), *The London Prodigall* (1605) STC 22333.

Shakespeare, William, *The Riverside Shakespeare*, ed. G. Blakemore Evans (Boston, Mass.: Houghton Mifflin, 1974).

The Second Part of King Henry IV, ed. Giorgio Melchiori (Cambridge: Cambridge University Press, 1989).

Coriolanus, ed. R. B. Parker (Oxford: Clarendon Press, 1994).

King Henry V, ed. T. W. Craik, Arden Shakespeare, 3rd series (London: Routledge, 1995).

King Henry VI Part 2, ed. Ronald Knowles, Arden Shakespeare, 3rd series (London: Thomas Nelson & Sons, 1999).

The First Quarto of King Henry V, ed. Andrew Gurr (Cambridge: Cambridge University Press, 2000).

King Henry IV Part 1, ed. David Scott Kastan, Arden Shakespeare, 3rd series (London: Arden Shakespeare, 2002).

King Richard II, ed. Charles R. Forker, Arden Shakespeare, 3rd series (London: Thomson Learning, 2002).

King Richard II, ed. Andrew Gurr, 2nd edn (Cambridge: Cambridge University Press, 2003).

The Taming of the Shrew, ed. Ann Thompson, rev. edn (Cambridge: Cambridge University Press, 2003).

Shapiro, I. A., 'Shakespeare and Mundy', *Shakespeare Survey* 14 (1961), pp. 25–33.

Shapiro, James, *1599: A Year in the Life of William Shakespeare* (London: Faber & Faber, 2005).

Shapiro, Michael, *Children of the Revels: The Boy Companies of Shakespeare's Time and Their Plays* (New York: Columbia University Press, 1977).

Sherman, Anita Gilman, 'The Status of Charity in Thomas Heywood's *If You Know Not Me You Know Nobody II*', *Medieval and Renaissance Drama in England* 12 (1999), pp. 99–120.

Sidney, Philip, *The Complete Works of Sir Philip Sidney*, ed. Albert Feuillerat, 4 vols. (Cambridge: Cambridge University Press, 1922–6).

Simpson, J. A. and E. S. C. Weiner (eds.), *The Oxford English Dictionary*, 2nd edn, 20 vols. (Oxford: Clarendon Press, 1989).

Skinner, Quentin, *The Foundations of Modern Political Thought*, 2 vols. (Cambridge: Cambridge University Press, 1978).

Slack, Paul, *Poverty and Policy in Tudor and Stuart England* (London: Longman, 1988).

Smallwood, R. L., '"Here, in the Friars": Immediacy and Theatricality in *The Alchemist*', *Review of English Studies* 32 (1981), pp. 142–60.

Smith, Henry, *A Preparatiue to Mariage* (1591) STC 22685.

Smith, Thomas, *De Republica Anglorum*, ed. Mary Dewar (Cambridge: Cambridge University Press, 1982).

Sohmer, Steve, *Shakespeare's Mystery Play: The Opening of the Globe Theatre, 1599* (Manchester: Manchester University Press, 1999).

Spenser, Edmund, *The Works of Edmund Spenser: A Variorum Edition*, ed. Edwin Greenlaw and others, 10 vols. (Baltimore, Md.: Johns Hopkins Press, 1932–49).

Starkey, Thomas, *A Dialogue between Pole and Lupset*, ed. T. F. Mayer, Camden Fourth Series, 37 (London: Royal Historical Society, 1989).

Stephens, John, *Essayes and Characters: Ironicall, and Instrvctive* (1615) STC 23250.

Stern, Tiffany, *Rehearsal from Shakespeare to Sheridan* (Oxford: Clarendon Press, 2000).

Stevenson, Laura Caroline, *Praise and Paradox: Merchants and Craftsmen in Elizabethan Popular Literature* (Cambridge: Cambridge University Press, 1984).

Stone, Lawrence, *The Crisis of the Aristocracy 1558–1641* (Oxford: Clarendon Press, 1965).

Straznicky, Marta, 'The End(s) of Discord in *The Shoemaker's Holiday*', *Studies in English Literature* 36 (1996), pp. 357–72.

Stubbes, Philip, *The Anatomie of Abuses* (1583) STC 23377.

Sullivan, Ceri, *The Rhetoric of Credit: Merchants in Early Modern Writing* (Madison, Wisc.: Fairleigh Dickinson University Press; London: Associated University Presses, 2002).

Sullivan, Garrett A., Jr., '"All Thinges Come Into Commerce": Women, Household Labor, and the Spaces of Marston's *The Dutch Courtesan*', *Renaissance Drama*, n.s., 27 (1996), pp. 19–46.

Sylvester, Richard S., and Davis P. Harding (eds.), *Two Early Tudor Lives* (New Haven, Conn.: Yale University Press, 1962).

Tawney, R. H., *Religion and the Rise of Capitalism: A Historical Study* (London: John Murray, 1926; repr. Harmondsworth: Penguin, 1972).

Tawney, R. H. and Eileen Power (eds.), *Tudor Economic Documents: Being Select Documents Illustrating the Economic and Social History of Tudor England*, 3 vols. (London: Longmans, Green, 1924; repr. 1951).

Thomas, Keith, 'Work and Leisure in Pre-Industrial Society', *Past and Present* 29 (1964), pp. 50–62.

(ed.), *The Oxford Book of Work* (Oxford: Oxford University Press, 1999).

Thomson, Leslie, '"As Proper a Woman as Any in Cheap": Women in Shops on the Early Modern Stage', *Medieval and Renaissance Drama in England* 16 (2003), pp. 145–61.

Thomson, Peter, *Shakespeare's Professional Career* (Cambridge: Cambridge University Press, 1992).

Tillyard, E. M. W., *Shakespeare's History Plays* (London: Chatto & Windus, 1944).

Timms, L. D., 'Dekker's *The Shoemaker's Holiday* and Elizabeth's Accession Day', *Notes and Queries* 32 (1985), p. 58.

Turner, Celeste, *Anthony Mundy: An Elizabethan Man of Letters* (Berkeley, Calif.: University of California Press; London: Cambridge University Press, 1928).

Tymme, Thomas, *The Figure of Antichriste, with the Tokens of the End of the World, Most Plainly Disciphered by a Catholike and Diuine Exposition of the Second Epistle of Paul to the Thessalonians* (1586) STC 24417.

Ure, Peter, 'Patient Madman and Honest Whore: The Middleton–Dekker Oxymoron', *Essays and Studies*, n.s., 19 (1966), 18–40.

Vale, Marcia, *The Gentleman's Recreations: Accomplishments and Pastimes of the English Gentleman 1580–1630* (Cambridge: D. S. Brewer; Totowa, Rowman & Littlefield, 1977).

Veeser, H. Aram (ed.), *The New Historicism* (New York: Routledge, 1989).

Vickers, Brian, 'Leisure and Idleness in the Renaissance: The Ambivalence of Otium', *Renaissance Studies* 4 (1990), pp. 1–37, 107–54.

Vitkus, Daniel, '"Meaner Ministers": Mastery, Bondage, and Theatrical Labor in *The Tempest*', in Richard Dutton and Jean E. Howard (eds.), *A Companion to Shakespeare's Works*, Vol. IV: *The Poems, Problem Comedies, Late Plays* (Malden, Mass.: Blackwell, 2003), pp. 408–26.

Voragine, Jacobus de, (*The Golden Legend*), tr. (William Caxton?) (1527) STC 24880.

Wack, Mary, 'Women, Work, and Plays in an English Medieval Town', in Susan Frye and Karen Robertson (eds.), *Maids and Mistresses, Cousins and Queens: Women's Alliances in Early Modern England* (New York: Oxford University Press, 1999), p. 51.

Waith, Eugene M., *The Herculean Hero in Marlowe, Chapman, Shakespeare and Dryden* (London: Chatto & Windus, 1962).

Weber, Max, *The Protestant Ethic and the Spirit of Capitalism*, trans. Talcott Parsons (New York: Charles Scribner's Sons; London: George Allen & Unwin, 1930; repr. 1956).

Weimann, Robert, *Shakespeare and the Popular Tradition in the Theater: Studies in the Social Dimension of Dramatic Form and Function*, ed. Robert Schwartz (Baltimore, Md.: Johns Hopkins University Press, 1978).

Author's Pen and Actor's Voice: Playing and Writing in Shakespeare's Theatre, ed. Helen Higbee and William West (Cambridge: Cambridge University Press, 2000).

Westfall, Suzanne R., *Patrons and Performance: Early Tudor Household Revels* (Oxford: Clarendon Press, 1990).

Whigham, Frank, *Ambition and Privilege: The Social Tropes of Elizabethan Courtesy Theory* (Berkeley, Calif.: University of California Press, 1984).

White, Paul Whitfield, *Theatre and Reformation: Protestantism, Patronage, and Playing in Tudor England* (Cambridge: Cambridge University Press, 1993).

White, Paul Whitfield and Suzanne R. Westfall (eds.), *Shakespeare and Theatrical Patronage in Early Modern England* (Cambridge: Cambridge University Press, 2002).

Whitney, Charles, '"Usually in the Werking Daies": Playgoing Journeymen, Apprentices, and Servants in Guild Records, 1582–92', *Shakespeare Quarterly* 50 (1999), pp. 433–58.

'The Devil His Due: Mayor John Spencer, Elizabethan Civic Anti-Theatricalism, and *The Shoemaker's Holiday*', *Medieval and Renaissance Drama in England* 14 (2001), pp. 168–85.

Wickham, Glynne, *Early English Stages 1300 to 1600*, 2nd edn, 4 vols. (London: Routledge & Kegan Paul, 1980–2002).

Wickham, Glynne, Herbert Berry and William Ingram (eds.), *English Professional Theatre, 1530–1660* (Cambridge: Cambridge University Press, 2000).

Wiles, David, *Shakespeare's Clown: Actor and Text in the Elizabethan Playhouse* (Cambridge: Cambridge University Press, 1987).

Williams, Gary Jay, *Our Moonlight Revels: 'A Midsummer Night's Dream' in the Theatre* (Iowa City, Iowa: University of Iowa Press, 1997).

Wilson, John Dover, 'Anthony Munday, Pamphleteer and Pursuivant', *Modern Language Review* 4 (1909), pp. 484–90.

The Fortunes of Falstaff (Cambridge: Cambridge University Press, 1943).

Wilson, Richard, *Will Power: Essays on Shakespearean Authority* (Hemel Hempstead: Harvester Wheatsheaf, 1993).

Winstanley, Gerrard, *The Works of Gerrard Winstanley*, ed. George H. Sabine (Ithaca, NY: Cornell University Press, 1941).

Woodbridge, Linda, *Women and the English Renaissance: Literature and the Nature of Womankind, 1540–1620* (Brighton: Harvester Press; Urbana, Ill.: University of Illinois Press, 1984).

Wright, Louis B., *Middle-Class Culture in Elizabethan England* (Chapel Hill, NC: University of North Carolina Press, 1935).

Wrightson, Keith, *English Society, 1580–1680* (London: Hutchinson, 1982).

Xenophon, *Xenophons Treatise of Hovseholde*, trans. Gentian Hervet (1534) STC 26073.

Youings, Joyce, *Sixteenth-Century England* (Harmondsworth: Penguin, 1984; repr. 1991).

Index

Act for the Punishment of Vagabonds, 31
Act for the Setting of the Poor on Work, 18, 93
actors and acting
  amateurism, 29, 46–7, 48, 49–50, 102–5
  apprentice actors, 28
  in character books, 26–7
  commercial nature of, 151, 155
  Coriolanus as actor, 150
  etymology, 26–7
  idleness of, 24, 26, 41–2, 43, 72–3
  licensing of, 28–9, 51
  masterlessness, 31
  Prince Hal as actor, 82
  Prince Hamlet as actor, 2, 117
  professionalisation of, 27–9, 45, 46–7, 48–9
  rehearsal, 45, 46, 50–3, 102–4, 141
  representation on stage, 44–54, 102–5
  touring, 30–2, 44, 47
  work of, 26, 33, 44–54, 87, 88, 117, 155–7
  see also child actors
Adam, 13
Admiral's Men, *see* Lord Admiral's Men
Aers, David, 11, 13, 16
Agnew, Jean-Christophe, 181n.73
Alfred, king of England, 12
Alleyn, Edward, 110
Antitheatricalism, 38–44, 150, 155
  see also Eutheo, Anglo-Phile; Gosson, Stephen; London, civic authorities; Northbrooke, John; Rankins, William; Salvianus; Stubbes, Philip
apprentices, 24, 36, 92, 93–4, 95, 122, 137–8, 139–40, 173n.15
Aquinas, Thomas, 13
Arab, Ronda, 8
Armin, Robert, 99
audiences, 24, 100–2, 109–10, 141–2, 155, 157
  as workers, 87
  see also playgoing
Ælfric, 12
Bacon, Francis, 16
Bale, John, 30
Ball, John, 13
Barber, C. L., 80
Barckley, Richard, 133
Barish, Jonas, 150–1, 167n.57
Barton, Anne, 29
Beaumont, Francis
  Knight of the Burning Pestle, The, 139–41
Becon, Thomas, 20
begging, 19, 42, 47, 145, 149, 150
Beier, A. L., 161n.30, 165n.25
Bentley, G. E., 28
Bevington, David, 29
Bible, The
  Ephesians, 7
  Exodus, 5
  Genesis, 13
  Matthew, 20, 39
  II Thessalonians, 5, 61–2, 73
Blackfriars boys, *see* Children of the Queen's Revels
Blackfriars playhouse, 24, 98, 99, 105, 109, 135–8, 139, 142, 154–7
Blanke, Thomas, Lord Mayor of London, 34, 37
Boethius, 12
Bolton, Edmund, 124
Bradbrook, Muriel, 28, 29, 39
Brayne, John, 36, 38
Bristol, Michael, 29
Brome, Richard, 98
Browne, John, 132
Buc, George, 24
Bullinger, Heinrich, 7
Burbage, James, 36, 37, 98, 99
Burbage, Richard, 109
Burghley, Lord, *see* Cecil, William
Burke, Peter, 114
Burton, Robert, 108, 116

calling *see* vocation
Calvin, John, 19
cares of state, 62, 74–7
carnival, 29, 65, 83–4
Castiglione, Baldassare, 8, 59
Cecil, William, first Baron Burghley, 35, 37
Chamberlain's Men, *see* Lord Chamberlain's Men
Chambers, E. K., 27–8, 29, 33, 38, 50
Chapman, Alison, 92, 96
Chapman, George
  Eastward Ho!, 135–8, 146
Chester, 9, 30
Chettle, Henry, 120
  Death of Robert Earl of Huntingdon, The, 53
  Downfall of Robert Earl of Huntingdon, The, 53
  Hoffman, 121
  Patient Grissil, 2, 110–13, 120
children's companies, 24, 99–106, 109–10, 111–12, 128, 135–41
Children of Paul's, 99
Children of the Queen's Revels (Children of the Chapel), 98, 99, 101, 105, 109
Cicero, Marcus Tullius, 21, 60, 66, 132
city comedy, 134, 139
Cleaver, Robert, 158n.12
Cocke, John, 26–7, 64
Cohen, Walter, 23
commerce, 18, 19, 76
  moral status of, 16, 131–3, 136–7
  representation on stage, 121–6, 132–41, 145
  social status and, 57, 123–4, 131–2, 137, 147, 150
Compendious or Brief Examination of Certayne Ordinary Complaints, A, 15
Conway, Edward, second Viscount Conway, 108
Cook, Ann Jennalie, 101, 109
Cooper, Lisa H., 123, 124
Cotta, John, 15
Coventry, 30, 31
Coverdale, Miles, 7
Covnsel to the Husband: To the Wife Instruction, 7
Crispin and Crispinian, Sts, 83–4, 88, 90, 91
Cromwell, Thomas, 30
Curtain playhouse, 36, 98

Dawes, Robert, 45
Day, John, 120
  Travels of the Three English Brothers, The, 121
decorum, 1
Dekker, Thomas, 120, 121
  Gull's Horn-Book, The, 108–9, 117, 152
  Honest Whore, The, 131, 145
  Patient Grissil, 2, 110–13, 120
  Roaring Girl, The, 121, 135
  Satiromastix, 2
  Shoemakers' Holiday, The, 2, 8, 89–96, 113, 138
  Westward Ho!, 135, 138–9
Deloney, Thomas, 89–90
Digges, Dudley, 131
Dod, John, 158n.12
Dollimore, Jonathan, 63
Drama
  control of in London, *see* London
  public disorder and, 34–7, 95–6
  Reformation and, 30–1
  social change and, 21–5
  see also actors and acting; audiences; playgoing; playhouses
Duby, Georges, 12
Dudley, Robert, Earl of Leicester, 23, 50, 59, 67
Dudley, Edmund, 59
Dutton, Richard, 23, 33

Earl of Leicester's Men playing company, 51
Earl of Worcester's Men playing company (later Queen Anne's Men), 120–35, 136
Edgar, Thomas, 158n.10
Edward VI, king of England, 15, 30, 61, 92
Eliot, T. S., 126
Elizabeth I, queen of England, 30, 50–1, 60, 62, 74
  Accession Day, 83, 89, 92
Elyot, Thomas, 15, 59, 60
enclosures, 17, 18
Engle, Lars, 147
Erne, Lukas, 88
estates, 11–14, 59–60, 65
Eutheo, Anglo-Phile
  Second and Third Blast of Retrait from Plaies and Theaters, A, 39, 41–2, 43, 45, 58, 152

Ferne, John, 123, 131
Forker, Charles, 47, 70, 73, 75, 77
Fortune playhouse, 37, 110, 120, 135, 136
Fougères, Stephen of, 12
Foxe, John, 30
Fraser, Russell, 41
Fulbecke, William, 15
Fumerton, Patricia, 9

Gair, Reavley, 100
Gardiner, Harold C., 30
Gawdy, Philip, 121

gentlemen and gentility
commerce and, 121–6, 147
definition of, 24, 56–7, 106–7, 150
idleness of, 6, 15, 56–8, 108–9, 116–17, 127–8, 137–8
playgoing, 108–9, 112, 137–8
supported by work of others, 143–4
work of, 56–62, 66–9, 116, 129, 139–40
see also estates
Globe playhouse, 97, 98, 105, 114, 142, 155
Gosson, Stephen, 39
Playes Confuted in Fiue Actions, 1, 42–3, 58, 152
Schoole of Abuse, The, 40, 43, 73
Greenblatt, Stephen, 23, 63, 172n.66
Greg, W. W., 50
Grindal, Edmund, 30, 36
guilds, 28, 29, 93
Gurr, Andrew, 32, 39, 73, 88, 98, 101–2, 110, 113, 120–1, 142, 174

Hall, Edward, 75
Harbage, Alfred, 101, 109
Harington, John, 128
Harman, Thomas, 150
Harrison, William, 57, 73, 106–7, 108
Hart, Alfred, 63
Haughton, William
Patient Grissil, 2, 110–13, 120
Helgerson, Richard, 68, 95, 171n.34
Henderson, Diana E., 129, 130
Henry VI, king of England, 29
Henry VIII, king of England, 30, 52, 53
Henslowe, Philip, 38, 53, 97, 110, 113, 120, 142
Heywood, Thomas, 120
Apology for Actors, 43
Four Prentices of London, The, 122, 139
Golden Age, The, 121
Gynaikeion, 8
If You Know Not Me You Know Nobody Part Two, 120, 121–2, 136
Rape of Lucrece, The, 121
Woman Killed with Kindness, A, 120, 126, 138
Hill, Christopher, 16, 17–18, 57, 92, 162n.33, 162n.35
Hill, Tracey, 45, 53
historicism and new historicism, 22–3, 62–5
Holbrook, Peter, 126
Holderness, Graham, 70, 71, 79, 80
Holinshed, Raphael, 73, 83
Holland, Thomas, 93
Homilies, Book of, 5, 14–15, 16, 22, 61
Shakespeare and, 63
see also idleness, Homily against
How a Man May Choose a Good Wife from a Bad, 120, 145
Hugh, St, 89–90, 92
Hugh of Lincoln, St, 83
humanism, 20–1, 150
Humphrey, Laurence 58–9, 60–1, 73, 75, 107
Hunt, Maurice, 6, 8
Hutson, Lorna, 7, 8, 20
Hutton, Matthew, 30

idleness
Falstaff and, 79–80
Homily against, 14–15, 61–2, 68, 73, 80, 85
madness as, 117
as misuse of time, 40, 41
of poetry, 40
Prince Hal, 80–3
Prince Hamlet, 114–18
private theatres and, 104–5, 137–8
Richard II, 72–4
of servants and clergy, 17
suicide as, 114–15
in *The Tempest*, 156
as treason, 85
see also actors and acting; gentlemen and gentility; playgoing; prodigals
inflation, 18
Ingelend, Thomas
Disobedient Child, The, 48
Ingram, William, 34, 35, 36–7

Jack Straw, 95
James I, king of England, 120
James, Mervyn, 59–60
Jewell, John, 62, 74
Johnston, Alexandra F., 30
Jonson, Ben, 2
Alchemist, The, 1
Cynthia's Revels, 101, 103, 109
Eastward Ho!, 135–8, 146
Every Man Out of His Humour, 88

Kastan, David Scott, 80, 94
Kemp, Will, 98–9, 111, 156
King's Men, *see* Lord Chamberlain's Men
Knowles, Ronald, 65, 68, 69
Knutson, Roslyn, 24, 109, 142, 168n.72
Kyd, Thomas
Spanish Tragedy, The, 138

Lady Elizabeth's Men playing company, 45
landlords, 18, 19
Langland, William, 17
Piers Plowman, 13–14, 16

Latimer, Hugh, 15, 17, 23, 58, 170n.24
Leicester, Earl of *see* Dudley, Robert, Earl of Leicester
Leinwand, Theodore B., 132, 134–5
Leggatt, Alexander, 97, 139, 140
Le Goff, Jacques, 13, 16–17
Lodge, Thomas, 41
London
  civic authorities, 28, 33–8, 46
  control of recreation in, 93–4
  development of commercial theatre in, 27, 32–8, 45, 99–106
London Prodigal, The, 110, 145
Lord Admiral's Men playing company (later Prince Henry's Men), 45, 53, 89, 97, 110–13, 120–35, 136, 142, 145
Lord Chamberlain's Men playing company (later King's Men), 49, 51, 87, 97–9, 113–18, 141–52, 154–7
Lord Chandos's Men playing company, 32
Lord Strange's Men playing company, 38
Lust's Dominion, see Spanish Moor's Tragedy
Luther, Martin, 19

MacLean, Sally-Beth, 23, 34, 50–1
Mankind, 29
manual work, 15, 16, 68, 76, 143–4
  medieval estates theory and, 11–14, 65
  Reformation and, 19
  representation on stage, 110–13, 121, 148–9, 156
  social status and, 15, 57, 106–7, 108, 112, 129, 148–9
Marlowe, Christopher, 145
  Edward II, 77–8
  Massacre at Paris, The, 95
Marston, John
  Antonio and Mellida, 100, 102, 105, 138
  Antonio's Revenge, 103, 104–5
  Dutch Courtesan, The, 9
  Jack Drum's Entertainment, 100, 102–3
  Eastward Ho!, 135–8, 146
  What You Will, 104
Master of the Revels, 23, 33, 35, 52
masterlessness, 18–19, 31
McLuskie, Kathleen, 37, 127
McMillin, Scott, 23, 34, 50–1
McNeill, Fiona, 9
Melchiori, Giorgio, 75, 168n.75
Merry Devil of Edmonton, The, 110
Middle Ages
  acting style of in early modern drama, 44, 46–8
  religious drama of, *see* mystery plays
  urbanisation in, 16–17
  work and social theory in, 11–14, 21, 59–60, 65, 66
  work as curse in, 6, 15
Middleton, Thomas
  Micro-cynicon, 111
  Honest Whore, The, 131, 145
  Roaring Girl, The, 121, 135
Montrose, Louis, 22
More, Thomas, 17, 21, 47–8
  Sir Thomas More (play) *see* Munday, Anthony
Mulcaster, Richard, 57, 107
Munday, Anthony
  Death of Robert Earl of Huntingdon, The, 53
  Downfall of Robert Earl of Huntingdon, The, 52–3
  John a Kent and John a Cumber, 45–7, 48
  Sir Thomas More, 45, 47–9, 52
  Wise Man of Westchester, The see John a Kent and John a Cumber
  see also Eutheo, Anglo-Phile
Munro, Lucy, 97, 104, 138
mystery plays, 29

Nashe, Thomas, 95
Newington Butts playhouse, 36
Northbrooke, John, 39–40
Norwich, 29–30, 31, 32

Ornstein, Robert, 79, 82

Paris Garden, 37
pastoral, 1
Patterson, Annabel, 114
Paul, St, 7, 58, 61–2, 73, 80
Paul's playhouse, 24, 99, 100, 105, 110, 135, 138
  see also Children of Paul's
Peacham, Henry, 131
Peasants' Revolt, 13
Perkins, David, 23
Perkins, William
  Treatise of the Vocations, A, 20, 22, 58
plague, 33, 35, 51
Plato, 40
play *see* Recreation
playgoing, 24, 34–7
  and idleness, 35–7, 40, 93, 108–9, 116, 137–8, 157
  see also audiences
playhouses
  growth of in London, 36–8
  work and workers in, 87, 94–9, 100–2, 125, 155–7
  see also actors and acting; audiences

Prince Henry's Men, *see* Lord Admiral's Men
Privy Council, 24, 30, 50–1, 98
  correspondence with London authorities over control of playing, 33–8, 50–1, 166n.42
prodigals, 137–8, 139–40, 145, 146
Puritanism, 17–18, 19, 50, 92, 151
Puttenham, George, 117

Queen Anne's Men, *see* Earl of Worcester's Men
Queen's Men playing company, 23, 28, 37

Rackin, Phyllis, 64, 65, 70
Rankins, William, 42–3, 73
recreation, 1–2, 50–1, 87, 93–5, 127–8, 137
Red Lion playhouse, 36, 38, 165n.32
Reformation, 6–7, 19–20, 30–1, 150
  gentility and, 57–8, 60–2, 107
  manual work and, 19
Rich, Barnaby, 108
Richard Whittington, 120, 121, 136
Riggs, David, 56, 66, 69, 80
Righter, Anne *see* Barton, Anne
Rose playhouse, 38, 89, 110, 120
Ruiter, David, 79, 80

Saint-Maure, Benedict of, 12
Salvianus, 41
Segar, William, 131
sermons, *see* Homilies, Book of
servants, 24, 36, 93–4, 96–7, 128, 143–4
Shakespeare, William
  gentleman status of, 6, 57
  works
    Antony and Cleopatra, 146
    Coriolanus, 61, 146
    history plays, 56
    Hamlet, 2, 81, 87, 112, 113–18, 142
    Henry IV Part One, 33, 75, 78–82
    Henry IV Part Two, 75–6, 78, 81–2
    Henry V, 75–6, 79, 82, 83–6, 87–9, 90–2
    Henry VI Part Two, 64, 65–9, 95
    Julius Caesar, 96
    Midsummer Night's Dream, A, 49–52, 82
    Richard II, 70–5, 76–8, 80, 157
    Richard III, 69
    Sonnets, 6
    Taming of the Shrew, The, 44, 49
    Tempest, The, 155–7
Shapiro, James, 83
Shapiro, Michael, 100
Shrove Tuesday, 89, 92, 93
Sidney, Philip, 59
  Defence of Poesy, A, 1, 26–7
Sir John Oldcastle, 120, 142
Sir Thomas More see Munday, Anthony
Sir Thomas Wyatt, 120, 142
Slack, Paul, 161n.30, 165n.25
sleeplessness, 67, 68, 69, 75–6
Smith, Henry, 159n.12
Smith, Thomas, 8, 108, 124
Smith, Wentworth
  Freeman's Honour, The, 142
Spanish Moor's Tragedy, The, 121
Spencer, John, Lord Mayor of London, 34, 97
Spenser, Edmund
  Faerie Queene, The, 114–15
sprezzatura, 117
Starkey, Thomas, 17
status, *see* gentlemen and gentility
Statute of Artificers, 18, 93
Stern, Tiffany, 45, 52, 103–4
Stevenson, Laura Caroline, 121–6
Stone, Lawrence, 56, 107, 147
Straznicky, Marta, 89, 94
Stubbes, Philip, 41, 43, 151
Sullivan, Ceri, 132
Sullivan, Garrett A., 8
Sunday playing, 37, 97
Swan playhouse, 35
Swinnerton, John, 142

Taming of a Shrew, The, 44–5, 49
Tarlton, Richard, 99
Tawney, R. H., 19, 162n.33
Theatre, Shoreditch, 32, 36, 38, 43, 98
Thomas, Keith, 1–2, 6
Thomas Lord Cromwell, 2, 142, 176n.67
Tillyard, E. M. W., 63, 78
Tymme, Thomas 62

unemployment, 18, 31
vagrancy, 18, 31
Veeser, Harold, 22
Virgil, 84
Vives, Juan, 116
vocation, 14–15, 16, 20, 36, 58, 61, 80

Wack, Mary, 9
Walsingham, Francis, 23, 37, 50
Weber, Max, 19
Webster, John, 26–7
  Westward Ho!, 135, 138–9
Weimann, Robert, 114
Westfall, Suzanne, 30, 31
Wever, R.
  Lusty Juventus, 48
Whitgift, John, 35
Whitney, Charles, 34, 93, 94–5

Wickham, Glynne, 29, 30, 36
Wiles, David, 99
Willoughby, Percival, 147–8
Wilson, John Dover, 78, 168
Wilson, Richard, 95, 97, 171n.34
Wimbledon, Thomas, 14
Winstanley, Gerrard, 16
women's work *see* work
Woodbridge, Linda, 8
Woodrofe, Nicholas, Lord Mayor of London, 34, 35, 38, 42
work
  demographics and, 18
  drama and, *see* actors and acting; audiences; playgoing; playhouses
  urbanisation and, 12
  etymology, 5, 159–160n.1
  repetitiousness, 2
  representation in playing company repertories
    children's companies, 99–106, 135–41
    Earl of Worcester's Men, 120–35
    Lord Admiral's Men, 110–13, 120–35, 145
    Lord Chamberlain's Men, 113–18, 141–52
  revenge as, 115–16
  social contingency of, 4–6, 7, 84, 86
  social control and, 18–19, 21, 93–4, 124–6
  social status and, *see* gentlemen and gentility
  social theory and, 11–21, 59–60, 84–6
  unpopularity as literary theme, 1
  women's work, 7–10, 91, 102, 129, 145
work, varieties of
  basket-making, 111, 112, 113
  brewing, 9, 101
  carrying, 2, 81, 113–18
  drapery, 131
  farming, 19
  gardening, 71–4
  government, 15, 20–1, 55–86, 106–7, 157
  gravedigging, 2
  hammering, 2, 115
  husbandry, 20–1
  kingship, 15, 20, 58, 62, 70–86
  laundry, 102
  law, 15, 16, 18, 106–7
  maid-service, 145
  medicine, 15, 106–7
  milking, 129
  poetry, 2, 155
  professions, 28
  prostitution, 8, 145
  religion, 11–14, 15, 16, 18
  sewing, 91
  shoemaking, 2, 19, 89–96
  shop-work, 2, 8
  smith-work, 19, 143–4
  studying, 2, 106–7, 111, 143–4
  warfare, 11–14, 59–60, 83, 106–7, 149
  watermen of London, 38
  writing, 116–17
  see also actors and acting; apprentices; commerce; servants; manual work; gentlemen and gentility
works, 19
Wulfstan, 12
Wyclif, John, 14

Xenophon, 7, 20

yeomen *see* landlords
York, 30
Yorkshire Tragedy, A, 110